I0896148

JOURNAL • OF MORAL THEOLOGY

TECHNOLOGY

Edited by James F. Caccamo and David M. McCarthy

JMT

JOURNAL • OF
M • O • R • A • L
THEOLOGY

Journal of Moral Theology is a peer-reviewed scholarly journal focusing on Catholic moral theology. Our mission is to publish scholarly articles in the field of moral theology, as well as theological treatments of related topics in philosophy, economics, political philosophy, and psychology. *Journal of Moral Theology* is published semiannually, with January and July issues.

Articles published in the *Journal of Moral Theology* will undergo at least two double blind peer reviews. Authors are asked to submit articles electronically to jmt@msmary.edu. Submissions should be prepared for blind review. Microsoft Word format preferred. Editors assume that submissions are not being simultaneously considered for publication in another venue.

ISSN 2166-2851 (print), ISSN 2166-2118 (online). *Journal of Moral Theology* is published by Mount St. Mary's University, 16300 Old Emmitsburg Road, Emmitsburg, MD 21727.

Pickwick Publications, An Imprint of Wipf and Stock Publishers, 199 W. 8th Ave., Suite 3, Eugene, OR 97401. www.wipfandstock.com. **ISBN 13: 978-1-4982-1928-0**

Note from the Issue Editors

For many of us, the electronic gadgets that are ever so popular as Christmas gifts still have a new and even futuristic feel to them. Yet, as we welcome 2015, we stand squarely in the midst of the digital era. Nearly 45 years after the invention of email, 25 years after the development of the World Wide Web, and more than 20 years after the advent of texting, digital communication and information technologies have become a part of the daily realities of people around the globe. As a marker, consider that as of 2013, there were more than 6.8 billion active cell phones, spanning developing and developed nations. That's 97 phones for every 100 people on the planet! Indeed, more people have cell phones than have access to clean toilets.[1]

While these new technologies have brought great benefits to our lives, they have also raised a host of questions that have profound moral implications. For instance, how are we to understand what it means for something to be "natural"? What does it mean to be human and carry out relationships with others? How do we understand and support sustainable, meaningful work in an era of objectification and hyper-commodification? What is privacy and is it really important? What is the role of information access in economic development? How does anonymity enhance or degrade civil society and social engagement? Can technologies be tools of protest, or will they inevitably be coopted by powers? Do our devices affect our ability to learn and understand the world? Does husbandry of devices compete with time for friendship and romance? For most of the twentieth century, "technology ethics" in the Catholic tradition focused on issues relating to medical interventions. Now that technology suffuses our lives, the moral implications seem endless.

Yet, for all of the challenges that technology offers us, it has not been taken up robustly within moral theology. While philosophers have been thinking about technology ethics for decades, and even engineers have several ethics journals of their own, scholarly articles and books in the theological disciplines are few and far between.

It is with great pleasure, then, that we bring to you this issue of the *Journal of Moral Theology* on the theme of technology ethics, the first of its kind in a theological journal in English. The issue begins with a pair of essays that explore the ways in which the experience of a technological culture is challenging fundamental categories in our human experience. Nadia Delicata examines the category of nature and how we might understand it in a technological age. Drawing on the insights

---

[1] United Nations, "Deputy UN Chief Calls for Urgent Action to Tackle Global Sanitation Crisis," UN News Centre (March 21, 2013), www.un.org/apps/news/story.asp?NewsID=44452&Cr=sanitation&Cr1=#.VHtZ-76Q02R.

of the philosophical and theological traditions, she suggests that, as part of the natural and divine work to continue God's creation, technological creativity is a profoundly "natural" phenomenon that can be understood under the rubric of natural law. Matthew John Paul Tan follows with an exploration of the concept of time in the age of Facebook, suggesting that social media's linear and episodic exposition of our lives offers challenges to the Christian experience of the divine unfolding of history.

Next, the issue follows with a pair of essays that probe two perennial issues in Catholic social ethics. Joseph Wolyniak digs into the issue of labor rights and the people who contribute their work to ensuring that we have devices in our pockets, backpacks, and offices. His analysis raises questions about those who mine the raw materials for electronics, put them together, and then dispose of them when we are done. Are they able to achieve integral human development? Do the material conditions of our enjoyment of electronics trade on conditions of poverty and oppression? Likewise, Patrick Flanagan goes on to examine the question of the relevance of unions in the online age, using the case of Pandora and its compensation of musicians.

Next, the issue offers a pair of articles that explore the ways in which common, but cutting edge technologies reveal underlying streams in cultural consciousness. Jana M. Bennett unpacks the issue of cochlear implants, which have become a point of controversy in the deaf community, not because they represent "trans-human" or "post-human" digital technologies, but because their use is predicated on the notion that difference is a medical problem that needs to be fixed. In the process, Bennett explores neutrality and narrative, as well as the social constructions of difference and disability. Kara N. Slade then wrestles with the important development of autonomous, artificial intelligence driven military drones, not in terms of *jus in bello* deliberations, but as an icon for a fundamental challenge that theological models of Christ and the human person pose for our ongoing understandings both of warfare and technology.

To close out our consideration of issues and areas of concern, we turn to probe what we might refer to as the "bread and butter" of the work of the moral theologian in the United States today: teaching and moral assessment. Mary E. Hess, a scholar in theological education, examines the issue of using digital communication and information technology in the college classroom. Neither a Luddite nor fetishist, Hess draws on both theological and pedagogical sources to suggest a way of understanding educational technology within the authentic human struggle for wisdom and community.

Finally, the issue closes with an essay by James F. Caccamo (co-editor of the issue) that takes up the issue of methodology in moral assessment of technology. Thus far, issues of the *Journal of Moral Theology* have tended to close with a review essay that surveys the landscape of the topic within moral theology. However, given the limited number of works published on technology ethics within the field this did not seem warranted, as it would end up more of a collection of book reviews than useful survey of key trends. Instead, Caccamo evaluates the competing theories of the influence of technology that are prominent in mainstream and scholarly writing on technology issues, suggesting an alternative approach that will enable technology ethicists to do analysis that fits more closely with wisdom of the Catholic moral tradition.

Before closing, we would be remiss if we failed to thank those who helped see this issue from creation to completion, especially Managing Editor, Gloria Balsley, as well as Anthony Ward and Alanna Cherry for the formatting and proofreading work.

— James F. Caccamo and David M. McCarthy

Journal of Moral Theology, Vol. 4, No. 1 (2015): 1-24

Natural Law in a Digital Age

Nadia Delicata

IN ITS THIRD CHAPTER DEDICATED TO "The Gospel of the Family and the Natural Law," the *Instrumentum Laboris* of the III Extraordinary General Assembly of the Synod of Bishops on "The Pastoral Challenges of the Family in the Context of Evangelization,"[1] recognized among the faithful "large-scale perplexity surrounding the concept of the natural law" (no. 20). More to the point, the document noted: "the concept of natural law today turns out to be, in different cultural contexts, highly problematic, if not completely incomprehensible. The expression is understood in a variety of ways, or simply not understood at all" (no. 21). As the document suggests, not only does science offer a materialist view of "nature," while many interpret the adjective "natural" subjectively to imply individual feelings or desires, but "law" tends to denote solely "positive law" that is *de facto* culturally relative (cf. nos. 22-6).

This "demise of the concept of the natural law" (no. 26) makes "some elements of Christian teaching" (no. 20), especially those relating to marriage and the family, increasingly "perplexing," "incomprehensible," "outdated" and completely ignored among the faithful.[2] Yet the "demise" of natural law among the faithful affects more than their appropriation of specific moral teachings.

Understood as the inherent God-given ability to reason morally, live righteously, and desire our ultimate end in God, natural law is a fundamental pillar for a robust theology of the Christian life. Even if natural law reflection relies on reason, it also assumes an entire edifice of revealed theology proper, anthropology, protology, and eschatology.[3] In a world marred by sin, the eyes of faith assume that natural law is perfected through the infused theological virtues and gifts of the

[1] General Secretariat of the Synod of Bishops, *Instrumentum Laboris* (June 24, 2014), www.vatican.va/roman_curia/synod/documents/rc_synod_doc_20140626_instrumentum-laboris-familia_en.html.

[2] As recently as 2009, the International Theological Commission issued a document on natural law: International Theological Commission, *In Search of a Universal Ethic: A New Look at the Natural Law*, 2009, www.vatican.va/roman _curia/congregations/cfaith/cti_documents/rc_con_cfaith_doc_20090520_legge-naturale_en.html.

[3] For an analysis of the theological foundation of medieval natural law see Jean Porter, *Natural and Divine Law: Reclaiming the Tradition for Christian Ethics* (Ottawa: Novalis, 1999), chs. 1-3.

Holy Spirit. In other words, as the school of the virtues preparing for ultimate beatitude, natural law is the moral dimension of the linchpin of all Christian dogma and revelation: the personal relationship between the human and divine. As *Veritatis splendor*,[4] the first encyclical "on the fundaments of the Church's moral teaching,"[5] noted thirty years ago, when natural law is disconnected from divine providence it drains moral theology of its properly theological character. Oppositely, if natural law in its Christian articulation is incomprehensible to the faithful, then one can only assume that much of Christian dogma and theologizing is equally mystifying. As the *Instrumentum Laboris* itself suggests, "a want of an authentic Christian experience, namely, an encounter with Christ on a personal and communal level, for which no doctrinal presentation, no matter how accurate, can substitute" (no. 15) makes meaningless the true foundation of Christian living and reflection, which is an ongoing commitment to becoming a disciple of Christ.

It follows that if the crisis of natural law among the Catholic faithful reflects a spiritual and existential crisis and not only a doctrinal and moral one, its retrieval as a robust foundation of the Christian life needs to face head-on other forces in human life that shape the "spirit" or *ratio* of our existence. As the Fourth Gospel iconically puts it, apart from the true "way" of Christ, there are the many, often false, ways of the "world." The ways of the world can be interpreted as the worldviews, horizons of meaning or "social imaginaries"[6] that, according to Bernard Lonergan, are the inevitable "biases" that shape a culture.[7] "Culture" is the *Gestalt* of implicit beliefs and assumed ways of doing things that mutually inform each other. Becoming inculturated is a process that molds the *sensus communis* through forming the powers of perception, imagination, memory, and intuition, thus enabling the immersion in, and partaking of, a constructed worldview. As the Ancient Greeks recognized, *paideia*, the word that denoted both

---

[4] Pope John Paul II, *Veritatis Splendor* (August 6, 1993), www.vatican.va/holy_father/john_paul_ii/encyclicals/documents/hf_jp-ii_enc_06081993_veritatis-splendor_en.html.

[5] This is Hittinger's translation of the encyclical's subtitle *De Fundamentis Doctrinae Moralis Ecclesiae*. See Russell Hittinger, *The First Grace: Rediscovering the Natural Law in a Post-Christian World* (Wilmington: ISI Books, 2003), xxxviii.

[6] As used by Charles Taylor, "social imaginaries" implies "the way that we collectively imagine, even pre-theoretically, our social life" in different historical and cultural contexts. Charles Taylor, *A Secular Age* (Harvard University Press, 2007), 146.

[7] Bernard Lonergan, *Insight: A Study of Human Understanding* (Toronto: University of Toronto Press, 1992). See in particular Chapter 7 "Common Sense as Object" that tackles the related issues of individual bias, group bias and general bias on a cultural level.

culture and education, is (or rather, should be) a process of "humanization."[8] Without an adequate *paideia*, man and woman remain somewhat less than human, since it is through being inculturated that we are formed morally, intellectually, and spiritually.[9]

In recent decades, much research in philosophy, theology, and jurisprudence has studied the shifting meaning of "natural law" in western history.[10] In the patristic age, that sought to transform Hellenic *paideia* to a *paideia tou Kyriou*, the popular Stoic conception of natural law started being Christianized, while in the Latin middle ages, Scholasticism as heir of Latin *humanitas* offered the most sophisticated Christian natural law reflection by theologians and jurists. This became increasingly secularized in modern jurisprudence,[11] with the effects reverberating on moral theology as well. Hence, mutations of natural law from the Greeks to modernity can be interpreted as culturally mediated; that is, reflecting how moral reflection and the biases of the culture that facilitate it are in "mutual self-mediation."[12]

In particular, as Yves R. Simon suggests, in western history natural law reflection shifts among three poles: as a matter of "practical cognition;" as "an issue of nature" and specifically of how human nature is "situated in a broader order of causality;" and lastly, as natural law is also construed as "the ordinance of a divine lawgiver."[13] A properly

---

[8] The classic study on Greek *paideia* is Werner Jaeger, *Paideia: the Ideals of Greek Culture*, vols. I-III, trans. Gilbert Highet (New York: Oxford University Press, 1943-1945).

[9] It is for this reason that Lonergan assumes the need for intellectual and moral conversions together with the religious conversion to Christ. Even more fundamentally, intellectual conversion implies the need for appropriating one's cognitive operations: paying attention, careful refection and the considered judgment of truth. Bernard Lonergan, "Self-transcendence: Intellectual, Moral, Religious," in *Philosophical and Theological Papers 1965-1980*, ed. Robert M. Doran and Robert C. Croken (Toronto: University of Toronto Press, 2005), 313-31.

[10] Even the International Theological Commission's document *In Search of a Universal Ethic: A New Look at the Natural Law* offers a historical development of the concept. Perhaps the first to analyze the difference between classical and modern understandings of natural law is Heinrich A. Rommen in his 1936 book, *The Natural Law: A Study in Legal and Social History and Philosophy*, trans. Thomas R. Hanley (Indianapolis: Liberty Fund, 1998).

[11] Edgar Bodenheimer, *Jurisprudence: The Philosophy and Method of the Law* 2nd Ed. (Cambridge, MA: Harvard University Press, 1974), 32-3.

[12] The phrase was used by Bernard Lonergan in his essay, "The Mediation of Christ in Prayer," delivered to the Thomas More Institute in September 1963. The essay was subsequently published in *Method: Journal of Lonergan Studies* 2/1 (March 1984): 1-20. In contemporary Lonerganian studies, the term is often associated with the way religion and culture "communicate" with, and in turn shape, one another. See for instance, John D. Dadosky, "Methodological Presuppositions for Engaging the Other in the Post-Vatican II Context: Insights from Ignatius and Lonergan," *The Journal of Inter-Religious Studies* 3 (March 2010): 9-24.

[13] Hittinger, *The First Grace*, 4, referring to Yves R. Simon, *The Tradition of Natural Law: A Philosopher's Reflections* (New York: Fordham University Press, 1999).

Christian understanding of natural law must include the third dimension, as philosophical reflection is supplemented by revelation. Nevertheless, even ancient Aristotelian and Stoic conceptions of natural law, emerging from an experience of the cosmos as charged with meaning, assumed a metaphysical and transcending order variously construed.[14] It is primarily modern western notions of natural law, shaped by a linear, perspectival sense of space and secular time, that tend to purposefully bracket (though not necessarily deny) the third understanding, reduce the significance of the second, and put disproportionate emphasis on the first. Eventually, in modern moral philosophy, natural law as practical cognition also ends up being eclipsed: on one hand, through the reaction of romanticism leading to emotivism; and on the other, through the rise of legal positivism.

We have now entered a new era shaped not by a modern "mechanistic" mindset, but by a digital one of "information." If digitality is the most obvious technological substratum of the new age, "information" is becoming its horizon of meaning. Just like its "modern" (or "typographical"), "classical" (or "literate"), and even Greek "oral" predecessors,[15] digital culture is creating its distinct social imaginaries. In particular, it inculcates its own sense of what is ordered, reasonable, and desirable (the foundation of the first sense of natural law) and of who the human is in relation to their environment (related to the second meaning of natural law). It also expresses its own particular intuition of what overall reality, and in particular transcendence, is like (the third level of natural law reflection). Accordingly, since the concept of natural law relies on these three categories of reason, anthropology, and metaphysics, if it is to be rehabilitated among the Christian faithful, it will need to consider digital culture's emerging cultural assumptions. Just like the Christian life is in a mutual self-mediation with the emerging digital culture, the contemporary understanding of natural law must also evolve to accommodate emerging sensibilities and expressions.

The first part of the article will present a hermeneutic of digital culture from a "media ecology" perspective. Media ecology, in particular through the work of the Thomist Marshall McLuhan, studies the way how human artifacts mediate, and therefore recreate, the sense of

---

14 See, for instance, Maryanne Cline Horowitz, "The Stoic Synthesis of the Idea of Natural Law in Man: Four Themes," *Journal of the History of Ideas*, 35 (1974): 3-16 and Owen Anderson, *The Natural Moral Law: The Good After Modernity* (New York: Cambridge University Press, 2012), 48-54.

15 The sensibilities of Greek "oral culture" are preserved in transcribed "oral encyclopedias" most famous of which are the Homeric epics. See Eric A. Havelock, *The Muse Learns to Write: Reflections on Orality and Literacy from Antiquity to the Present* (New Haven: Yale University Press, 1986).

what reality is like by altering the balance of the *sensus communis.*[16] Based on this insight, I will suggest that in this past century, electronic and digital media have been creating a novel cultural imaginary of "information." As a new "ontology"—indeed being called such by "philosophers of information"[17]—the imaginary of information is reflected in emerging anthropological assumptions,[18] as well as in our

---

[16] The eclectic discipline of "media ecology," in particular through the thought of Marshall and Eric McLuhan, is chosen to interpret emerging phenomena as "imaginaries" primarily because, as a robust grammar of "all things" it is highly compatible with the Catholic and traditionally Thomistic understanding of natural law that relies on the mutual interpretation of the "Book of Nature" and the "Book of the Scriptures." Yet, as a contemporary retrieval of the classical grammarian mindset it considers not only the Book of Nature as given, but also the Book being written through human ingenuity. For a brief introduction to media ecology see Lance Strate, "President's Message: Understanding MEA," *In Medias Res* 1 (1999): 1-2, www.media-ecology.org/publications/In_Medias_Res/v1n1.pdf.

[17] A sub-discipline of "philosophy of technology," the main exponent of a "philosophy of information" is University of Oxford's Luciano Floridi. For a brief overview of his thought see "Trends in the Philosophy of Information," in *Philosophy of Information* Vol. 8 ed. Pieter Adriaans and Johan van Benthem in the series *Handbooks of the Philosophy of Science* (Elsevier, 2008), 113-31. For a more developed argument see his book *The Philosophy of Information* (New York: Oxford University Press, 2011).

[18] While it is beyond the scope of this article, the key emerging anthropological assumption is of the posthuman. N. Katherine Hayles' now classic *How We Became Posthuman: Virtual Bodies in Cybernetics, Literature, and Informatics* (University of Chicago Press, 1999) notes that "the posthuman appears when computation rather than possessive individualism is taken as the ground of being, a move that allows the posthuman to be seamlessly articulated with intelligent machines" (34). In distinction to modern notions of the human, the determining characteristics of the posthuman include: "emergence replaces teleology; reflexive epistemology replaces objectivism; distributed cognition replaces autonomous will; embodiment replaces a body seen as a support system for the mind; and a dynamic partnership between humans and intelligent machines replaces the liberal humanist subject's manifest destiny to dominate and control nature" (288).

The philosopher of information Floridi agrees with this general description of the posthuman. However, following the presupposition that the new ontology is information and that the new ecology is an "infosphere", he describes the posthuman as an "inforg": "connected informational organism." See Luciano Floridi, *Information: A very short introduction* (New York: Oxford University Press, 2011), 70-2.

Moreover, since the "inforg" actively participates in the infosphere through "distributed cognition" among humans and machines, Floridi also calls for an analogous concept of "distributed morality". "The increasing pervasiveness and autonomy of artificial agents and of hybrid multiagent systems [from corporations to software] … able to perform morally relevant actions, independently of the humans who engineered them" in itself calls for an expanded understanding of "moral agency" to consider and include the analogous "agency" of the non-human. See his paper "Distributed Morality in an Information Society," *Science and Engineering Ethics* 19 (September 2013): 727-43.

"Distributed morality" can be understood as a reflection on pervasive or ecology-wide expressions of good and evil analogous to what the Catholic tradition terms structural or systemic sin. However, while increasingly "intelligent" artifacts raise the question

culture's belief that the manifestation of intelligence is best captured by the quest for technological perfection: the ability to quite literally re-fashion all that exists.

Thus, I will argue that in a digital culture shaped by the imaginary of information, natural law reflection cannot ignore the technological human, imbued with a desire to make things and to tinker with their environment as they deem fit. Natural law reflection must be extended to offer a robust way to evaluate the goodness or otherwise of the fruit of human making, just as it already is the ground for judging the goodness or otherwise of human acting in general. However, to properly consider natural law through its three pillars of reasoning, understanding of the human, and divine ordinance, *techne* must be studied anthropologically as well as theologically. Hence, in the second part, I will present a theo-anthropology of *techne* through the thought of the seventh century Father of the Church St. Maximus the Confessor. Maximus' reflection on *techne* as a postlapsarian "garment of skins" offers the contours for distinguishing between mere making and authentic human creating.

Through this pivotal distinction, in the third part, I will argue how *techne* could be incorporated within a Christian understanding of natural law in at least three ways: as the virtue of rightly ordered, and not merely efficient, creating; as oriented to fulfilling the properly human inclination of being co-creators with God; and lastly, as demanding a conception of practical wisdom that extends beyond considering human personal and social responsibility to the cosmological responsibility of tending creation. Through human action and creative labor, the entire created realm is brought, in the power of the Holy Spirit, to a "cosmic liturgy."[19]

THE EMERGING "DIGITAL" CULTURE

Gaudium et spes, the Second Vatican Council Constitution on the Church in the Modern World, inaugurated the project "of scrutinizing the signs of the times and of interpreting them in the light of the Gospel." This entails the duty to "recognize and understand the world in which we live, its explanations, its longings, and its often dramatic

---

of distributed morality more sharply, if the media ecology tradition is correct in claiming that *all* human artifacts have ecological effects beyond those initially willed by their creator, then the more fundamental question is how to order human "making" itself.

[19] As Balthasar notes, "cosmic liturgy" is the key imaginary of the hope for the new creation in Maximus the Confessor's thought. Hans Urs von Balthasar, *Cosmic Liturgy: The Universe according to St. Maximus the Confessor* (San Francisco: Ignatius Press, 2003).

characteristics" (no. 4).[20] The interdisciplinary field of "media ecology," in particular through the thought of Marshall and Eric McLuhan, attempts such "recognition" of cultural dynamics by facilitating awareness of how artifacts that become our second nature, alter the way we perceive and, hence, the way we make sense of reality.[21] Just as speech, as an all-immersive event, demands and, therefore, trains holistic perception, while alphabetic literacy shapes the mind to focus on figures to the exclusion of the ground, so every human artifact, but in particular tools that facilitate the quintessential human characteristic of "communing" with one another, can have more or less pronounced effects on the *sensus communis* to dramatically recreate cultural imaginaries.[22]

This emphasis on how the effects of artifacts on the human psyche remain mostly unconscious—what McLuhan famously encapsulates in the adage "the medium is the message"—has often led to the accusation of technological determinism. Yet, as a Catholic convert and life-long student of the patristic and medieval tradition, McLuhan strongly believed that "there is no inevitability so long as we are willing to contemplate what is happening."[23] That contemplation of things, which for the Catholic McLuhan, is through faith and reason, becomes the fundamental stance for seeking to understand how artifacts are morally significant precisely because they are "the extensions of man." As the McLuhans put it: "In tetrad form, [that is, through the laws of media] the artifact is seen to be not neutral or passive, bur an active *logos* or utterance of the human mind or body that transforms the user and his ground."[24] Artifacts are the means through which the human interrelates in his or her environment (i.e. they are "media") and indeed, are constitutive elements of that constantly regenerated ecology. Thus, if the "natural" raison d'être for making artifacts, and therefore of human *techne* itself, is to promote human and ecological

---

[20] Vatican II, Pastoral Constitution on the Church in the Modern World *Gaudium et spes* (December 7, 1965), www.vatican.va/archive/hist_councils/ii _vatican_council/documents/vat-ii_cons_19651207_gaudium-et-spes_en.html.

[21] Key texts include: Marshall McLuhan, *Understanding Media: The Extensions of Man* (McGraw-Hill, 1964) and Marshall McLuhan and Eric McLuhan, *The Laws of Media: The New Science* (University of Toronto Press, 1992). Marshall McLuhan's Cambridge doctoral dissertation, defended in 1943, also situates his later work that interprets the effects of media to shape culture as grounded in his study of classical grammar in western culture. See his recently published doctoral work: *The Classical Trivium: The Place of Thomas Nashe in the Learning of His Time* (Berkeley: Gingko Press, 2009).

[22] The most well-known work on the relation between methods of communication and the development of cultural imaginaries is that by McLuhan's student, the Jesuit Walter J. Ong, *Orality and Literacy: The Technologizing of the Word* (London: Methuen and Company, 1982).

[23] In Marshall McLuhan and Quentin Fiore, *The Medium is the Massage: An Inventory of Effects* (New York: Bantam Books, 1967), 25.

[24] McLuhan and McLuhan, *The Laws of Media*, 99.

flourishing, than the measure of flourishing itself would be the crucial criterion by which the goodness or otherwise of human creation is to be judged.[25]

Judgment of truth and goodness however, must rely on holistic perception and correct understanding. Yet if, by being the very glasses through which we experience the world, media destabilize our sensorium, then we require tools for waking us up from our narcosis to properly perceive and interpret artifacts' pervasive effects.[26] The work of Marshall McLuhan, taken over by his son Eric McLuhan, culminated with the "four laws of media," or "tetrad," as probes to help bring to awareness the multiple effects of tools on the human and their social, cultural, and physical environment. Reminiscent of the Christian assumption that the Book of Nature can be read like the Book of the Scriptures, the four laws suggest that an analogous Book of Culture, or of the "ecology" created by human artifacts, can also be read in as fine a detail as we are capable (or willing) to study.[27]

As extensions of the capabilities of the human body, especially of the senses that mediate between internality and externality, self and other, the true content of every medium is always the user himself or herself.[28] Media effects recreate cultural imaginaries precisely by shaping the way we reason, understand ourselves, and make sense of reality: the three pillars of natural law reflection. At the same time,

---

[25] McLuhan is famous for his claim that "the moralist typically substitutes anger for perception," (Lewis H. Lapham quoting McLuhan in the "Introduction" to the MIT Press edition of *Understanding Media: The Extensions of Man* published in 1994, xiv). Prudential judgment and decision-making should not be confused with mere moralizing: a superficial judgment based on erroneous perception and insufficient understanding, precisely because it fails to truly "contemplate" and deliberate the ultimate teleological significance of what is going on. Hence, instead of moralizing, McLuhan first utilizes "probing" as an exercise that breaks the spell of mindless mediation. Only then can the discipline of unbiased attending be cultivated to enable intelligent consideration, objective judgment and finally, truly creative, moral action.

[26] See McLuhan, *Understanding Media*, chapter 4, "The Gadget Lover: Narcissus as Narcosis." Contra Freud, McLuhan argues that the root of Narcissus' pathology was not to fall in love with himself, but to not realize that the image he became obsessed with was merely a reflection (or extension) of himself and not of another. Likewise, we do not fully appreciate how our tools are part of us, an extension of our physical and psychic presence in the world.

[27] Analogous to the Aristotelian four causes that seek to explain the 'why' of things, and to the medieval four senses of scripture that seek to ponder the multiple hidden meanings of a text, the four laws of media are a retrieval of the ancient art of *grammatica* as the art of interpreting all phenomena. See McLuhan and McLuhan, *The Laws of Media*, 215-39.

[28] As he explained in his 1971 letter to Edward T. Hall, Marshall McLuhan notes "The user of the electric light—or a hammer, or a language, or a book—is the content. As such, there is a total metamorphosis of the user by the interface. It is the metamorphosis that I consider the message." In *Letters of Marshall McLuhan*, eds. Matie Molinaro, Corinne McLuhan and William Toye (New York: Oxford University Press, 1987), 397.

while the four laws of media alert us to a myriad of probable technological effects, the effects themselves take time to emerge to an extent significant enough as to radically change culture.[29] That is, the laws have both diagnostic (what is going on) and prognostic (what will continue to happen) value. This implies that they enrich our understanding not only of current hidden imaginaries and presuppositions, but of emerging ones as well. In this way, they open the possibility for human intelligent "ordering" and responsible cultural transformation.

The McLuhans formulated the four probes/questions thus:[30]

1. What does the medium enhance?
2. What does the medium obsolesce?
3. What does the medium retrieve that had been obsolesced earlier?
4. What does the medium flip into when pushed to extremes?

If we apply the four laws to today's electronic and digital technologies, it becomes immediately evident why the emerging culture is obsolescing modernity as typographic hyperliteracy that emphasized atomization and linear causality. Electronic and digital technologies accelerate ubiquitous connectivity and pervasive proximity, recreating a "global," but nonetheless "village"-like interaction.[31] What is novel about this face-to-face way of interacting, however, is that it is divorced from the persons' flesh or physical presence. The thrust of communication technologies since the telegraph has been to improve real time connectivity to retrieve the immediacy of speech as paradigmatic human communication/communing experience. However, while new technologies enable real time exchange of thoughts and experiences, even of mutual hearing and seeing, their net effect is to create an alter or "virtual" environment for the mutual encounter of "souls," more than, properly speaking, of embodied selves. Essentially, we have succeeded in creating an alternate reality through tools that extend our ears, eyes, skin and thoughts/memories beyond the immediate personal body or context.

---

[29] Interestingly however, Marshall McLuhan stresses how "Unlike previous environmental changes, the electric media constitutes a total and near-instantaneous transformation of culture, values and attitudes." In Eric Norden, "A Candid Conversation with the High Priest of Popcult and Metaphysician of Media," *Playboy Magazine* (March 1969): 26-7, 45, 55-6, 61, 63.

[30] McLuhan and McLuhan, *The Laws of Media*, 227-8.

[31] Hence, why McLuhan coined the now iconic phrase "global village," to stress that in the electric age, human interaction is not only increasingly global, but also retrieving tribe-like dynamics that undermine modern individualism. Interestingly, later on in his career, he substituted the phrase for "global theatre," to stress how all human beings are active agents in a global web-like relationality. See Marshall McLuhan, "At the moment of Sputnik the planet became a global theater in which there are no spectators but only actors," *Journal of Communication* 24, no. 1 (1974): 48-58.

Of course, this experience has been nothing short of magical and in many ways reminiscent of the realm of the intangible "sacred" that the "great disembedding"[32] of secularity profoundly denied. Hence, it is not surprising that the Internet as infrastructure and the Web as mode of distributing/accessing data—especially Web 2.0 that prioritizes interaction and digital presence—is experienced as exciting and even awe-inspiring. In many ways, digital technologies not only retrieve the sense of an altered, even "spiritual" reality traditionally associated with the sacred, but also make me and those with whom I interact virtually other-worldly. Online we are all new beings, quite literally, spiritual beings. And just like other watershed technologies in human evolution, this new inebriating experience of innovation, creative opportunities, and extraordinary power makes us more likely to succumb to the quintessential hubris of believing that we are "god-like" or even "gods."[33]

We are now in a new phase of this novel way of being together, as reversal effects become more palpable and the true form of the foundational medium starts emerging. The form of the medium emerges precisely through its effects on the toolmaker, who increasingly takes on the likeness of the tools made.[34] In particular, humanity and everything that surrounds us mimic, or takes on the form of, electricity itself and its primordial language of presence/absence, on/off, wave/particle. This language is translated most paradigmatically in digital technologies that speak a universal language of zeros and ones. Image, sound, 3D shapes, heat, pressure, or any other happening that can be captured through our senses (or myriad technological extensions thereof) is translated and recorded in the same binary form—making each kind of information communicable, and indeed even mutually translatable, into the other. Quite literally, all reality, whether physical or virtual—the distinction does not hold anymore—is increasingly understood as communicating "information" that can be read, analyzed, and even reconfigured as we deem fit. This is evident in the "internet of things" that allows homes, neighborhoods, towns, and cities to be read, responded to, and altered intelligently. Likewise, the "semantic web" allows for the reconstruction of our very experience of the world through customized information access. "Things" become "code," just

32 Taylor, *A Secular Age*, 146-58.

33 Marshall McLuhan interprets scriptural narratives like the Tower of Babel as repeating the original sin of Eden, but this time mediated by delusions of grandeur stemming from new technological achievements. See *Understanding Media*, 114.

34 "We become what we behold. We make our tools and our tools shape us." While this anecdote is often attributed to Marshall McLuhan, it is actually not found in any of his published writings. Rather it is found in an article that John Culkin, S.J., a Professor of Communications and close friend of McLuhan's wrote about his friend. John M. Culkin, "A schoolman's guide to Marshall McLuhan," *Saturday Review* (March 18, 1967): 51-3, 71-2.

as intelligent design, not only of experiences or "software," but of matter or "hardware" (as epitomized in 3D printing, whether on physical or biological substrata), implies that "code" makes "things"—or even living beings.

As the distinction between physical and virtual, actual and potential, matter and form is progressively dissolved, so humanity's very essence is increasingly perceived as, and mediated through, this foundational new language and *ratio* for digital culture: the "information code."[35] In their contemporary form of code, "words" are making a comeback as generative principle: a retrieval of the Stoic *logos spermatikos* that presupposes that all reality is inherently meaningful and emerging. In turn, we increasingly utter who we are as human beings, not just through speech or the sharing of ideas, but through our "making." From engineering matter, to engineering genes, to engineering selves and everything in between, configuring, crafting and "making" become the quintessential expressions of being human.

"Skillful making," *techne*, and not just "reasonable uttering," *logos*, is the mark of participation in a global theatre, where we all are encouraged to become, in Pope Paul VI's evocative phrase, "artisans of [our] destiny."[36] Just like in classical and medieval literacy, rhetoric transformed the art of memorable sayings and songs retrieved from an oral age, so in a digital age artisanry is retrieving (and transforming) the mechanization impulse of the typographic age. Yet, if wisdom demands that we carefully distinguish between sophistry and oratory—with the latter, according to Cicero and Quintilian, being the mark of the good, virtuous man[37]—so must we be able to distinguish between mere making and truly reasonable creating that produces the fruit of true technology analogous to the truthful, beautiful words that "teach, delight and move."

A THEO-ANTHROPOLOGY OF *TECHNE*

The emerging digital imaginary of "information" prioritizes code over matter, assuming that the same information can inhere unchanged in multiple physical substrata. For the emerging digital culture, it seems to matter not whether I read a paperback or an ebook, chat with my best friend online or in person, or indeed whether I reveal who I am most profoundly through my physical presence, virtual avatars, or

---

[35] For a very detailed historical study of the rise of information as cultural imaginary see, James Gleick, *The Information: A History, A Theory, A Flood* (New York: Pantheon, 2011).

[36] Pope Paul VI, Encyclical on the Development of Peoples, *Populorum Progressio* (March 26, 1967), no. 65, www.vatican.va/holy_father/paul_vi/encyclicals/-documents/hf_p-vi_enc_26031967_populorum_en.html

[37] Cicero's ideal in *De Oratore* of the *doctus orator*, the "learned orator" is further idealized in Quintilian as the *vir bonus dicendi peritus*, "a *good* man skilled in the art of speaking." See McLuhan, *Classical Trivium*, 71.

even digital footprint. In the iconic words of the father of cybernetics, mathematician Norbert Weiner, "Information is information, not matter or energy."[38] In contrast, while the traditional Thomistic understanding of natural law also appreciates that the human is both body and soul-reason, it resolutely does not separate them. Rather, in line with traditional Christian teaching that lauds the goodness of the flesh, the human is understood properly as an enfleshed spirit. Thus, natural law as participation in eternal law is expressed through our own distinctly human inclinations that are both bodily and spiritual. In continuity with the order of enfleshed beings, the human is a physical substance that desires to maintain its integrity, and the human is an animal that desires to propagate itself. At the same time, what makes the human *imago Dei* is precisely the quintessential human characteristic to transcend our bodily reality through being reasonable.[39] Hence, while the soul-reason might be the form of the human, nonetheless as enfleshed spirits, our ultimate beatitude is participation in Christ's own resurrection in the flesh through our own particular resurrected bodies.

Moreover, as the *Catechism of the Catholic Church* puts it, this spiritual-bodily finality does not just include human individual embodiment, but also the transformation of the cosmos as a whole:

> At the end of time, the Kingdom of God will come in its fullness. After the universal judgment, the righteous will reign forever with Christ, glorified in body and soul. *The universe itself will be renewed. ... Revelation affirms the profound common destiny of the material world and man* (nos. 1042, 1046, my emphasis).[40]

The common destiny of world and human implies that, as condensed in such scriptural metaphors as the "new heaven and new earth" (2 Pet 3:13; Rev 21:1) or "the holy city, the new Jerusalem" (Rev 21:2), ultimate human fulfillment in a renewed creation includes the "universal resurrection that synthesizes and really restores one humanity *as the subject of the achievements of history*, although in a different dimension of being."[41]

Our eschatological hope marries God's eternal plan for the fulfillment of creation with human and divine interventions in history, that is, with God's perfecting of the fruit of humanity's labor as a proper divine-human co-creation. As *Gaudium et spes* notes:

---

[38] Norbert Wiener, *Cybernetics: Or the Control and Communication in the Animal and the Machine*, 2nd ed. (MIT Press, 1961), 132.

[39] Thomas Aquinas, *Summa Theologiae*, trans. Fathers of the English Dominican Province (2nd and rev. ed., 1920), I-II, qq. 90-108.

[40] *Catechism of the Catholic Church* (Libreria Editrice Vaticana, 1993), www.vatican.va/archive/ENG0015/_INDEX.HTM.

[41] Sergius Bulgakov, *The Bride of the Lamb*, trans. Boris Jakim (Eerdmans, 2002), 344 (my emphasis).

> Far from diminishing our concern to develop this earth, the expectancy of a new earth should spur us on, for it is here that the body of a new human family grows, foreshadowing in some way the age which is to come. That is why, although we must be careful to distinguish earthly progress clearly from the increase of the kingdom of Christ, *such progress is of vital concern to the kingdom of God*, insofar as it can contribute to the better ordering of human society (no. 39, my emphasis).

It follows that if human craftsmanship and technological accomplishments not only have the potential to contribute to the human search for truth and the "better ordering of human society" in history, but also to "foreshadow" the eschatological age, then the question of ultimate human beatitude should have as its foundation, not just what it means for humanity to desire God in Godself or to live as human communion in imitation of God's *koinonia*, but also how humanity is called to being co-creators through our technological prowess.

This implies a robust theo-anthropological reflection, not only on the human created *imago Dei* to "have dominion" over the earth and its creatures (Gen 1:28) and "to till [the Garden of Eden] and keep it" (Gen 2:15), but also on the fallen human, the human banished from Eden, but nonetheless divinely "clothed" with "garments of skins" (Gen 3:21) who becomes a city dweller (cf. Gen 4:17) and a maker of tools. Just as the ecclesial tradition of moral and spiritual reflection has contemplated what it means to become holy through becoming wise and virtuous so, in our digital age of technological tinkering and radical ecological re-configuration, the church needs to consider seriously what it means to desire holiness through contributing as artisans to the making of a more integral creation. Thus, a theo-anthropology of *techne* becomes necessary for a Christian retrieval of natural law that takes seriously the contemporary cultural imaginary of information relying on the tinkering of *techne*.

This exercise, however, is not as simple as it sounds, since our infatuation with "technology" and practical making is relatively recent in the western intellectual tradition. Consequently, in the long history of philosophical and theological reflection, considerations of *techne* have been sparse. From the Athenian philosophers to the high middle ages, *techne* was considered with ambivalence, in particular because of its dependence on the "baseness" of material reality.[42] The great philosophers, from Plato and Aristotle to the Stoics, still recognized the reasonability of *techne*, precisely by interpreting it as a form of knowledge (*episteme*) beyond mere experience (*empeiria*), since the craftsman can give a rational account of the method behind the making

42 Joshua Lollar, "*Pathos* and *Technê* in St Maximus the Confessor," in *Knowing the Purpose of Creation through the Resurrection*, ed. Maxim Vasiljevic (Alhambra, CA: Sebastian Press, 2013), 223-38.

and even teach his or her craft.[43] The Stoics, in their account of the unity of the soul and overarching emphasis on conformity to the cosmological Logos, go a step further, characterizing virtue itself (*arête*) as a form of *techne*: the ability to apply to concrete situations knowledge of human nature and therefore, to actuate reasonable deeds. Indeed, Cicero famously describes prudence as the "art" of living well (*vivendi ars est prudentia*). Yet in Plotinus, the immediate philosophical precursor of the fourth century Church Fathers immersed in Neoplatonism, *techne* is mostly dismissed, since the contemplation of things giving rise to the rational principle is in itself deemed to be creative. Artists and craftsmen merely produce copies of things, even if Plotinus acknowledges that they are still responsible for the beauty of the objects they make through giving them form.[44]

The Christian tradition inherited this ambiguity and even found justification for it in the Scriptures. Paradigmatic narratives like the building of the tower of Babel "to make a name for ourselves" (Gen 11:1-9) or even the fascinating point raised by Genesis that the children of Cain, murderer of his brother, were the first city dwellers, tool makers, artisans, and musicians (Gen 4:17-22), can be contrasted with how craftsmanship under the guidance of God saved Noah and the remnants of creation from the deluge (Gen 6:9-22) and how God himself "called by name" and filled "with divine Spirit" master craftsmen to build the ark of the covenant and fashion all necessary materials for the proper worship of God (Exod 31:1-11). The Scriptures give us the most pivotal key to interpret the theo-anthropological status of *techne*: *techne* under God's rule saves and glorifies the world, but *techne* that is fruit of human *hubris* is disordered and leads to death.

The fourth century Cappadocians offered an initial theological exposition of this inherent ambiguity of *techne* through their interpretation of the "garments of skin" with which God clothed the first man and woman after the fall (Gen 3:21).[45] The theology of the "garments

---

[43] As Aristotle puts it: "there is no craft [*techne*] that is not a state involving reason concerned with production [*meta logou poiētikē*], and no such state that is not a craft. Hence a craft is the same as a state involving true reason concerned with production [*meta logou alēthous poiētikē*]" (*Nicomachean Ethics* VI, 3.3). Quoted from Michael L. Morgan, ed., *Classics of Moral and Political Theory*, 5th ed. (Indianapolis: Hackett Publishing, 2011), 309.

[44] Richard Parry, "*Episteme* and *Techne*," in *Stanford Encyclopedia of Philosophy* (Fall 2014), http://plato.stanford.edu/entries/episteme-techne/.

[45] See: Gregory of Nyssa, *Life of Moses*, trans. Abraham Malherbe (Paulist Press, 1978) and *On the Making of Man*, 7, www.ccel.org/ccel/schaff/npnf205.x.ii.-ii.viii.html; St. Basil the Great, "Question 55" in "The Long Rules," *St. Basil: Ascetical Works*, trans. M. Monica Wagner (Catholic University of America Press, 1962), 330-7 and *On the Human* Condition, trans. Nonna Verna Harrison (Crestwood, NY: St Vladimir's Seminary Press, 2005); and Gregory the Theologian (of Nazianzus), Oration 45 "The Second Oration on Easter," 8, www.ccel.org/ccel/schaff/npnf207.iii.-

of skin," that serves as counterpart to the other theo-anthropological themes of the theology of Christ as Archetype of humanity and the Genesis metaphor of being created in the "image and likeness of God," reflects on human nature, not as originally intended by the Creator, but as corrupted by sin. Most crucially, while the "garments" of *pathos* and *techne* are a mark of human nature's mortality and corruption that blemishes creation, at the same time, they are also a sign of God's infinite divine mercy and his desire to offer us a pedagogy for our conversion.

Maximus the Confessor develops further this theology of the "garments of skin," in particular when it comes to reflecting on *techne* as postlapsarian anthropological reality. His commentary in *Ambiguum* 45 on Gregory the Theologian's understanding of Adam as created *atechnos* offers a robust foundation to consider *techne* both as mark of sin and as gift for humanity, and therefore to distinguish morally between true *techne* that accomplishes beauty and mere making that perpetuates the fall's disorder in creation.[46] This reflection on *techne* must also be read in conjunction with the long ecclesial monastic and natural law tradition of reflecting on *pathos*, since for Maximus it is evident that *techne* is a gift offered both in response to, and certainly in conjunction with, *pathos*.

In *Ambiguum* 45, Maximus offers three "contemplations" or interpretations of Gregory's famous verse in the oration *On Pascha*: "He (i.e., Adam) was naked in his simplicity and in a life devoid of artifice, and without any kind of covering or barrier. For such was fitting for the primal man." In each contemplation, Maximus reflects on how *techne* is a response to a specific postlapsarian reality of brokenness and need.

---

xxvii.html and Oration 38 "On the Theophany," (also known as "Birthday of Christ"), 12, www.ccel.org/ccel/schaff/-npnf207.iii.xxi.html.

More recently Orthodox theologians like Sergius Bulgakov, (in particular in his *The Bride of the Lamb*, Sections II "The Church, History and the Afterlife", 253-378 and Section III "Eschatology", 379-526), Panayiotis Nellas, *Deification in Christ: The Nature of the Human Person*, trans. Norman Russell (Crestwood, NY: St. Vladimir's Seminary Press, 1987) and Nikos A. Nissiotis, "Secular and Christian Images of Human Person" *Theologia* 33 (1962): 947-89; *Theologia* 34 (1963): 90-122, have also offered theologoumena on *techne* as part of their theo-anthropologies. As Nellas explains, a theological reflection on "the natural state of man," and therefore on how the human created *imago Dei* is, according to the Fathers, in a state of *apatheia* and *atechnos*, "without artifice", cannot suffice, for: "It does not provide a complete answer, since experience proves that the historical reality of man is different from that which we have seen to be defined by the phrase 'in the image.' In the Christian perception of things this is to be ascribed to the fact that the historical reality develops within the unnatural situation in which man has found himself since the fall" (43).

[46] Maximus the Confessor, *The Ambigua: On Difficulties in the Church Fathers*, vols. 1 and 2, ed. and trans. Nicholas Constas (Cambridge, MA: Harvard University Press, 2014). *Ambiguum* 45 is in the second volume, 192-201.

In the first contemplation, Maximus stresses the close relation between *techne* and *pathos*, since it is precisely because the original human possessed *apatheia*, dispassion, that he had no need for artifacts. As the original humans lived in perfect harmony with their environment, they experienced no bodily needs and desires and, thus, felt no necessity to make artificial things that would mediate between the human body and a harsh environment to make it better suited to their needs and better molded to conform to their desires. *Techne* is thus a gift that enables survival in the new creaturely reality of necessity and even makes possible human thriving as a measured, intelligent response to ordered desires. This is what the dawn of culture and civilization (ideally) reflects and why civilization itself is understood as a sign of progress.

The second contemplation takes it a step further. Before the fall, it was not just human bodily reality that was in perfect harmony with its environment. The human spirit was also perfectly ordered by focusing all its energy for becoming on its ultimate finality: God in Godself. It is this "unconditioned motion" of love to God that ordered human relationality in all its aspects: in the relationship between human persons and through Adam and Eve's harmony with the rest of the divinely created environment. This harmony was so complete that man and woman experienced, not only no physical needs, but also no intellectual curiosities, since Adam was endowed with the original gift of knowing reality wholly and perfectly. Thus, he was able to name all creatures (cf. Gen 2: 20-22), including his own companion whom he recognized as exactly like him, "bone of my bones and flesh of my flesh" (Gen 2: 23), and to "till and keep" the Garden of Eden with ease (Gen 2:15; cf. Gen 1:28-30). Responsible stewardship, rather than making was the mark of the original human.

Yet, the fallen humans who experience bodily and spiritual needs, not only utilize *techne* for their survival and to thrive in a harsh reality. *Techne* itself often becomes a response to disordered desire and, as the insights of the media ecology tradition perfectly illustrate, can even perpetuate disordered desire through shaping our sensibilities. This is what Maximus implies when he says that the human can be driven not only by "irrational fantasies of passions," but also by being "*engrossed* in the principles of technical skills" or by "investigating natural principles derived from the law of nature in order to acquire knowledge." While the exercise of reason, in both its speculative and technical dimensions, is a gift, nonetheless it requires the ordering that comes through practical reason to be in service of the truly good, and thus to glimpse truth with authenticity and to create beauty with integrity. Indeed, as the Christian tradition illustrates, it requires even more than practical reason, since it is only through eyes opened by the Holy Spirit, and thus through the infused theological virtues of faith, hope and love, that the human can arrive to true knowledge of reality as revelatory of the Creator and therefore, fulfill in perfect harmony their role as co-creators with God.

Put *in nuce*, in a postlapsarian reality, *techne* must be ordered through a patient pedagogy to acquire and be open to receive infused virtues. On the contrary, as Maximus notes in his final contemplation, the original human had no need for a pedagogy to acquire virtues, because they were already perfectly and naturally virtuous: their will to growth to their finality in the likeness of Christ as the God-human was perfectly animated by the Spirit of God within them. Hence, the divine ordering of creation, the eternal law, including the ordering of their very nature, was perfectly self-evident to the original human, and thus their living was marked by profound harmony with all there is.

Yet, it is precisely the sin of disobedience, the mark of breakdown in the human's ordering of his nature to its absolute finality in God, that disrupts this connaturality and introduces confusion, not only in human nature, but in the created realm as a whole. As microcosm of the created macrocosm, humanity's distance from God is manifested in the vices of ignorance, pride and violence, that is, in their "original sin" that accentuates chaos in the created realm itself. As human *logos* is disordered through shifting its attention away from Logos, as the fallen Adam is now unable to rule his passions or to know reality as it is, he is also unable to steward creation to bring it to its fulfillment. Thus, Maximus illustrates perfectly how an obfuscated natural law requires not only the right ordering of the passions, but also the right ordering of *techne*.

In fact, according to Maximus, postlapsarian reality is properly speaking a "technical" reality, where the human is by necessity an artificer of "extensions" for their bodily and spiritual faculties. As the human is gifted by a greater awareness of their frailty, both bodily and spiritual, so they compensate for their nakedness through making "tools" that mediate and transform their experience and knowledge of the rest of creation. Through artifacts, they seek to fulfill not only their bodily and spiritual desires, but also to accomplish their original destiny of being microcosm, and thus to bring all of creation to reflect the splendor of the nature of God.

Maximus' three contemplations on Gregory's *atechnos*, unpack the crucial difference between original human nature and the postlapsarian condition that corrupted our nature, while not radically depraving it. Even if the Son-made-flesh brings absolute salvation and restores creation's potential for receiving grace, until the *eschaton*, the heavy garments of *pathos* and *techne* remain essential means for fulfilling our destiny as microcosm to return the macrocosm—all of creation—to God. If the passions are the subjective dimension of how the human seeks to survive and to thrive in their new harsh environment, their technologies are the permanent, objective, mark of their efforts to cultivate the cosmos to become a resplendent mediation of God. Human artifacts constantly seek to fix what appears broken, to facilitate what seems difficult, to beautify what is perceived as ugly, to make existence on earth more favorable to life and to flourishing in authentically human relationships.

Yet this ongoing effort to technologize, to create artifacts that mediate a more "human" existence, are completely dependent on what the human perceives to be their, and creation's, ultimate good. In their original state, human beings "had nothing mediating God—mediation [according to Maximus] being the ultimate motion of the contemplation of nature."[47] But in their postlapsarian reality, the body itself burdened by the passions is the foundational—and decisive—mediator and veil to the divine. Analogously, *techne* as extensions of the body, can both thicken the mist the separates us from God, as well as allow rare glimpses of the divine. Indeed, it is precisely this fundamental distinction—between *techne* as mediating divine reality and *techne* as obscuring further divine reality—that needs to ground our moral reflection on human creativity and its fruits.

Techne and Natural law reflection in a Digital Age

In Maximus' three contemplations, three nuances of *techne* emerge: as a means to fulfill all our desires; as necessary for tending the earth to its finality; and as a key mode of human reasoning in our postlapsarian—but saved in Christ—world. It is also evident that as a means to fulfill our desires and to accomplish our purpose as co-creators, *techne* is in itself desirable, in itself a good. Indeed, as an essential human good, it can also distract us from our ultimate Good. In particular in its promise of progress, of crafting a better way of life, *techne* can seem to be an end in itself instead of a means. This is, in fact, the predicament of the emerging "information" imaginary, where coding, crafting and experimenting become ends in themselves. The world becomes like a giant *Lego* with humans being its playful engineers. However, the Christian tradition reminds that *techne* is not merely procedural know-how and thus the key to playful tinkering, but also crucial to ultimate human and creaturely becoming. Hence, it is imperative that *techne* be morally evaluated and directed through right reasoning (*recta ratio*) illumined by grace.

Maximus' three ways of understanding *techne* could be appropriated within the Thomistic framework of Christian natural law reflection, precisely to offer a robust method for evaluating *techne* morally. His three insights could be presented thus: as the response to *pathos* and thus as oriented to fulfilling in a harsh world all human inclinations, bodily and intellectual; as the virtue of rightly ordered, and not merely efficient, human making; and lastly, as demanding a fuller con-

[47] Lollar, "*Pathos* and *Technê* in St Maximus the Confessor."

ception of practical wisdom that considers the cosmological responsibility of tending creation. This would also offer a corrective to today's tendency to equate *techne* itself with human reasoning.

Techne as fulfilling human inclinations

In his first contemplation, Maximus stresses how as a postlapsarian "garment of skins," *techne* is a concrete response to human *pathos* in all its forms. If the human desires life over death, then the human creates multiple means to safeguard life in the harshest of circumstances. From clothing to architecture, to farming and techniques of division of labor, to medicine and all the other arts that enable a better quality of life, the human attempts to cheat death, live long and prosper. Likewise, humanity applies its craftsmanship, from techniques of communication, to the arts of teaching and learning, to propagate the species and its opportunities for thriving. In our days, this also includes the many technologies that facilitate (or limit) human reproduction itself. All this implies the human thirst for knowing the truth about reality, which the human also seeks to discover through devising tools, arts and techniques that extend their senses and reasoning abilities for a more accurate grasp of the secrets of the cosmos. And if the human as social animal desires to live in communion, then their technological masterpieces are precisely centered on creating "society" itself: a whole "artificial" environment mediated through human artifacts that cultivates culture and civilization. Even the desire for transcendence is technologically mediated: whether for the worship of the divine or in the search for the spiritual, the arts of beauty that transcend the human spirit, imply and respond to the quintessential human orientation to know God even in a postlapsarian existence.

Yet, as it seeks to actualize human desires and potential through extending human faculties, *techne* must be properly disciplined in the same way *pathos* or desire itself is disciplined through reason. Thus, just as in the Thomistic natural law schema, practical reason determines which actions respond rightly to human inclinations—that is temperately, courageously and justly, following the principle of the mean—and thus reason demands the inculcation of such "good" actions over less desirable ones, so *techne* and the artifacts it produces can be judged on whether they are a reasonable response to human needs and desires and, if judged to be so, selectively chosen to propagate more "human" lifestyles and cultures. In this sense, if technological prowess externalizes and concretizes our intelligence in artifacts to quite literally "humanize" the world, prudence determines what artifacts are truly worth making and what crafts are to be reasonably pursued because they are truly reflective of human dignity. The criterion for judging the legitimacy of *techne* would thus be human nature itself as it flourishes in an environment of its own making: civilization.

Hence, the ordering of *techne* according to natural inclinations opens the possibility for conceiving of "making" as a key aspect of "acting". In the same way we can prudentially judge if an action is intrinsically evil, good, or—as is often the case—a complex amalgam of human impure desires and more or less fitting deeds to fulfill those intentionalities, so distinct artifacts and procedures could be judged as legitimately fulfilling human desires or as perpetuating disordered desires. If *pathos* accentuates our perception of brokenness and, in its disordered expression, binds us more tightly to the flesh, so *techne* can be the expression of disordered desire that perpetuates it: not only as a learned, inculcated behavior, but as a behavior extended and accentuated precisely through the tool that enables it. Hence, just as prudence must determine what is reasonable making in view of the human and creation's finality, it must also determine how disordered desire that makes artifacts to satisfy multiple human inclinations, is in itself perpetuated through those very same artifacts. This is because, as the material and enduring expressions of human desires—ordered or not—artifacts remain as permanent marks on our environment creating multiple complex ecological effects. Hence, a proper "ecological" prudence, or a prudence that considers the present and future well-being of the global environment is necessary, in particular for the more drastic technological innovations possible today.

Techne as intellectual virtue ordered to the New Creation

From the above it is evident that, as an intellectual virtue, *techne* is both a form of knowledge like *episteme*, but also practical in its orientation, like *phronesis*. The pivotal difference between *phronesis* and *techne* however, is that if in determining right action, *phronesis* effectively shapes the actor into a prudent person, what *techne* accomplishes, its product, has usually been perceived as external to the artisan or technician. Yet what the media ecology tradition implies, what Maximus seems to confirm, and what is evident if *techne* does not only respond to desires but in itself perpetuates desires, is that this distinction is not as clear-cut as it immediately appears. For if human products are properly "extensions" of the body, then, not only do they recreate the milieu through which men and women are called to fulfill their destiny, but like all actions, they also re-create the human himself and herself.

Thus, the reasonability of *techne* is not simply a matter of method and efficient causality. It must also be considered from the point-of-view of its finality, that is, through the inherent intelligibility and beauty of what it makes—ultimately the re-creation of the human and the cosmos itself. In this latter sense, *techne* is less like *episteme*, knowledge or know-how, and more like *phronesis*, practical wisdom. For just as practical reason always deals with the particular circumstance, but in view of ultimate human flourishing, so making the right individual "extensions" of the human must be understood as contributing to overall cultural and cosmic flourishing.

After all, it is conceivable to be very skillful at surgically cutting the human body and to apply that skill, not in a hospital theatre, but to traffic human organs. Based on his or her skill, is that person properly speaking a "surgeon"? Or do they, notwithstanding their procedural know-how, betray the craft of surgery as a form of medicine precisely through producing horror rather than health? It is likewise possible to be perfectly knowledgeable of the art of manipulating the properties of chemicals and to use that skill to create addictive recreational drugs rather than medicine. Yet on which criterion is one to be properly called a "pharmacist"? Based on mere skill, or also on the right application of that skill to produce healing products? And if one is to take the analogy with moral reasoning a step further, how, indeed, are the products themselves to be judged as "good"? Based on the quality of material or skill put into producing them? Or based on their form and purpose—their desirable "humanizing" effects on the created *oikos*?

In this regard, the desire to create can be properly understood within a natural law framework as a crucial, properly human inclination, analogous to our intellectual inclination to seek knowledge about ultimate reality and our personalist orientation that desires relationship with the other. It would then follow, that if knowledge seeks ultimate truth and relationship delights in the goodness of the absolute other, so *techne* is the intellectual virtue that accomplishes things, not merely efficiently, but with elegance that makes more resplendent creation's inherent beauty.

Moreover, just as in a postlapsarian world our human capabilities must be perfected through grace and the theological virtues, in the same way that our knowledge of truth must be perfected through the supranatural virtue of faith and justice through the supranatural virtue of love, so *techne* would necessitate hope that God's world is being reborn as the New Creation. More specifically, the Holy Spirit's gifts of knowledge, piety and fear of the Lord, would inspire proper awareness of reality as, first and foremost, God's creation and thus, reverence for creation itself as God's work. In this sense, awe, respect and humility would transcend human technological prowess as ultimately serving, not human needs and desires, but God's very commandment to participate as co-creators in his project of rebirthing creation. The *Logos* as artificer of creation would be properly considered as the Master Craftsman, the Teacher, who honors humanity as beloved apprentice or disciple in their artisanry of the cosmos.

Techne demanding a new human who reasons "cosmologically"

An understanding of *techne* rightly ordered to the New Creation and perfected through grace, makes glaringly obvious the perversity of the technological or "efficient" mindset that emerges in modernity to dethrone "dialogue" or discursive reasoning oriented to wisdom.[48] Even more aberrantly, the emerging "information" mindset eradicates the very boundaries between knowing, making and becoming: all knowing is today a potential (re)making, since knowing itself is purely for the sake of "manipulating." Yet this raises the more fundamental question of how to properly consider the "reasonable" human being, indeed of what "reason," human "dignity" and human "nature" actually are. As we are navigating in novel cultural imaginaries, that are re-forming notions of human cognition and intelligence, of ontology and even ultimacy—the three building blocks of natural law reflection from the Greeks to modernity—then the retrieval of natural law in the Church today must also confront these fundamental biases of the emerging culture and offer a strong corrective.

Natural law reasoning—or reasoning that is inherently teleological and analogical, seeking to conform human becoming to ultimate desirable standards of being—is in itself a radical challenge to the assumption of the human as merely *Homo faber*. In fact, reason as *phronesis* ordering reason as *techne* retrieves *Homo sapiens*, the "wise" human being, who is properly desirous of the ultimate good, ultimate truth and ultimate beauty—of Being itself. Without this teleological foundation, on which the Christian natural law tradition is properly founded, *techne* can become the primary expression of *hubris*, especially in our times where our technological prowess is way more advanced that our ability to reason morally in face of much complex novelty.

Hence, natural law reasoning must not only appropriate *techne* and order it teleologically. It must also be augmented in its specifics to consider secondary and tertiary principles of acting and crafting that speak to contemporary reality. Moreover, a retrieval of natural law as *recta ratio* that takes *techne* seriously, must also consider how the understanding of our natural inclinations is in itself being transformed through our technological prowess.

For instance, the fundamental inclination to existence changes its meaning when what is perceived to exist is increasingly both physical and virtual, both actual and potential, with the lines increasingly blurring between the two. Hence, why new phenomena like identity theft and cyber bullying are today considered to be acts of violence as serious as their physical equivalents. Similarly, the inclination to perpetuating the species through reproduction and parenting changes its meaning when technology is increasingly dictating *bios* through "creating life" and redefining death. For instance, the very meaning of motherhood and fatherhood as gender-specific identities and biological phenomena is stretched to its limits when practices like in-vitro

[48] See Walter J. Ong, *Ramus: Method and the Decay of Dialogue* (Chicago: University of Chicago Press, 2005).

fertilization, surrogacy, and donor eggs and sperm become increasingly the norm. And of course, the desire for knowledge and for communing can be experienced and fulfilled in radically novel ways in an environment where the entire ecology is of interconnected minds and intelligent machines that can read all of reality as pregnant with "information."

These considerations—very simplistic when considering the immense possibilities for change that new technologies are constantly inviting us to experiment with—highlight how it is our very self-understanding and the world itself that have changed—changes that are not going to be simply erased or annihilated, but that demand that they be prudently directed to reflect more authentic flourishing. Thus, it becomes poignantly obvious that while a personal and social ethic remain necessary—albeit altered to reflect emerging understandings of personhood and relationality—they are also increasingly not sufficient. If as humanity, as one global culture, we are to order complex ecological changes effected through human (and possibly even non-human) agency and manipulation, natural law reasoning must be more profoundly cosmological. This implies, that natural law must consider as much as possible, the "total ecology" in view of its finality as New Creation, but also our human obligation to steward the flourishing of creation in all its rich, inter-dependent diversity.

The final word can perhaps be left to Maximus the Confessor, who in his own understanding of virtuous human becoming ordered through natural law offers this succinct summary of authentic human formation, that when illuminated by the Holy Spirit is a true human divinization:

> Thus it cannot be doubted that those who, by means of a philosophical principle, wish to raise themselves up from the forefather's fall, begin by completely negating the passions, after which they cease busying themselves with the principles of technical skills, and finally, peering beyond natural contemplation, they catch a glimpse of immaterial knowledge, which has absolutely no form susceptible to sense perception or any meaning that can be contained by spoken words. Then, just as God in the beginning created the first man, they too will be naked in the simplicity of their knowledge, in their life free of distractions, and in their mortification of the law of the flesh (*Ambiguum* 45).

Conclusion

We are living in strange times marked by a crisis of truth, a truncated sense of freedom, at the same time that we are being faced by radically new technological challenges that raise profound moral dilemmas. Throughout I have suggested that a retrieval of natural law would be particularly valuable in our times, in particular if, as *recta ratio*, it offers a corrective to the emerging cultural imaginary of "information" where all "knowing" is potentially a "making" (or "remaking") but that has no objective ground for considering whether it actually fulfills or approximates authentic human "becoming." Paradoxically, a culture of "coding" is perhaps in a better position to appreciate the necessity for "pattern recognition" and thus for discerning, once again, intelligibility in human "nature" and in the creaturely realm itself. Perhaps, the emerging hope in a culture of "making" is precisely a re-appreciation for the whole—the final "product"—that is larger than the method or materials that brought it into being. In this sense, a greater appreciation for "making" as part of natural law reflection could actually enhance the possibility of retrieving practical wisdom, and thus, for re-grounding moral reflection in authentic human and creaturely becoming.

Yet, from a Christian perspective, human becoming is always mediated through divine grace to actualize a finality that is ultimately in God himself. Thus, a properly Christian retrieval of natural law reflection must necessarily be theo-anthropological, considering not only human original creation, but also human becoming in a broken postlapsarian existence. In fact, as the Christian tradition has been teaching, *techne* itself is a divine gift of mercy to assist our flourishing even in the harshness of broken reality. It is the concrete application of our human intelligence taking flesh in the things we make to extend our governance of the world. Hence, precisely because of the responsibility of such governance, *techne* itself must be guided by wisdom; *techne* itself must be ordered by the divine intelligibility of the cosmos that makes it properly God's creation. It is this consideration that must order our human becoming in a digital world where brokenness is increasingly a "random" making, an experimental "playing God" with little consideration for cosmic flourishing. M

Journal of Moral Theology, Vol. 4, No. 1 (2015): 25-35

Faith in the Church of Facebook

Matthew John Paul Tan

THIS ARTICLE WILL INVESTIGATE THE IMPACT of Facebook's timeline format and the implications of having the church traverse through this format, given Facebook's current status as an indispensable point of dissemination of all manner of information. More specifically, this article will focus on the time that this timeline format embodies. The significance of time can be gleaned from Scott Bader-Saye's essay entitled, "Figuring Time: Providence and Politics."[1] In it, Bader-Saye writes that "time, community and politics interweave in significant ways," so much so that "the ways we experience, name, and interpret time contribute to the kinds of communities we imagine and inhabit."[2] Conversely, it is also true that the practices and communities that we adopt and move within also constitute an acceptance of modes of time as one's own.

What this article also seeks to demonstrate is that this link between time, community and practice is of great theological significance for the Christian. Dispensing with this burden will require demonstrating how the church works under the lordship of a time very different from that in social media. It will also require this article to show how, as a result of this difference in times, the traversing of the church within a space under the lordship of a different time will have an impact on the way that faith is received and operationalized. In elaborating on these points, what will become apparent is the need to highlight the relationship between memory and God's providence, and show how this relationship looks in the church, and how that relationship differs in the church as it traverses through Facebook's timeline. In outlining this article's case, a key theological touchstone will be *Lumen fidei*, the encyclical by Pope Francis on "the light of Faith."[3]

FAITH AND TRAVERSE

Before analyzing the nexus between the church, Facebook and faith outlined above, it is necessary to first establish the case for the

---

[1] Scott Bader-Saye, "Figuring Time: Providence and Politics," in *Liturgy, Time and the Politics of Redemption*, ed. Randi Rashkover and C.C. Pecknold (Grand Rapids: Eerdmans, 2006), 96.

[2] Bader-Saye, "Figuring Time: Providence and Politics," 95, 98.

[3] Francis, *Lumen fidei* (June 29, 2013), w2.vatican.va/content/francesco/en/encyclicals/documents/papa-francesco_2013-0629_enciclica-lumen-fidei.html.

relationship between faith and the spaces we occupy. To this end, attention must be drawn to three things one might not necessarily associate with Facebook. The first is paragraph 31 of the Dogmatic Constitution of the Church, *Lumen gentium*.[4] Speaking of the laity, the document brings out the spatial dimension of evangelization, and the church's positioning of itself in order to fulfil that task. In speaking specifically to the laity, paragraph 31 is indicative of an evangelical methodology for huge swathes of the church when it calls on the church to engage in a "sanctification of the world from within as a leaven," and "in this way they may make Christ known to others."[5] From this, one can observe one aspect of the relationship between faith and space and the church's placing within that relationship, that the spread of the faith is dependent not on a church's situating itself over and above the secular sphere. Indeed, *Lumen gentium* no. 31 makes clear that the spread of the faith actually is tied intimately with an embedding of the church within the secular sphere, and especially so through the laity.

A second noteworthy point is that Pope Francis also hints at this methodology in his Apostolic Exhortation, *Evangelii gaudium*, in which he equates obedience to God's call to spread the gospel with going "out of our own comfort zone in order to reach all the 'peripheries'."[6] In terms reminiscent of the Dogmatic Constitution, the Apostolic Exhortation emphasizes the spread of the gospel as thus one which must "evangelize cultures in order to inculturate the Gospel,"[7] thereby making the Word of God "incarnate *in* the peoples of earth."[8] Although there is no explicit mention of the internet as an avenue of evangelization, *Evangelii gaudium* does make a more general reference to "the media" which nonetheless highlights the link between media and space, a link that has an impact on the embedding of the gospel within a culture, as highlighted in *Lumen gentium*. In a section pertaining to "urban cultures," *Evangelii gaudium* speaks of "vast new expanses" which act as "interpreters and generators of meaning." These consist of "languages, symbols, messages and paradigms which propose new approaches to life," which are sustained via the "influence of the media."[9] This influence of the media is relevant due to the

---

[4] *Lumen gentium: Dogmatic Constitution on the Church* (1964), www.vatican.va/-archive/hist_councils/ii_vatican_council/documents/vatii_const_19641121_lumen-gentium_en.html.

[5] *Lumen gentium*, no. 31.

[6] Francis, *Evangelii gaudium: Apostolic Exhortation on the Proclamation of the Gospel in Today's World* (2013), no. 20, w2.vatican.va/content/francesco/en/a-post_exhortations/documents/papa-francesco_esortazione-ap_20131124_evangelii-gaudium.html.

[7] *Evangelii gaudium,* no. 69.

[8] *Evangelii gaudium,* no. 115. Emphasis added.

[9] *Evangelii gaudium,* no. 73.

fact that it is precisely these "places where new narratives and paradigms are being formed,"[10] places which constitute the "privileged locus of the new evangelization."[11] To tie this more immediately to the topic at hand, we can glean from *Lumen gentium* (and by extension, *Evangelii gaudium*) an ecclesial imperative, as the body of Christ, to facilitate the encounter with Christ by immersing oneself within the space of social media, particularly Facebook.

Thirdly, this link between the embedding of the church and the spread of the faith is coupled by another spatial observation which is made in *Lumen fidei.* The spatial dimension of *Lumen fidei* is different from that raised by *Lumen gentium* because while the first speaks to the *spreading* of the faith, the second speaks to the *operationalization and maintenance* of faith at the same time that the faith is embedded within secular space. Because of *Lumen fidei's* focus on the operationalization of faith, it is this encyclical that will form the primary touchstone for this article. Paragraph 9 is particularly important here, for it explicitly identifies a spatial dimension to faith, challenging overly spiritualized or purely cognitive approaches to contemporary Christianity. Paragraph 9 does so with the notion that "faith *sees* to the extent that it journeys."[12] With this, paragraph 9 does not equate faith to a mere assent to ideas. Instead, faith is a result of a twofold process. First, faith is something that is received, and received insofar as it acts as a way of seeing. Secondly, faith as a form of seeing emerges from a journeying through space.

Put another way, faith is not merely a series of propositions, but a collage of events and conditions that mark one's life in this world. Such conditions are not just objects that we see, they are also lenses *through which* we see. In *The Social Construction of Reality*, Peter Berger and Thomas Luckmann speak of every action and decision being refracted through a rubric of what they call "plausibility structures," socially distributed practices and institutions which act as subtle guides by which one comes to regard certain things or ways of seeing things as persuasive or plausible.[13] In similar terms, Pierre Bourdieu speaks of how the concrete forms of space and the positioning of an agent within such spaces create fore-structures called a "field." This field, for Bourdieu, then creates a *habitus,* a set of dispositions to accept particular presumptions about the cosmos (which he calls *doxa*) as real.[14] Such dispositions are not the result of any prior process of

---

[10] *Evangelii gaudium,* no. 74.

[11] *Evangelii gaudium,* no. 73.

[12] *Lumen fidei*, no. 9. Emphasis added

[13] Peter L. Berger and Thomas Luckmann, *The Social Construction of Reality: A Treatise in the Sociology of Knowledge* (London: Penguin, 1967), 154-5.

[14] Pierre Bourdieu, *The Field of Cultural Production* (Cambridge: Polity, 1993), 162; Bourdieu, *Outline of a Theory of Practice* (Cambridge: Cambridge University Press, 1977), 35.

discernment, but are in a sense pre-cognitively accepted as one moves through the warp and weft of everyday life. What is theologically significant is that these dispositions are unseen and yet accepted at a pre-theoretical level.[15] Thus, at a very fundamental level, the acceptance of these fore-structures as a precursor to any action, however unconscious, can be considered an act of faith, insofar as faith is defined as the belief in "the evidence of things unseen" (Heb 11:1).

Timeline and Time

Even after identifying the spatial dimension of faith, the question must be asked concerning what this has to do with the specific phenomenon of the church's moving through Facebook's timeline format. At one level, the timeline format is just another of many format changes brought about by the corporation on Facebook accounts around the world. Be that as it may, a more profound change is taking place. From the set of pictographic and textual data on a front page, Facebook has mimicked Twitter's mode of rationalizing everything in a user-profile—from statuses, posts, citations and photo uploads—into a single thread of events, and weaving them together with similarly rationalized threads of other user-profiles. This interwoven series of feeds are then fed through a single endlessly-cascading feed on one's screen, with no distinction made between one type of post and another apart from its timing. Only the latest posts stay within eyeshot, and earlier ones disappear from sight and are retrievable only with considerable effort. A further tweak on this update has even removed the requirement for strict chronological sequencing between posts, though the rule still remains in force that posts beyond a certain time frame are removed from view.

Anything the church seeks to make manifest through its traversing of cyberspace, in particular the social medium of Facebook, would have to be reformatted to adapt to the timeline platform. What needs to be focused upon here is the kind of time that the Facebook timeline presumes and externalizes, and investigate how Facebook is an artifact of a particular kind of time. In doing so, the article wishes to show the difference between Facebook's version of time and that of the church. Having noted this difference, the article will go on to demonstrate how the church's traversing through Facebook operationalizes a lordship of a particular time, one that may be antithetical to a distinctly Christian conception of time. It will then demonstrate how, if this preceding argument is correct, the practice of Christian faith would become undermined.

---

[15] Berger and Luckmann, *The Social Construction of Reality*, 65.

CHRONOS AND *KAIROS*: TIME AND FAITH

Chronos

Attention must now turn to the type of time that one must submit to while traversing in Facebook. Insofar as the internet is inextricably hooked to the infrastructure of the computer, which runs on the time set by a clock, one can argue that the internet also operates on "clock time," which is a very Modern conception of time. This is significant, because "clock time" is premised upon the ability to conceive of one moment being followed by another. It is a scientifically quantifiable time, with discernible units of measure. Yet, in order for time to become a unit of scientific measure, it must be turned into what Walter Benjamin calls "homogeneous, empty time."[16] Time must be homogeneous because scientific measurements of any kind require all units of measure to be absolutely identical to one another. And time must be empty because the most consistent way of ensuring such homogeneity is to strip these units of time of any substantive content.[17] The kind of time you can set your watch to, according to Robert Gibbs, has to be such that each moment has to be made to pass by and pass away, which can only be so if the moment had no significance in and of itself.[18] Thus, while contemporary clock time is characterized by a march of moments, it is a march of the same type of moment—the "uniform mathematic moment,"[19] with that same type of empty moment brought before you over and over again. It is the march of one godforsaken moment after another.

Under conditions where time is emptied and laid out on a string, what time becomes is a disposable commodity in which culturally, what matters is the intensity of the present moment. Indeed, Graham Ward argues that contemporary culture is one that "idolizes the present, the seizure of the present," because in idolizing the "present as such," one is experiencing a secular version of "eternity as the fullness of time."[20] In order to create the "present as such," however, it becomes necessary to change the relationship between past, present and future in such a way that no one moment has a real and organic relationship with another. To authentically experience the present, the past has to be excised from the present, reduced to a moment that is to be

---

[16] Walter Benjamin, *Illuminations* (New York: Schocken Books, 1968), 263–4.

[17] With reference to novels, Benedict Anderson argues that "nothing better shows the immersion of the novel in homogeneous, empty time than the absence of those prefatory genealogies." This can easily transfer to contexts outside that of the novel. See Benedict Anderson, *Imagined Communities* (London: Verso, 2006), 26.

[18] Robert Gibbs, "Eternity in History: Rolling the Scroll," in *Liturgy, Time and the Politics of Redemption*, ed. Randi Rashkover and C.C. Pecknold (Grand Rapids: Eerdmans, 2006), 128.

[19] Gibbs, "Eternity in History," 128.

[20] Graham Ward, *Cities of God* (London: Routledge, 2000), 154.

seized, lived, and then tossed aside. This conception of time in theory is what underpins the experience of Facebook posts in practice. For whether it is in status updates, photo uploads or articles, Facebook harnesses the fullness of the present in order for the posts themselves to be fully experienced within the timeline. However, the fact that these posts are framed within the timeline infrastructure also means that there is no discernible link between one post and those that are lined up before or after it, and no narrative framework to connect the posts as a whole. This is the case even when posts are lined up within the same user-profile.

The idolization of the present which excises the present from other moments and forbids any narrative to cohere these moments, will also have an impact on the way the future is apprehended. As each moment becomes isolated from another, the future becomes a moment whose contours remain completely unknown, because there is no real basis from which one can apprehend the future, except insofar as it is a repetition of the present. This repetition—the "recurrence of the same"—is identified in our day by Friedrich Nietzsche in works like his *Notes on the Eternal Recurrence*. It is a state where "everything has returned," and where "all that has existed countless times will return again countless times."[21] If that were true, however, then any attempt to imagine the future as anything different from the present would appear to be a pretentious illusion.

Moreover, any attempt to transform the present to project it into the future is but a novelty, which is ephemeral and thrown into the ash heap of history as soon as it arrives. The Protestant poet, Kathleen Norris, has taken notice of the effects of living under a cultural condition marked by a unilinear structure of time.[22] In her *Cloister Walk*, Norris speaks of living in such a time as a "death-in-life… when my capacity for joy shrivels up."[23] But the effects do not stop at the level of culture, for if the church were to uncritically immerse itself in such a culture, the practice of faith as a belief in things unseen would be effected as well. This ties back to paragraph 13 in *Lumen fidei*, a line of which reads: "in refusing to await the time of promise, his life-story disintegrates into a myriad of unconnected instants."[24]

It is worth considering how *Lumen fidei's* notion of life as a series of "unconnected instants" links up with the notion of faith under the lordship of time conceived as a string of disconnected, un-narrated

---

[21] Karl Jaspers, *Nietzsche: An Introduction to the Understanding of His Philosophical Activity* (Baltimore: Johns Hopkins University Press, 1997), 352.

[22] For a detailed display of this point, see Matthew John Paul Tan, "St. Evagrius of Pontus and Redeeming Time in Postmodernity," *The Church and Postmodern Culture* (September 23, 2013), http://theotherjournal.com/churchandpomo/2013/-09/23/stevagrius-of-pontus-and-redeeming-time-in-postmodernity/.

[23] Kathleen Norris, *The Cloister Walk* (New York: Riverhead, 1996), 130-1.

[24] *Lumen fidei,* no. 13.

moments. To do this, one must turn to the issue of how memories of past events are apprehended, particularly when done so within a unilinear structure of time. This is important for two reasons. More generally, it is important because *Lumen fidei* makes an explicit tie between faith and the memory of the past. In paragraph 4, *Lumen fidei* calls faith "a light coming from the past, the light of the foundational memory of the life of Jesus."[25] Elsewhere, Francis makes an important tie that faith has to truth. And thus faith, like "the question of truth is really a question of memory," dealing "with something prior to ourselves and can succeed in uniting us in a way that transcends our petty and limited individual consciousness."[26]

The interactions between faith and memory—and the changes to that relationship when the unilinear structure of time in a digital environment becomes normalized—now assume greater importance. This is because understanding the changes in time structure also leads us to a greater understanding of the changes in our apprehension of faith in God's goodness. In a structure of time where only the present is both the only real moment and also a disposable moment, the past can never be a reality as such. It is instead a specter, a ghost of an experience that comes to the forefront of one's mind, but can never be *really* experienced. It remains but a mirage which disappears upon arrival. Memory becomes mere nostalgia, an irretrievable mental museum piece. Under such conditions, what faith becomes is but a belief in museum pieces. When faith becomes a belief in things lost in the past, then faith in God's goodness in the now is reduced to mere optimism, because it has no real basis apart from a distant, unconnected specter of God's goodness in an irretrievable past.

Under such conditions, one should not be surprised to find—to echo Norris—that joy shrivels up. This is because the joy of God's intervention in history becomes sporadic, momentary, arbitrary and finally, isolated and disconnected from any other occasion of God's providential action. Moreover, whenever joy does come, it is a joy that instantly becomes distant in a past that is never retrievable in the present in any real way. All one is left with is the norm, that is, the constant stream of one godforsaken moment after another, and the eternal recurrence. As Walter Benjamin noted, homogenous empty time defined as this unchanging stream of unchanging moments is also a time when radical transformation to that time, or what he calls the "Messianic cessation of happening"[27] is snuffed out. This has the effect of curbing faith in God's goodness, defined in terms of the expectation of God radically transforming an otherwise repetitive sequence of

---

[25] *Lumen fidei*, no. 4.
[26] *Lumen fidei*, no. 25.
[27] Benjamin, *Illuminations*, 283.

events, or at best, expecting such a transformation to be sporadic and momentary interruptions to a normality where joy is absent.

Kairos

If this flattened streamlining of time as *chronos* can render the apprehension of providence into pleasant but episodic interruptions to a joyless normality, how is it any different to a Judeo-Christian conception of time, time as *kairos*? Normally, the notion of *kairos* has been explained in terms of every moment being an "eternal present." This is true at one level, since every moment is *the* time, so *kairos* can interrupt *chronos'* cataloging of moments as merely *a* time. Be that as it may, such an interruption does not get to the more fundamental challenge of transforming the present's relationship to the past and future in a unilinear structure of time. Indeed, insofar as the relationship between the past and future is left unconsidered, and a real connection between past, present and future is never made, the notion of "eternal present" may even serve to reinforce the fetishization of the present under the lordship of "clock time."

One way of understanding the apprehension of time and faith in divine providence in a *kairotic* register would involve apprehending time in a Hebraic register. To this, Rabbi Edward Feld's commentary on the Psalms entitled *Joy, Despair and Hope*[28] provides a wonderful insight on the psalmic confusion of time. In a commentary on the confusion of tenses in Psalm 92, Feld makes reference to the prophetic experience of an ahistorical God's concern for his very historical creatures. For Feld, the prophetic imagination becomes paradigmatic of the psalmic apprehension of God's operations in the world, and by extension, becomes paradigmatic of the way God's time and operations enter ours.

For the prophets, Feld says, the experience of God's involvement in the world is not one that is sporadic, occurring in a single, arbitrarily chosen moment and then lost irretrievably to the past. Rather, in the prophetic imagination, God's work so penetrates the fabric of time that, when it makes contact with and is experienced in the present, it goes beyond the present and weaves its way into the past such that, for the prophet, the present becomes linked to the past through the golden thread of God's providential operations.[29] Moreover, this golden thread becomes so woven into both past and present that one becomes another. In the psalms and prophetic writings, this interweaving comes out in utterances where tenses become confused in the same stanzas.[30] Feld notes that the prophets experience the works of God so viscerally

---

[28] Edward Feld, *Joy, Despair, and Hope: Reading Psalms* (Eugene: Cascade, 2013).

[29] Feld, *Joy, Despair, and Hope*, 139.

[30] Feld, *Joy, Despair, and Hope*, 141.

that they speak of it as already having happened in the past.[31] Moreover, in the prophetic imagination, the future is framed in the past tense, so long as they remained anchored in the providential action of God, which again are felt so intensely that even before they are experienced in the present, they have already broken into the past. In Feld's words: "Prophetic poetry sees God's expected, yet unaccomplished acts so vividly that the past tense is used to describe an activity of God that is yet to be performed.... Future possibility has become fact – the future is not openended but already determined."[32]

Indeed, in the prophetic imagination, God's operations in the past constitute the very superstructure by which the present is experienced and the future is understood, with references to the past and passages in the psalms that are read in the past tense actually refer to a future promise of providence. This then feeds back onto our experience of the present. Seen in the light of the prophetic imagination, the present is not the joyless norm that is interrupted by the joy of God's providence. Rather, under the lordship of the *kairos,* it is the joy of the Messianic in the now that is the norm and joylessness that is the aberration. Seen in this register, the anxiety we have regarding the future shows the extent to which we are yet to be under the lordship of God's time. God's time is the aegis under which Benjamin's "Messianic cessation of happening" takes hold in history.

Conclusion: Facebook and Recitation

To reiterate what we have covered above, Facebook is not just a newsfeed. It is a space. Even more than that, it is an infrastructure that manifests certain commitments about the world, and by extension, certain predispositions pertaining to time. The acceptance of certain lordships of time are not just abstract, they lay the foundation of forming certain predispositions pertaining to faith in God's providence. Traversing through such a space, therefore, cannot help but become formative of a person's faith. Thus, if traversing through the space of Facebook can become erosive of faith in terms of the expectation of God's providence in everyday life, then the church's exclusive traversing through Facebook is arguably harmful to the church's mission in becoming a contact point for God's providence in an enduring fashion.

It would seem that, if faith is to be nurtured, it has to be done so as the church traverses through a space that militates against faith, just as it has in every age, and just as it must now in the space of social media. If that were so, then there must exist a mode of travelling by which the adulteration of faith under the lordship of clock-time, as is institutionalized in Facebook, can be countered. This mode consists in having

[31] Feld, *Joy, Despair, and Hope*, 139.
[32] Feld, *Joy, Despair, and Hope*, 139.

the church's traversing of clock time parallel a traversing within a prophetic imagination described above, an imagination that operates under the aegis of God's time. This imaginary is operationalized through the practice of liturgy, and this concluding section would focus on the practice of recitation as a fundamental element of liturgy.

William Cavanaugh's *Theopolitical Imagination* is a primer on how liturgy, in particular the Eucharistic liturgy, provides a concrete site that transgresses "spatial and temporal barriers" to unite "all times and places in eternity."[33] In such liturgical transgressions of time, one becomes immersed in a space whereby the past and future are all collapsed into the present. A supplement to the Eucharistic mode of transgressing time can be found in contemporary rabbinical literature, in particular that of Feld. Feld speaks of the seemingly mundane practice of recitation and proclamation of Scripture as the concrete means of actualizing the prophetic imagination. For Feld, recitation with one's lips is not just a neutral instrument by which words on a page are made audible to an audience. Rather, recitation is a practice of emplacement, that is, the creation of a space and the placing of a body within that space. As the body—namely the lips—recites the word of the psalms, one is moving one's body through that space.

The act of corporeally moving through space thereby plants the seeds of faith as a present apprehension of past memory and future expectation via the act of traverse, as highlighted in *Lumen fidei*, no. 9. This corporeal element is indispensable for the nurturing of faith so defined because, as Conor Sweeney has argued, the body stands as a point of convergence between the past, present and future.[34] In a similar vein, Feld argues that the act of recitation is an act of faith because it is corporeally enacting, in the present, the future as depicted in the psalms. Recitation plants the seeds of faith because the act of recitation constitutes a foretaste of future reality. In Feld's words, the bodily "intonation of the psalm is both an announcement about future hope and also the creation of that future moment in the present."[35]

In short, it is in the practice of recitation that one grounds the prophetic imagination, which in turn acts as the locus of resistance to the lordship of clock time in Facebook. In the first instance, recitation places the one at prayer in the locus of that imagination, "the house of

---

[33] William T. Cavanaugh, *Theopolitical Imagination: Discovering the Liturgy as a Political Act in an Age of Global Consumerism* (New York: T&T Clark, 2004), 118.

[34] Conor Sweeney, "A Baptismal Theology of Relation: Overcoming the Intra-cosmic Temptation," Presentation at the Transcending Dualisms Conference, John Paul II Institute for Marriage and Family in Melbourne (May 2014). Although Sweeney uses the language of signification in his coverage on the body, the signification here does not imply an absence of a real presence in that signification. Rather, Sweeney implies a sacramental imagination in which the sign is organically making present what is signified.

[35] Feld, *Joy, Despair, and Hope: Reading Psalms*, 145.

God." The act of recitation is the embodied experience of the providence of God in the here and now, and it stretches that space to other bodies via the communication of experience to those that have ears to hear.[36] In the second instance, through the practice of recitation, one is doing more than merely indulging in cognitive fantasy. Indeed, one is actively resisting the inevitability of lordship of "clock-time" by creating a real space, with a real field of dispositions whereby another time, God's time, is made perceivable here and now. In so doing, the practice of recitation is one, but not the only, practice whereby the adulterating effects of traversing through the church of Facebook can be resisted, and the "doing of that new thing" (Isa 43:19), where God's providence is made present, and where faith in that future providence is vindicated in the now. M

[36] Feld, *Joy, Despair, and Hope: Reading Psalms*, 145.

Journal of Moral Theology, Vol. 4, No. 1 (2015): 36-64

Progress and *Progressio*: Technology, Self-betterment, and Integral Human Development

Joseph G. Wolyniak

> Let men make all the technical and economic progress they can, there will be no peace nor justice in the world until they return to a sense of their dignity as creatures and sons of God, who is the first and final cause of all created being. Separated from God a man is but a monster, in himself and toward others; for the right ordering of human society presupposes the right ordering of man's conscience with God, who is Himself the source of all justice, truth and love.
>
> John XXIII, *Mater et magistra,* no. 215

IN A RECENT COMMERCIAL ADVERTISING the HTC Droid DNA smartphone, a man is prepped for a procedure in a futuristic surgical theater.[1] Seated in a chair and fitted with a device that envelops his right arm and thorax, a smartphone placed in the center of his chest activates the surgical apparatus—presumably functioning as an artificial heart. "Droid DNA augmentation initiated," announces an android surgeon, triggering the injection of nanoids that begin bionically hybridizing the subject's DNA in a strand displacement cascade. As the treatment takes effect, sequential progress is audibly chronicled: "neural speeds increasing to 4G LTE;" "brain upgrading to a quad-core processor;" "predictive intelligence with Google Now complete." The augmentative sequence finalized, the man (now *trans*-human? cyborg?) lifts his gaze out onto a horizon of new, endless possibility. A narrator concludes: "It's not an upgrade to your phone; it's an upgrade to yourself."

Debatable science and marketing hyperbole aside, the ad encapsulates a familiar promise of technology. Not only is *it* getting better all the time, but because of it *so are we*. Our technological devices enable us to manipulate and maneuver our world with ever-greater efficiency, expedience, and expertise—facilitating what would otherwise be inconceivable. To the extent that work is necessary for human dignity, technology offers a means by which the human person can effectuate her labor, her God-given vocation, her self-realization within a God-ordered creation. It does not seem outlandish, therefore, to assume

[1] Verizon: HTC Droid DNA. "Hyper Intelligence." Television advertisement. Psyop, Inc., directed by Laurent Ledru, 2012. See: http://vimeo.com/56384500.

technology can be essential to human flourishing. Being both a result of human innovation and vital to the human vocation, it is understandable that we might assume that technological progress *is* human progress—that an upgrade to our phones might well be an upgrade to ourselves. But is it?

That is the question at the heart of this essay. Looking first at the general contours of Catholic social doctrine regarding human and technoscientific progress, it is then necessary to note the difficulty of thinking Christianly about technology. Focusing on the particular device of the mobile phone—specifically the way in which it is sourced, manufactured, and disposed of—the concentration is placed on one illustrative, seemingly innocuous, and increasingly constitutive aspect of our ordinary existence. The phone is thus an exemplification of what sociologist Mike Michael calls the "technoscientific artefacts" that "operate as the facilitative backdrop to the doing of everyday life" wherein "the norms, expectations, conventions of social interaction are in part enacted with, and mediated through, all manner of mundane technologies."[2] Reflecting on the device in light of the effective conditions for its realization, we can better appreciate how the goods of the mobile phone are bound up in a rather complicated web of relationality. Our devices may well connect us with others in ways far deeper than we generally acknowledge, which in turn requires that we reconsider the question of progress with respect to the whole. Returning to the concept of "integral human development" will therefore offer the frame of reference needed to assess the potential for technology as a means for human advancement.

The Promise of Progress: Prospects, Portents, and Provisos

Can a particular technological device entail progress for its possessor? It is a seemingly straightforward question, ostensibly about the myriad feats a given device enables us to perform, the power it accordingly affords us, and the prospect of self-betterment it offers in turn. Right from the start, though, we must recognize how deceptively difficult it can be to hazard an answer, with matters muddled by rather slippery conceptions of the good(s) in question. A mobile phone undoubtedly makes us better at performing certain tasks, but does it make us better? To even approach such a question, we need a comprehensive moral framework. Catholic social doctrine offers just that, with an especially fecund tradition of reflection on technology, progress, and self-betterment—perhaps most comprehensively in the notion of integral human development, which will be addressed in detail below. Before turning to that particular tenet, however, some general contours

[2] Mike Michael, *Technoscience and Everyday Life* (New York: Open University Press, 2006), 37.

of magisterial teaching bear consideration here: 1) the consistent affirmation of the legitimate goods science and technology offer, 2) the need to situate such legitimate goods (and their limits) in context, and 3) the dangers of an unchecked trust in the promise of technoscientific progress.

It is especially notable that many of the modern encyclicals reference developments in science and technology as an occasion for a recapitulation of Church teaching in the first place. Pope St. John XXIII, for instance, situates *Mater et magistra* (1961) in the lineage of Pope Leo XIII's *Rerum novarum* (1891), with "subsequent changes" prompting the need "to confirm and make more specific… the mind of the Church on the new and important problems of the day."[3] Foremost among such notable changes are a variety of technoscientific developments including:

> The discovery of nuclear energy, and its application first to the purposes of war and later, increasingly, to peaceful ends; the practically limitless possibilities of chemistry in the production of synthetic materials; the growth of automation in industry and public services; the modernization of agriculture; the easing of communications, especially by radio and television; faster transportation and the initial conquest of interplanetary space.[4]

Such advances open up new horizons, requiring rearticulation of the gospel anew. Yet, despite a still-pervasive conflict myth concerning the Church's relationship to science and technology, the general tenor of magisterial response is neither reactionary nor reproving. Quite the contrary, it is rather optimistic—even celebratory. Various papal fathers consistently acclaim the advancement of science and technology and the potential goods such progress might entail for the betterment of the individual person and human family.

In point of fact, John XXIII suggests that the "present advance in scientific knowledge and productive technology" offers "to a much greater degree than ever before" an opportunity to "reduce imbalances;" indeed, "scientific and technical progress" has already given rise to "greater productive efficiency and a higher standard of living," leading to an "increase in social relationships," "mutual ties," and "development in the social life of man."[5] The Holy Father accordingly affirms the quest "to deepen and extend [humankind's] dominion over

---

3 John XXIII, *Mater et magistra* (1961), nos. 46, 50, www.vatican.va/holy_father/john_xxiii/encyclicals/documents/hf_j-xxiii_enc_15051961_mater_en.html.

4 *Mater et magistra*, no. 47.

5 *Mater et magistra*, nos. 54, 59-60.

Nature," noting with approval how the "progress of science and technology that has already been achieved opens up almost limitless horizons."[6]

The Second Vatican Council's Pastoral Constitution on the Church in the Modern World, *Gaudium et spes* (1965), offers similar approbation:

> Man judges rightly that by his intellect he surpasses the material universe, for he shares in the light of the divine mind. By relentlessly employing his talents through the ages he has indeed made progress in the practical sciences and in technology… [and] has won superlative victories, especially in his probing of the material world and in subjecting it to himself.[7]

Moreover, the Council Fathers affirm how "man has ceaselessly striven to better his life" and, chiefly with "the help of science and technology," has "extended his mastery over nearly the whole of nature" such that "many benefits once looked for, especially from heavenly powers, man has now enterprisingly procured for himself."[8]

In *Laborem exercens* (1981), Pope St. John Paul II likewise lauds efforts towards "subduing the earth" by an "immense development of technological means" that he unequivocally regards "an advantageous and positive phenomenon."[9] Insofar as technology offers humankind "a whole set of instruments"—an *omnium gatherum* that "facilitates," "perfects," "accelerates," and "augments" human work—it is "undoubtedly man's ally."[10] In fact, the Holy Father opens his encyclical by advocating the "continual advance of science and technology," equating the fruits thereof with our "daily bread" as "the bread of science and progress" that humankind has produced by the "work of [his] hands" and "sweat of his face."[11]

Blessed Pope Paul VI similarly sees science and technology as vital to human advancement, suggesting in *Populorum progressio* (1967) that industrialization is essential to "human progress" as "both a sign of development and a spur to it."[12] He specifically commends the "dint

---

[6] *Mater et magistra*, no. 179.

[7] Vatican II, Pastoral Constitution on the Church in the Modern World (*Gaudium et spes*, 1965), no. 15, www.vatican.va/archive/hist_councils/ii_vatican_council/documents/vat-ii_const_19651207_gaudium-et-spes_en.html.

[8] Vatican II, *Gaudium et spes*, no. 33

[9] John Paul II, *Laborem exercens* (1981), no. 10, www.vatican.va/holy_father/john_paul_ii/encyclicals/documents/hf_jp-ii_enc_14091981_laborem-exercens_en.html. Provided that, John Paul II notes, when it comes to the human vocation "the objective dimension of work does not gain the upper hand over the subjective dimension, depriving man of his dignity and inalienable rights."

[10] *Laborem exercens*, no. 5

[11] *Laborem exercens*, no. 1.

[12] Paul VI, *Populorum progressio* (1967), no. 25, http://www.vatican.va/holy_father/paul_vi/encyclicals/documents/hf_p-vi_enc_26031967_populorum_en.html.

of intelligent thought and hard work" by which "man gradually uncovers the hidden laws of nature and learns to make better use of natural resources"—assuming "control over his way of life," pioneering "new investigations and fresh discoveries," and taking "prudent risks" in "new ventures." Such sentiments echo his predecessor, who called for addressing inequality via "development" fostering "the best possible adjustment of the means of production to the progress of science and technology" in keeping with "the demands of the common good."[13] Urging the faithful "to take an active part" in facilitating "man's self betterment,"[14] John XXIII argues "it is not enough for Our sons to be illumined by the heavenly light of faith and to be fired with enthusiasm," for amidst "a culture and civilization… so remarkable for its scientific knowledge and its technical discoveries," engaging the world requires an apostolate that is "scientifically competent" and "technically capable."[15]

At the same time, the magisterium insists on a circumscribed conception of technoscientific products and potential—often in the same breath as praises are sung. While in *Sollicitudo rei socialis* (1997) John Paul II approvingly notes how "technological civilization" contributes to "human liberation," granting that humankind "needs created goods and the products of industry… enriched by scientific and technological progress," he insists on its "limits," the "danger of the misuse," the "appearance of artificial needs," and the imperative to subordinate "the possession, dominion and use [of such goods] to man's divine likeness and to his vocation to immortality" which is "the transcendent reality of the human being."[16] Paul VI correspondingly argues human advancement "necessarily comes up against the eschatological mystery of death," at which point only faith in the "death of Christ and his resurrection and the outpouring of the Spirit" is able to "help man to place his freedom, in creativity and gratitude, within the context of the truth of all progress and the only hope which does not deceive."[17] Technologies that humans conceive, create, and employ offer a real but range-bound freedom and power.

What's more, an unchecked assurance in technoscientific progress risks obscuring the dangers of a despotic techno-utopianism. Paul VI

[13] *Mater et magistra*, no. 78-9. Importantly, the demand of the common good necessitates concern "not merely to the present generation but to the coming generations as well."

[14] *Pacem in terris*, no. 147.

[15] *Pacem in terris*, no. 148.

[16] John Paul II, *Sollicitudo rei socialis* (1987), nos. 7, 29, http://www.vatican.va/holy_father/john_paul_ii/encyclicals. /documents/hf_jp-ii_enc_30121987_sollicitudo-rei-socialis_en.html. Here Pope John Paul II cites: *Gaudium et spes*, nos. 19, 57; *Populorum progressio*, no. 41.

[17] Paul VI, *Octogesima adveniens* (1971), no. 42, http://www.vatican.va/holy_father/paul_vi/apost_letters/documents/hf_p-vi_apl_19710514_octogesima-adveniens_en.html.

states unequivocally: "Every kind of progress is a two-edged sword. It is necessary if man is to grow as a human being; yet it can also enslave him, if he comes to regard it as the supreme good and cannot look beyond it."[18] In the Apostolic Letter *Octogesima adveniens* (1971), the pope similarly warns against a totalizing credo of "ceaselessly renewed and indefinite progress" marked by a "new positivism" of "universalized technology as the dominant form of activity, as the overwhelming pattern of existence, even as a language, without the question of its meaning being really asked."[19] Progress, wrongly taken to be "the condition for and the yardstick of human freedom," risks becoming "an omnipresent ideology" that oppresses despite its promise to liberate.

Paul VI thus introduces a new term, technocracy, to the encyclical lexicon in a sober warning:

> It is not enough to develop technology so that the earth may become a more suitable living place for human beings.... The reign of technology—*technocracy*, as it is called—can cause as much harm.... Man is truly human only if he is the master of his own actions and the judge of their worth, only if he is the architect of his own progress. He must act according to his God-given nature, freely accepting its potentials and its claims upon him.[20]

In resistance to technocracy, Paul VI again urges the "deep thought and reflection of wise men in search of a new humanism, one which will enable our contemporaries to enjoy the higher values of love and friendship, of prayer and contemplation," for only this "will guarantee man's authentic development—his transition from less than human conditions to truly human ones."[21]

Such authentic humanism transcends a "narrow humanism, closed in on itself and not open to the values of the spirit and to God who is their source," typified by an overestimation of technology's "apparent success" in "organizing terrestrial realities without God."[22] Ostensible advances will ultimately languish if "closed off from God," for humanistic aspirations and attainments "closed off from other realities" will "end up being directed against man" and instead become "inhuman."[23] It is, therefore, only in an expansive notion of progress—what Paul VI calls "integral development"—that we find the true ends of

---

[18] *Populorum progressio*, no. 19.

[19] *Octogesima adveniens*, nos. 41, 29.

[20] *Populorum progressio*, no. 34.

[21] *Populorum progressio*, no. 20 (emphasis mine).

[22] *Populorum progressio*, no. 42.

[23] Paul VI is here citing Henri de Lubac, *Le Drame de L'Humanisme Athée*, 3rd ed. (Paris: Spes, 1945), 10. In a much-quoted line, Paul VI adds: "Man is not the ultimate measure of man. Man becomes truly man only by passing beyond himself."

human advancement.[24] Real progress is that "authentic development" which is "well rounded" and fosters "the development of each man and of the whole man."[25]

John XXIII encapsulates the foregoing in his observation that while science and technology can be "gigantic forces for good," they can all too easily become "engines of destruction."[26] If "scientific and technical progress is to be used in the service of civilization," it must acknowledge the "supreme importance of spiritual and moral values." Quoting Pius XII's 1953 Christmas Eve address,[27] John XXIII notes the incoherence of an age "marked by a clear contrast between the immense scientific and technical progress and the fearful human decline" where the human is at risk of devolving into a "*monstrous masterpiece*" through "transforming man into a giant of the physical world at the expense of his spirit."[28] He further maintains that while it is "claimed that in an era of scientific and technical triumphs… man can well afford to rely on his own powers, and construct a very good civilization without God," in truth "these very advances in science and technology frequently involve the whole human race in such difficulties as can only be solved in the light of a sincere faith in God, the Creator and Ruler of man and his world."[29]

Thus, the Holy Father extols the faithful "not to allow their consciences to sleep," for while "the Church teaches—and has always taught—that scientific and technical progress and the resultant material well-being are good things and mark an important phase in human civilization," so too does She teach "that goods of this kind must be valued according to their true nature: as instruments used by man for the better attainment of his end." The pope concludes: "May these warning words of the divine Master ever sound in men's ears: 'For what doth it profit a man, if he gain the whole world and suffer the loss of his own soul?'"[30]

Such sentiments are, of course, nothing new. They can be traced at least as far back as St. Augustine's *City of God*, Book XXII, wherein he notes with praise how:

---

[24] *Octogesima adveniens*, no. 34.

[25] *Populorum progressio*, no. 14.

[26] *Mater et magistra*, no. 210.

[27] Pius XII, "Radio Message, Vigil of the Nativity of Our Lord Jesus Christ, 1953," AAS 46 (1954) 10, www.vatican.va/archive/aas/documents/AAS%2046%20-[1954]-%20-%20ocr.pdf.

[28] *Mater et magistra*, nos. 243-44 (emphasis mine). John XXIII also describes this condition as "idolatry" wherein "men are losing their own identity in their works."

[29] *Mater et magistra,* no. 209. Psalm 126.1 is later quoted to reinforce the point: "Unless the Lord build the house, they labor in vain that build it" (no. 217).

[30] *Mater et magistra*, nos. 245-46.

> There have been discovered and perfected, by the natural genius of man, innumerable arts and skills which minister not only to the necessities of life but also to human enjoyment. And even in those arts where the purposes seem superfluous, perilous and pernicious, there is exercised an acuteness of intelligence of so high an order that it reveals how richly endowed our human nature is. For, it has the power of inventing, leaning and applying such arts.[31]

It is remarkable that, according to Augustine, even when human *techné* veers into the perilous and pernicious it still reveals the greatness of human abilities—endowments worthy of celebration insofar as they reveal the greatness of the endower. Augustine thus has no compunction about celebrating the "progress and perfection which human skill has reached" in "astonishing achievements," nor the "completeness of scientific knowledge [which] is beyond all words and becomes all the more astonishing when one pursues any single aspect of this immense corpus of information."[32]

Yet, he does so within the context of acknowledging the God-infused "capacity for reasoning and intellection."[33] Such cognizance of "the Creator of this noble human nature" gives rise to a worship of "the true and supreme God whose providence rules all that He has created, whose power is unlimited, and whose justice is infinite."[34] Indeed, in a passage immediately preceding the quote above, Augustine hails "those supernatural arts of living in virtue and of reaching immortal beatitude which nothing but the grace of God which is Christ can communicate to the sons of promise and heirs of the kingdom."[35] Magisterial teaching stands in this vein, celebrating legitimate techno-scientific progress within the *regnum hominis* while reminding us of the *regnum Dei* beyond.

What are we to make of all this? On the one hand, the magisterium repeatedly reminds us of the necessary limits of technological prowess and the destructive potential that technology can represent if such bounds are heedlessly ignored. To disregard the limits of technology, we are reminded, is to refuse to acknowledge what it cannot do and thus to distort what it can. On the other hand, magisterial teaching is anything but hidebound when it comes to technology. Instead, the papal fathers repeatedly stress the real and potential goods that technology can procure, arising out of and further facilitating human work. The magisterium commends the role that technology has historically

---

[31] St. Augustine, *City of God*, Books XVII-XXII, trans. Gerald G. Walsh and Daniel J. Honan, The Fathers of the Church vol. 24, (2008; repr., Washington, D.C.: Catholic University of America Press, 1954), 484.

[32] Augustine, *City of God*, 484-85.

[33] Augustine, *City of God*, 484.

[34] Augustine, *City of God*, 485.

[35] Augustine, *City of God*, 484.

played in the development of humankind, especially in its rightful assertion of dominion over creation and the triumph of the spirit over matter. The faithful—and indeed all people of good will—are accordingly encouraged in their various scientific and technological pursuits. On balance, perhaps we could say the magisterium generally adopts an affirmative position: that which is not against me is with me.

In constructive and critical pastoral guidance, the tradition certainly offers extensive resources germane to the present concern: whether and to what extent a given technological device might be a means for self-betterment, especially in terms of the authentic humanism and integral development noted above. Before considering exactly how Catholic social doctrine might illumine matters, however, it is worth contemplating the givenness of the given device in question. Like all technological devices, the mobile phone in not simply a given—it is a product, which is to say it is produced. That might seem like inconsequential semantics, but philosopher George Parkin Grant (1918–1988) explicates the importance—and difficulty—of carefully attending to that which makes our given devices possible. His groundbreaking contribution is worth recapitulating in some detail, especially in terms of its theological import.

THE DIFFICULTY OF THINKING CHRISTIANLY ABOUT TECHNOLOGY

"In each lived moment of our waking and sleeping," begins George Grant in his seminal essay on technology, "we are technological civilization."[36] In making this claim, Grant endeavors to illuminate the extent to which "we have encompassed ourselves within technology" such that "our political and social decisions are interwoven with the pursuit and realization of technological ends."[37] This development is not a matter of mere happenstance, for "we westerners willed to develop a new and unique co-penetration of the arts and sciences, a co-penetration which has never before existed."[38] The "co-penetration of knowledge and making" is not "simply an extension of human making through the power of perfected science," but "a new account of what it is to know and make." Indeed, this new account of knowing and making—epitomized by the writings of Francis Bacon (1561-1626) and René Descartes (1596-1650)—was explicitly distinguished from the ancient science and was animated by "the faith that the mastery of nature would lead us to the overcoming of hunger and labor, disease and war… [and] could build the world-wide society of free and equal

[36] George Grant, "Thinking about Technology," *Technology and Justice* (Notre Dame, IN: University of Norte Dame Press, 1986), 11.
[37] Grant, "Thinking about Technology," 15.
[38] Grant, "Thinking about Technology," 12.

people."[39] Acknowledging the legitimacy of such aspirations, Grant nevertheless contends that "progress is a more complex matter than was envisaged by those who had believed that a better society would arise ineluctably from technology."

Grant is particularly concerned with highlighting the novelty of our technological civilization, a paradigm in which we are so deeply embedded it can be hard to see it for what it is. Carefully examining default assumptions about technological progress, for instance, he exposes the extent to which we take the givenness of the predominant paradigm and its products for granted. Usually construed as "a great step forward in the systematic application of reason to the invention of instruments for our disposal," the supposed progress is shown to arise out of a much larger narrative.

> Human beings have from their beginnings developed instruments to help them get things done (indeed in our era many distinguish human beings from other animals by calling us the tool-making animals). The word "instrument" is not confined simply to external objects such as machines or drugs or hydropower, but includes such development of systems of organisation and communication as bureaucracies and factories. Technology is then thought of as the whole apparatus of instruments made by man and placed at the disposal of man for his choice and purposes.[40]

While Grant concedes that this story is to a certain extent "undeniable," he is concerned that it obscures the novelty of the technological civilization in which we find ourselves.

That novelty is perhaps best exposed by scrutinizing a commonplace claim: that our given technological devices are neutral and do not impose on us the ways they should be used. This prevalent assumption construes technological devices as mere instruments whereby "the morality of the goals for which they are used is determined outside them," where "capacities have been built into them by human beings... who operate those machines for purposes they have determined."[41] Yet this commonsense notion does not allow such devices "to appear before us for what they are," naïvely assuming their givenness "as if they existed in abstraction from the events which have made possible their existence."[42]

What events make possible their existence? Grant notes how our technological devices are comprised of:

---

39 Grant, "Thinking about Technology," 14-15.
40 Grant, "Thinking about Technology," 19.
41 Grant, "Thinking about Technology," 20.
42 Grant, "Thinking about Technology," 21.

> a vast variety of materials, consummately fashioned by a vast apparatus of fashioners. Their existence has required generation of sustained effort by chemists, metallurgists and workers in mines and factories… [and] have been made within the new science and its mathematics. That science is a particular paradigm of knowledge and, as any paradigm of knowledge, is to be understood as the relation between an aspiration of human thought and the effective conditions for its realization.[43]

Our order of things is "so taken for granted as the way things are" that it is given "an almost absolute status," and as such it becomes "our civilizational destiny"—and "like all destinies, they 'impose.'"[44] Grant suggests that his attempt here is to be descriptive; he is not necessarily aiming to advance any particular normative claims. In fact, he concedes that it may well be, as is often supposed, "that the development of that paradigm is a great step in the ascent of man" and "the essence of human liberation."[45] His stated intention is simply to show how particular technological devices are inseparable from the paradigms that produce them, arguing that to assume a given device is neutral (and therefore does not impose) is to erroneously abstract it "from the destiny that was required for its making."[46]

Part of the destiny required for its making entails the advent of institutions that can generate the requisite research and development needed to produce such technologies in the first place, such that "the 'ways' that automobiles and computers can be used are dependent on their being investment-heavy machines which require large institutions for their production."[47] Such technical devices "can be built only in societies in which there are large corporations," which are "instruments with effect beyond the confines of particular nation states" and risk becoming (perhaps inevitably) "the instruments of the imperialism of certain communities towards other communities." The institutional requirements for the production of technological devices, which "exclude certain forms of community and permit others," exemplify how modern technology and modern society are coproduced by "the same account of reasoning."[48] The question of a particular technological device, therefore, quickly becomes a question about the ideational and institutional paradigm that produced both the given device and the effective conditions for its realization.

Theorizing technological devices as merely neutral instruments becomes increasingly difficult, for it requires conceding that they are

---

43 Grant, "Thinking about Technology," 21 (emphasis mine).
44 Grant, "Thinking about Technology," 21-2.
45 Grant, "Thinking about Technology," 22.
46 Grant, "Thinking about Technology," 23.
47 Grant, "Thinking about Technology," 24.
48 Grant, "Thinking about Technology," 27.

governed "according to standards of justice which are reached outside of the existence of the [devices] themselves."[49] If, however, we see how both the device and the effective conditions of its realization are inseparable, we can begin to see how the "instruments and the standards of justice are bound together, both belonging to the same destiny of modern reason." This destiny and its standards of justice are in turn related to "modern conceptions of goodness," wherein the good becomes "our free creating of richness and greatness of life and all that is advantageous thereto."[50] Grant suggests that this conception of goodness, this "liberation of human desiring from any supposed excluding claim," is concomitant with the "liberation in which men overcame chance by technology—the liberty to make happen what we want to make happen."[51] If it is not already obvious, such accounts of goodness and freedom, justice and reason, have a particular genesis and trajectory. If Grant's assessment is allegedly descriptive, it is nonetheless clear the normative does not lag too far behind.

Grant's attempt to lay bare "the novelness of our novelties" challenges the supposition that the technologies functioning as the backdrop of our existence are utterly anodyne.

> When we represent technology to ourselves as an array of neutral instruments, invented by human beings and under human control, we are expressing a kind of common sense, but it is a common sense from within the very technology we are attempting to represent. The novelness of our novelties is being minimized. We are led to forget that modern destiny permeates our representations of the world and ourselves. The coming to be of technology has required changes in what we think is good, what we think good is, how we conceive sanity and madness, justice and injustice, rationality and irrationality, beauty and ugliness.[52]

We accordingly tend to think about technology in terms of its own rationale. Whereas we may think we are thinking about, say, the employment of one neutral instrument (such as a mobile phone), in reality we "have bought a package deal of far more fundamental novelness than simply a set of instruments under our control… a destiny which enfolds us in its own conceptions of instrumentality, neutrality and purposiveness."

In light of this, "deliberating in any practical situation our judgement acts rather like a mirror, which throws back the very metaphysic of the technology which we are supposed to be deliberating about in

[49] Grant, "Thinking about Technology," 28.
[50] Grant, "Thinking about Technology," 30.
[51] Grant, "Thinking about Technology," 31.
[52] Grant, "Thinking about Technology," 32.

detail."[53] We tend to inevitably adopt a default "decision for further technological development," which "exalts the possible above what is" and therefore compromises "our ability to think that there could be knowledge of what is in terms of which the justice of every possible action could be judged in advance of any possible future."[54] Instead of an ethics marked by "*a posse ad esse non valet consequentia*," we are left with an ethics of "when you see something that is technically sweet you go ahead and do it" and merely "argue about what to do about it only after you have had your technical success." Thus Grant concludes: "technology is the ontology of the age."[55] Amidst such a technological ontology, he contends, there is "a pressing need to understand our technological destiny from principles more comprehensive than its own."[56]

Grant's account helps us to see the predicament of thinking theologically amidst a predominant technological ontology. While it is difficult for us to see our technological devices as anything other than given neutral tools that users must employ and allocate properly, Grant exposes the way in which our devices are bound up in the ideational and institutional paradigms that produce them. Our mobile phones are not just little pieces of magic wrapped in plastic and glass that arise out of nowhere.[57] Their existence is predicated on ideas and institutions—certain forms of community in relation to other communities, ways of being in relation to others—which require our attention if we are to adequately assess the possibility of progress they offer. It shows us just how convoluted our seemingly straightforward questions about technology can be, how difficult it is to think about technology with principles more comprehensive than its own. Perhaps the point is best expounded via a concrete example, returning to our question about the mobile phone. If we look more closely at the systems and structures that give rise to our mobile phones—part of the effective conditions for their realization—we can underscore the necessity of devoting our theological attention not just to the givenness of the device itself but also to the wider paradigm that produces it.

The effective conditions for the realization of The Mobile phone

In his song "Ain't No Reason," Brett Dennen laments his own acquiescence to world in which "slavery is stitched into the fabric of [our] clothes."[58] I want to likewise suggest that exploitation is stitched

[53] Grant, "Thinking about Technology," 33.
[54] Grant, "Thinking about Technology," 34.
[55] Grant, "Thinking about Technology," 32.
[56] Grant, "Thinking about Technology," 34.
[57] I am grateful to my friend, Fr. Christopher Adams, for this way of wording the matter.
[58] Brett Dennen, "Ain't No Reason," *So Much More* (Dualtone, 2006).

into the very fabric of our phones, produced and discarded within an all-too-common complex of global capitalism. It is imperative to examine the sourcing, manufacturing, and disposal of mobile phones if we are to adequately reflect on what Brian Brock calls the "material artifact" aspect of the "technology assessment."[59] As Grant has shown us, a given device is never merely given but always also produced. And the effective conditions for the realization of our technological artifacts, as we shall see, are bound up in a rather complex and compromising web of social, political, and economic entanglements.

The story begins in Numbi, within the war-torn Democratic Republic of Congo (DRC), where coltan—a black, metallic ore—is mined. From this ore, tantalum ($_{73}$Ta) is extracted: an element critical for the production of electrolytic capacitors that store and release our phones' electricity. Crucial as these processors are for the functions we demand of our devices, the mining of the ore on which they are predicated is lucrative business; lucrative business that, in turn, has funded and fueled one of the deadliest conflicts in the world over the last century. Numbi, in the South Kivu region of the DRC just west of Rwanda, is the epicenter of coltan mining—accounting for nearly 80% of the world's supply. For years it has been (not coincidentally) one of the most violent regions within one of the most violent regions of the world, including the site of the bloody Ituri Conflict.[60] When in the aftermath of the 1994 Rwandan Genocide, the Hutu perpetrators fled westward to the DRC, groups such as the FDLR (Forces démocratiques de libération du Rwanda) assumed control of several of the Kivu region's most productive and profitable mines—gaining and maintaining their jurisdiction through utter brutality. But this is the story of just one region, with a similarly sad tale replicated throughout the DRC.

Zainab Hawa Bangura (special representative on sexual violence to the United Nations) notes that "in 2013, rebel groups in the Democratic Republic of the Congo generated almost $1bn from minerals extracted from mines in conflict zones," with "civilians unlucky enough to live near deposits of conflict minerals… driven from their homes, subjected to horrific human rights abuses, and sometimes

---

[59] Brian Brock, *Christian Ethics in a Technological Age* (Grand Rapids: Eerdmans, 2010), 15.

[60] Megan Camm calls the 1999 Ituri Conflict as a "war within a war" (i.e., the Second Congo War), gruesomely "fought between consortiums of local tribal militias and proxies…. Disorganized bands, often armed only with machetes, clubs, lances, and bows and arrows descended on civilian populations, killing, raping, and burning as they went. Victims, including women and children, were often brutally mutilated." Megan Camm, "Conflict in Congo," *World Policy Journal* 28.4 (December 2011), 70-80.

forced into slave labour."[61] Armed groups that control these mines perpetuate systematic sexual violence: "Rape in this context is not the collateral damage of warfare—it is the direct result of the illicit trade in conflict minerals." While Bangura acknowledges that "most companies are five to seven layers removed" from the "violent phase" of a mineral supply chain that is "complex," she unequivocally emphasizes that the "link between sexual violence and conflict minerals is not: the international demand for these minerals fuels a vicious cycle of rape and war." Because of the dual threat of armed conflict and systematic sexual violence, the DRC is considered one of the most dangerous places in the world to be a woman.[62] Suffice to say that the extraction of coltan is at the geopolitical center of an unfathomably monstrous conflict, leaving aside issues pertaining to the environmental impact of extracting this "natural resource."[63]

Advocacy groups have sufficiently pressured some multinational corporations into stemming their use of conflict minerals and there have also been some legislative strides within particular nation-states—i.e., provisions in the 2010 U.S. Dodd-Frank Act.[64] However, a recent report from the UN Group of Experts on the DRC addressed to the UN Security Council noted "while progress has been made to promote due diligence and traceability for [conflict materials]… many problems remain with respect to production and trade."[65] Persistent "violations of international humanitarian law" include: "recruitment and use of child soldiers, summary executions, sexual violence and the targeting of civilian populations."[66] Indeed, even in areas where there

---

[61] Zainab Hawa Bangura, "Sexual Violence and Conflict Minerals: International Demand Fuels Cycle," *The Guardian* (June 18, 2014), www.theguardian.com/sustainable-business/sex-violence-conflict-minerals-supply-chain.

[62] TrustLaw, "Factsheet—The world's most dangerous countries for women," Thompson Reuters Foundation (June 15, 2011), www.trust.org/trustlaw/news/factsheet-the-worlds-most-dangerous-countries-for-women.

[63] The concept of "natural resources" requires theological appraisal. See Matthew Whelan, "Have You Ever Seen What They Do to Valuable Natural Resources?: Agriculture, Language, and Wendell Berry," *The Other Journal* (August 25, 2011), http://theotherjournal.com/2011/08/25/have-you-ever-seen-what-they-do-to-valuable-natural-resources-agriculture-language-and-wendell-berry.

[64] A recent report by the Enough Project highlights impacts of the Dodd-Frank Wall Street Reform and Consumer Protection Act (no. 1502): Fidel Bafilemba, Timo Mueller, and Sasha Lezhnev, "The Impact of Dodd-Frank and Conflict Minerals Reforms on Eastern Congo's Conflict" (June 10, 2014), www.enoughproject.org/reports/impact-dodd-frank-and-conflict-minerals-reforms-eastern-congo's-war.
Regarding corporate efforts, see: Don Clark, "Apple Reports on Its Sources of 'Conflict Minerals,'" *The Wall Street Journal* (May 29, 2014), http://online.wsj.com/articles/apple-reports-on-its-sources-of-conflict-minerals-1401405074.

[65] UN Security Council, "Final Report of the Group of Experts on the Democratic Republic of Congo," (January 23, 2014), www.un.org/sc/committees/1533/e-group.shtml.

[66] UN Security Council, "Final Report," 4.

have been gains made against rogue armed groups, the national defense forces charged with protecting the Congolese people (known as the Forces Armées de la République Démocratique du Congo, or FARDC) have themselves further perpetuated the domination, exploitation, and violence that has engulfed this region.[67]

What becomes of this coltan once mined? It, along with other conflict minerals, is sold in underground markets, processed through smelters and refiners, and shipped together with various constituent parts to assorted manufacturers across the world.[68] Two-fifths of mobile phones are then assembled by the world's largest electronics manufacturer: the Taiwan-based multinational Hon Hai Precision Industry Company, which trades as the Foxconn Technology Group. With over a million employees—nearly half of whom work in a sprawling plant in Longhua, Shenzhen—Foxconn is the largest private employer in China.[69] An extensive press deluge in recent years noted numerous human rights violations: workers hired or fired on a moment's notice, deplorable working conditions, excessive hours, insufficient vacation and leave, unrealistic production quotas, unremunerated overtime, worker exhaustion, and widespread clinical depression.

An independent investigation by the Fair Labor Association in the spring of 2012 found over fifty violations of the FLA Code and Chinese labor law, including: working hours (weekly averages exceeding legal limits, with stints of seven days or more without a minimum 24-hour break), health and safety (unreliable policies, procedures, and practices compounding generally compromised worker wellness, including exposure to harmful chemicals and a deadly explosion at one facility), worker integration and communication (reported alienation from workplace committees, management-appointed committee nominations, unresponsive top-down communication), and inadequate compensation (unpaid/unscheduled overtime, variable benefits, and required co-pay into insurance programs that did not benefit workers).[70]

---

[67] UN Security Council, "Final Report," 3-4. The many foreign and domestic armed groups fighting within the region include: the Mouvement du 23 mars (M23), the Nduma Defense of Congo (NDC), the Forces de résistance patriotiques en Ituri (FRPI), the Lord's Resistance Army (LRA), and the FDLR.

[68] As one commentator frames matters: "The tantalum capacitors might come from Australia or the Congo. The nickel in my battery probably originated from a mine in Chile. The microprocessor chips and circuitry maybe came from North America. The plastic casing and the liquid in the LCD were manufactured from petroleum products from the Gulf, Texas, Russia or the North Sea, and moulded into shape in Taiwan." John Agar, *Constant Touch: A Global History of the Mobile Phone* (Cambridge: Icon Books, 2004), 14.

[69] Joel Johnson, "1 Million Workers. 90 Million iPhones. 17 Suicides. Who's to Blame?," *Wired.com* (Feb. 28, 2011), www.wired.com/2011/02/ff_joelinchina.

[70] Fair Labor Association, "Independent Investigation of Apple Supplier, Foxconn" (March 2012), www.fairlabor.org/report/foxconn-investigation-report.

Angela Bao, writing about the attraction of China's rural poor to urban manufacturers like Foxconn, describes how the "motivation to break the cycle of poverty spurs millions of farmers to make the frantic, often desperate leap from rural to urban life."[71] Complicating migrant workers' quest for self-betterment, an arcane "household registration system" known as *hukou*—originally devised in the 1950s to keep farmers from migrating to urban centers after the Soviet Union ended industrial support to China—"gradually evolved into what is now an invisible and all but insurmountable barrier for farmers to achieve equal rights as urban dwellers," preventing the rural poor from establishing official residence in cities and denying access to various forms of government welfare (including education and healthcare).[72] The result is a "severely skewed dual structure," not just between rich and poor but also between the urban and rural poor. Compounding matters further, the Chinese Central Government's 1978 "Reform and Opening-Up" campaign "laid out the welcome mat for its rural poor looking to strike it rich" in urban industrial centers, though the two-tiered *hukou* system remained intact and severely restricted the migrants' basic rights.[73] At roughly the same time, "at least 40 to 50 million farmers had their arable land confiscated by the government under the guise of urban development."[74] Nearly a quarter of the land-deprived farmers, who had to "depend largely on planting crops and vegetables to make a living," were now expected to survive "after being chased from the land their family has plowed and cultivated for generations." Within two decades, China's urban population "soared from 170 to 450 million."[75] Millions of the displaced rural poor sought work by any means necessary; a vast number turned to low-skill, low-wage manufacturing jobs.

The pressures placed on workers in Foxconn plants are not just physical. Acute mental and emotional burdens exacerbate the physical toll. The displaced rural poor often migrate great distances to urban centers in search of work, straining and often severing ties with their families and social networks. The rupture workers experience further aggravates the aforementioned difficulties, with a notable compound effect. In point of fact, after a string of on-site suicide attempts by

[71] Angela Bao, "Endless Road in China: From Country to City and Back," *World Policy Journal* 27.23 (Winter 2010/2011), 23-31.

[72] Bao, "Endless Road," 24.

[73] Bao, "Endless Road," 25.

[74] Bao, "Endless Road," 27.

[75] Bao, "Endless Road," 25.

Foxconn workers in 2010—resulting in the installation of safety lattices, or "suicide nets," around the perimeter of its factories[76]—investigations pointed to various motivating factors including overwhelming workloads, degrading conditions, and deplorable recompense. Yet, Terry Gou (Foxconn's founder and chairman) suggested that "personal emotional problems" were at the root of numerous suicide attempts; or as Bao suggests, the workers suffered not just on account of "the lack of external security" but perhaps especially because of "the lack of a sense of internal belonging"—a displacement, detachment, and disconnectedness that led to despondency.[77] While the corporeal toll is significant, Bao maintains "the emotional cost is equally dramatic." Such alienation, itself a symptom of the strained social ties caused by the migration in the first place, flies in the face of conventional cultural wisdom: "As Chinese Confucian philosophy has it, 'A prosperous society is impossible without stable families as its foundation.'"[78]

With elements mined, parts manufactured, and devices assembled, our mobile phones are then packaged, distributed, marketed, and consumed. They serve their purpose in our employment—at least until an upgrade is available—and then we haphazardly discard them. Where do they end up? More likely than not, in a place like Agbogbloshie on the outskirts of Ghana's capital, Accra, which is home to the world's largest technotrash landfill. In his photobook, *Permanent Error*, Pieter Hugo vividly documents what he calls the "global waysides that we might know only as 'away', as in 'we threw it away.'"[79] In this "away," local Ghanaians sift through technotrash in search of precious metals that can be sold to recyclers for profit. Keyboards, screens, motherboards, batteries, and wires dot a desolate landscape of entwined organic and inorganic matter. Diseased and emaciated cattle graze alongside human persons sorting through the remnants of our discarded devices. It is a place so bleak that those who call Agbogbloshie home tellingly refer to it as "Sodom and Gomorrah."[80]

According to a 2013 statement from the UN Working Group on Business and Human Rights, the landfill is "populated mainly by the

---

[76] See, for instance: Tom Randall, "Inside Apple's Foxconn Factories," *Bloomberg.com* (March 30, 2012), www.bloomberg.com/slideshow/2012-03-30/inside-apple-s-foxconn-factory.html#slide9.

[77] Bao, "Endless Road," 26. She cites, for example, the massive increase witnessed in holiday travel: "In 2009, some 192 million passengers hit the rails during the 40-day Spring Festival travel—the largest human migration in history."

[78] Of course, there are neoliberal retorts. See, for instance, Tim Worstall, "Apple and Foxconn are the Best Thing that's Ever Happened to Chinese Labor," *Forbes.com* (Nov. 30, 2012), www.forbes.com/sites/timworstall/2012/11/30/apple-and-foxconn-are-the-best-thing-thats-ever-happened-to-chinese-labour/.

[79] Pieter Hugo, *Permanent Error* (Munich: Prestel Art, 2011), 97.

[80] Samantha L. Stewart, "Ghana's e-waste dump seeps poison," *Newsweek.com* (July 25, 2011), http://www.newsweek.com/ ghanas-e-waste-dump-seeps-poison-68385.

poorest in society and economic migrants."[81] The e-waste—stemming primarily from other parts of the world, especially the Americas, Europe, and Asia—customarily enters Ghana marked as second-hand goods for resale. But the shipments commonly contain inoperative and obsolete electronics misleadingly labeled in order to circumvent high recycling costs. Women, men, and children comb through the graveyard of outmoded devices with little recourse to alternative employment, their livelihood essentially dependent on a life-threatening trade. Unsurprisingly, the land is almost uninhabitable—"heavily contaminated from [the] burning and disposal of toxic waste, with harmful effects on the health of the communities." The sentiments of one worker are illustrative:

> "I came here from Tamale [in northern Ghana] five years ago…. I make between two and five cedis [approximately $1.50] each day, and each month I send 50 cedis [$15] back to my family in the north. I would like to go back home, but my family needs the money, so I stay. We get too many problems here—sometimes I have to go to the hospital. It's not good for us."[82]

Many of the workers, routinely exposed to toxic chemicals, will not live past thirty years old. In one of the most polluted cities in the world, the occupational hazards are as bad as they can get.

Yet, the destitution of workers that propelled them to the dump in the first place often keeps them there—hoping that the castoffs from the developed world keep coming. As another worker put it: "This is not a good place to live. But we don't want the people in Europe and all those places to stop sending the waste…. This is a business centre, and we are using the money we make here to help our families to have a better life."[83] The poorest of the poor glean out of necessity (if to their detriment) the castoffs of our upgrades, in a perverse juxtaposition of superdevelopment and subsistence. As Pieter Hugo describes it, Agbogbloshie is a place where the "fallen icons of our proud Information Age lie as rotting fruit, the progeny of centuries of technological advancement."[84] An away place "where the notions of progress and obsolescence collapse, where memories and information stored in countless hard drives turn into black smoke and molten plastic."[85]

---

[81] UN Working Group on Business and Human Rights, "Statement at the end of visit to Ghana" (July 17, 2013), www.ohchr.org/EN/NewsEvents/Pages/DisplayNews.aspx?NewsID=13547.

[82] Afua Hirsch, "'This is not a good place to live': inside Ghana's dump for electronic waste," *The Guardian* (Dec. 14, 2013), www.theguardian.com/world/2013/dec/14/-ghana- dump-electronic-waste-not-good-place-live.

[83] Hirsch, "Not a good place," np.

[84] Hugo, *Permanent Error*, 97.

[85] Hugo, *Permanent Error*, 9.

The tagline of a onetime leader in the mobile phone industry encapsulates a central aim of our devices: "Connecting people."[86] By glimpsing at the sourcing, manufacturing, and disposal of our phones, we discover a twisted irony in this stated aim. We are indeed connected to others by our devices, though in ways far more profound than we generally imagine. Numbi, Shenzhen, and Agbogbloshie offer glimpses into the effective conditions for the realization of our technological products, revealing deep and disturbing disorders. Such sophisticated devices require immense institutions for their realization, institutions that in turn promote certain forms of community while prohibiting others. To the extent that we consume, employ, and discard the devices on offer, we participate in particular ways of relating to those whose lives are—whether or not we realize it—closely linked with ours. The average consumer may be "seven layers removed," but the exploitation is no less real. Blind or desensitized to such exploitation, we mistakenly assume that violence is the exception rather than the rule.[87] The unsettling underbelly of the supposedly neutral device forces us to face and rethink the assumptions about the neutrality of our devices, which offer a promise of progress to possessors with no strings attached. By glancing at the disordered formation and afterlife of our devices, we can begin to see how we—the producers and possessors of mobile phones—are inextricably ensnared in a matrix of exploitation. The devices we unquestioningly employ implicate us within a web of relations in ways we never imagined or intended. Their neutrality is anything but neutral, their givenness anything but a given. Whatever they do, they certainly impose.

It is important to bear in mind, though, that the effective conditions for the realization of our devices are not merely material and institutional but also ideational and spiritual. Our technological objects and their requisite institutions are coproduced according to the same account of reason and being, a story we are told and sold. That which makes possible the existence of our devices includes more than miners, manufacturers, and gleaners—essential as they are as inessential cogs of commerce. It includes postulations about the world as it is and ought to be. The evermore-ubiquitous mobile phone assumes and extends a co-penetrated conception of making and knowing, constantly updated and upgraded in a way that exalts the possible over what is under the guise of progress. So constitutive of our present existence—

[86] Nokia, a Finland-based multinational, was once the world's leading vendor of mobile phones and developed one of the world's first handheld devices in the Mobria Cityman 900. Microsoft acquired Nokia's Devices & Services division in April 2014, ending Nokia's direct involvement in the device sector.

[87] Matthew Whelan, "Violence and the Ordinary," Paper presented at New Wine, New Wineskins Symposium (Notre Dame, IN: University of Notre Dame, July 31–August 3, 2014).

an exemplary mundane artifact "related to the everyday in its micro-social guise as a process of taken-for-granted ordering"[88]—the mobile phone is anything but an innocuous tool for us to employ and allocate well. It is part of the modern story about what it is to know or make or be, laying claim to conceptions of the good and the better. It is a paradigmatic example of our technological ontology.

Situating our technological devices against the backdrop of the effective conditions for their realization exposes the complexity of thinking Christianly about technology. Without that backdrop, it is difficult if not impossible to even see a given device for what it is. Our very way of knowing and making and being is mediated and constituted by technology—ever increasingly so, perhaps inescapably so. As the late Walter J. Ong puts it, technology is "a phenomenon far more complex" than we generally assume, "more operative within us than outside us," living "deep within us in the very concepts it enables us to form."[89] So fundamental to our way of being, he cautions that it is "too easy to impute to technology all of the threats and evils in the world" just as it is "too easy to look at technology for all of the blessings available to mankind."[90] To "localize evil in one phenomenon or movement or even one ideology," he warns, "is to blind oneself to what evil is—and to what good is." He accordingly calls our attention to a concept of the good that is "Catholic," which "in the strict sense… does not mean 'universal' ('inclusive,' a bounding concept) but, in its exact Greek etymology, 'through-the-whole' (a totally positive, non-bounding concept)," a good that "must penetrate all." To where might we turn for such a conception?

Integral human development: Progress in the Scope of Things

Notably absent from the earlier overview of magisterial teaching on technology was any mention of Pope Benedict XVI's contribution, intentionally left to the last as it is his analysis of technology that ties the foregoing together. Benedict XVI engages the question of technology more frequently and systematically than perhaps any previous pope, drawing on the abovementioned magisterial tradition to further advance the concept of integral human development.[91]

Its relevance is multifarious, but it is especially illumining in two primary respects. First and foremost, it insists on a grammar—and therefore an ontology—that is not in the final analysis technological

[88] Michael, *Technoscience*, 37.

[89] Walter J. Ong, "Technology Outside Us and Inside Us," *Communio* 5.2 (Summer 1978), 100-121.

[90] Ong, "Technology," 121.

[91] For an excellent overview and analysis of *Caritas in Veritate*, see: Miguel J. Romero, "Liberation, Development, and Human Advancement: Catholic Social Doctrine in *Caritas in Veritate*," *Nova et Vetera*, 8.4 (2010): 923-57.

but theological. Second and following from this, it insists on a theological grammar of love (*caritas*) and grace (*cháris*) "received and given" as the beating heart of the Church's social teaching, whose "source is the wellspring of the Father's love for the Son, in the Holy Spirit" and whose principle (*caritas in veritate*, "love in truth") "takes on practical form."[92] This twofold insistence sums up and ties together all that I have been gesturing towards in this essay, for Benedict XVI's reassertion a theological grammar helps set the possibility of technological progress within the framework of "*integraque progressio libertatem*"—necessarily entailing an integral conception of the liberation, advancement, and betterment on offer.[93] It is, therefore, derivative upon a vision wherein persons as "objects of God's love" become "subjects of charity," called to "make themselves instruments of grace, so as to pour forth God's charity and to weave networks of charity" throughout the world.[94]

The practical form of charity-in-truth includes justice, even if "*charity goes beyond justice*, because to love is to give, to offer what is 'mine' to the other; but it never lacks justice, which prompts us to give the other what is 'his,' what is due to him by reason of his being or his acting. I cannot 'give' what is mine to the other, without first giving him what pertains to him in justice."[95] Thus, "charity demands justice" if it also "transcends" and "completes" it in "the logic of giving and forgiving" characterized by "relationships of gratuitousness, mercy, and communion." Furthermore, "to desire the *common good* and strive towards it *is a requirement of justice and charity*."[96] The demands of justice and charity therefore explicitly require devotion of our attention and efforts towards addressing and alleviating those structures of social sin that prevent right relationship, the common good, and human flourishing. For, "to love someone is to desire that person's good and to take effective steps to secure it." On a personal level, that might also entail "an effective shift in mentality" away from "hedonism and consumerism" and towards "the adoption of *new lifestyles*" which take into account our being in relation to one another and the whole of creation.[97]

---

[92] Benedict XVI, *Caritas in veritate* (2009), nos. 3, 6, www.vatican.va/holy_father/benedict_xvi/encyclicals/documents/hf_ben-xvi_enc_20090629_caritas-in-veritate_en.html.

[93] *Caritas in veritate*, no. 17 (Latin Version).

[94] *Caritas in veritate*, no. 5.

[95] *Caritas in veritate*, no. 6 (emphasis in original).

[96] *Caritas in veritate*, no. 7 (emphasis in original).

[97] *Caritas in veritate*, no. 51. Benedict XVI adds: "Every violation of solidarity and civic friendship harms the environment, just as environmental deterioration in turn upsets relations in society."

Yet, Benedict XVI insists "charity without truth would be more or less interchangeable with a pool of good sentiments."[98] In such a world, "there would no longer be any real place for God" and charity would be "confined to a narrow field devoid of relations… excluded from the plans and processes of promoting human development of universal range, in dialogue between knowledge and praxis." Such a charity cannot realize its full potential, including attending to the effects of sin. To be sure, "the Church's wisdom has always pointed to the presence of original sin in social conditions and in the structure of society;" however, the "conviction that man is self-sufficient and can successfully eliminate the evil present in history by his own action alone has led him to confuse happiness and salvation with immanent forms of material prosperity and social action."[99] Such self-reliance is "thereby deprived of *Christian hope*, deprived of a powerful social resource at the service of integral human development."[100] As hope is "already present in" and "called forth by faith" marked by love, charity-in-truth "feeds on hope and, at the same time, manifests it" as an "absolutely gratuitous gift of God" that "bursts into our lives as something not due to us, something that transcends every law of justice." It is all and only gift. And as a gift, "by its nature goes beyond merit, its rule is that of superabundance."

Such an emphasis on the primacy and finality of God and God's manifest charity-in-truth, mediated by the Church and known in and through a "*charity, illumined by the light of reason and faith*," makes possible the pursuit of "development goals that possess a more humane and humanizing value."[101] What Benedict XVI calls an "authentic development" requires "the sharing of goods and resources," including our technological goods and the resources they help us cultivate, but it is "not guaranteed by merely technical progress and relationships of utility, but by the potential of love that overcomes evil with good, opening up the path towards reciprocity of consciences and liberties." Therefore, progress-as-*progressio* (in the sense of *integraque progressio libertatem*) enfolds into one the concepts of progress, advancement, and development within the framework of integral human freedom and liberation. The authentic freedom and liberation on offer, to which we bear witness through charity-in-truth, is not one that we can or will achieve by relying on technology alone. It is always and only given and received in Christ. In other words, technology has never and will never advance the human person beyond her material condition. It will not attain for her that which she seeks in her transcendent pursuits. Technology may well facilitate the human

[98] *Caritas in veritate*, no. 4.
[99] *Caritas in veritate*, no. 34.
[100] Emphasis in original. Benedict XVI is here citing *Spe salvi* (2007), no. 17.
[101] *Caritas in veritate*, no. 3 (emphasis in original).

search for that which is good, beautiful, and true; but the full realization thereof is ultimately discovered only by divine self-disclosure, a gift to be received and shared not an emolument to be achieved and hoarded.

Herein lies the threat of technology: human advancement, progress, and development "goes awry if humanity thinks it can re-create itself through the 'wonders' of technology" in and of itself.[102] When technology assumes "supremacy" in the human imagination, it "tends to prevent people from recognizing anything that cannot be explained in terms of matter alone."[103] According to Benedict XVI, however,

> all our knowledge, even the most simple, is always a minor miracle, since it can never be fully explained by the material instruments that we apply to it. In every truth there is something more than we would have expected, in the love that we receive there is always an element that surprises us. We should never cease to marvel at these things.[104]

Benedict XVI acknowledges "technology is highly attractive because it draws us out of our physical limitations and broadens our horizon."[105] Yet, in order to see rightly, to see most fully, "requires new eyes and a new heart, capable of *rising above a materialistic vision of human events*, capable of glimpsing in development the 'beyond' that technology cannot give."[106]

This does not diminish the legitimate goods that technology offers. Benedict XVI, with his predecessors, praises technology properly understood and used. Technology is (as the pope emphasizes) "a profoundly human reality" and is "linked to the autonomy and freedom of man."[107] In and through it "we express and confirm the hegemony of the spirit over matter," allowing the human spirit to be more easily enraptured in "worship and contemplation of the Creator."[108] It "enables us to exercise dominion over matter, to reduce risks, to save labour, to improve our conditions of life," and "touches the heart of the vocation of human labour" for in technology ("seen as the product of his genius") "man recognizes himself and forges his own humanity." It "is a response to God's command to till and to keep the land." Yet, "technology is never merely technology" for "it reveals man and his aspirations towards development, it expresses the inner tension that impels him gradually to overcome material limitations."

---

[102] *Caritas in veritate*, no. 68.
[103] *Caritas in veritate*, no. 77.
[104] *Caritas in veritate*, no. 77 (emphasis mine).
[105] *Caritas in veritate*, no. 70.
[106] *Caritas in veritate*, no. 77 (emphasis in original).
[107] *Caritas in veritate*, no. 69.
[108] Benedict XVI is here citing Paul VI, *Populorum progressio*, no. 41. Compare Vatican II, *Gaudium et spes*, no. 57.

Benedict XVI's account, therefore, addresses what Brian Brock identifies as the problem with the standard technology assessment—serving as "a classic example of secular rationality in that it has no methodological place for divine action or for substantive moral or ontological claims" and thereby "assumes the practical irrelevance of God's past and present working."[109] In such accounts, "humanity shoulders the responsibility of finding a way forward amidst a chaotic context from which a future must be secured" and thus "moral being and moral deliberation assume a specific and describable shape in which the power of technology plays a central role in framing human aspirations." As David L. Schindler similarly suggests, we are problematically locked in an assumptive technological ontology that "abstracts from the logic of love proper to created being, and in so doing assumes a version of power that can only become in the end a caricature of the power of God, a power not of love but of a technical manipulation tending ultimately toward tyranny."[110] This ontology is thus essentially "semi-Pelagian" in that, "however unintentionally, [it] assigns to man the wrong sense of priority in actualizing his relation to God that most properly characterizes his meaning as a creature, and thereby assigns to man the wrong sense also of what it means to be a creature and to act *in and by himself* and hence in a legitimately autonomous way (*iusta autonomia*)."[111]

In short, Benedict XVI's reassertion of integral human development demands a wide frame of reference to measure the promise of technological progress. To assess whether a given technology might make good on its promise requires that we take into account the fullness of what it is to know, make, and be. For Benedict XVI, questions about goodness or betterment cannot be asked in abstraction from the transcendental unity of the good, the beautiful, and the true in all created being—which in turn requires reference to the Uncreated Being, the one true God. We cannot expect to answer the questions posed by technology if we assume the practical irrelevance of God, with attendant moral and ontological claims excluded. Benedict XVI seeks to turn the predominant logic of technology on its head, insisting on the absolute relevance of transcendent truths to our most immanent

---

109 Brock, *Christian Ethics*, 23.

110 David L. Schindler, "America's Technological Ontology and the Gift of the Given: Benedict XVI on the Cultural Significance of the *Quaerere Deum*," *Communio* 38.2 (Summer 2011), 237-278.

111 Schindler, "America's Technological Ontology," 244-5. Schindler suggests this semi-Pelagianism, or "ontological pelagianism," is marked by "voluntaristic freedom, instrumentalist intelligence, and positivistic religion or religiosity" (245). While he suggests that the human action in and through technology is not a "theological pelagianism that signifies a heresy in the formal sense," a Pelagian specter nevertheless "lies at the root… as its ontological infrastructure" (246).

questions. This includes an insistence on the right relationships between creatures and other creatures, creation, and their Creator—relations marked by justice, charity, and love. It includes the recognition of limits that allow our tools to do what they are meant to do without being compromised by attempting to achieve what they cannot. It includes an insistence on the ultimacy of the ultimate, the "subsistent Love and Truth."[112] Only an integral progress-as-*progressio* can conclusively achieve what we humans universally long for: not just palliation but salvation.

CONCLUSION: HOW NOT TO BECOME A MONSTROUS MASTERPIECE

So can an upgrade to our phones occasion an upgrade to ourselves? It is a seemingly straightforward if deceptively difficult question. An adequate answer requires we first acknowledge the tangible and genuine goods that technological devices, born of human ingenuity, can and do offer. Arising out of and further facilitating the human vocation, they enable otherwise inconceivable feats, promote human flourishing, and offer advanced abilities to their possessors. The mundane, ubiquitous mobile phone serves an exemplary case in point—a device that facilitates connectivity, communication, organization, navigation, and so on. Such dexterities are definite goods that, with successive upgrades, offer consistent improvements to our way of doing things. Whether the device might offer an upgrade to oneself, however, is a question that becomes complicated by the effective conditions for the realization of our devices. The phone, part of a presumptive paradigm that is both ideational and institutional, can no longer be seen as a merely neutral tool with beneficent potential. Even just glimpsing at the institutional requirement for its realization, which promotes certain forms of relating while prohibiting others, exposes deep disorders. The violence of the ordinary unsettles assumptions about the supposedly unadulterated goods of our innocuous devices. Couched in the evils inherent to structures of social sin, the requirements of right relationship and the common good are seriously compromised with the offered advancement derivative upon the use and abuse of others. Such disconcerting realities call for a more careful consideration of the promised progress.

The concept of integral human development offers a frame of reference attuned to the often-unacknowledged entanglements of our ostensibly inoffensive implements. Positing a wider frame of reference, the notion of integral human development offers not so much a direct answer to specific questions about particular devices but the possibility of seeing them for what they are. By seeing our devices for what

[112] *Caritas in veritate*, no. 52.

they are, we can begin to think Christianly about technology's inexorable presence in us and us in it. We can call certain ways of knowing and making to account, naming and resisting the violent and nihilistic ontology on which predominant paradigms trade. We can reassert a grammar of creation, gift, and grace that can help us to see our tools and ourselves rightly. Seeing our tools and ourselves in an integral light, we can attend both to the inherent relationality of the human person and the tendency of all created goods, manufactured products, and private possessions towards the commons—acknowledging that our good and our goods are inescapably bound up with the good of the other. We must therefore attend to the malformations inherent in the ordinary as a precondition to entertaining the prospects of technological self-betterment, a muddle which more technology or better allocation cannot itself solve. If we can better see matters as they are, we might be able to resist the ease with which our tools—developed out of the human vocation to till the ground and keep it—become a means whereby we rise up against our brothers and sisters.[113]

The wider frame of the integral necessitates attention to the effective conditions for the realization of our devices, exposing the exploitive nature of our transactional and contractual relationships. This, in turn, complicates claims to personal self-betterment insofar as we realize our good is always bound up with the good of other creatures and all creation. Technology, in this regard, has not, cannot, and will not fulfill its promise of progress on a grand scale. The particular goods it does offer must be set within the continuum of all that is needed for human development—progressing from less to more fully human conditions, advancing the whole person and all persons. Technology can and does make us better at doing certain things, helping us achieve and attain legitimate ends, but it cannot and will not make us better in an ultimate sense. For our definitive betterment we must look beyond technology, even beyond addressing structures of social sin, to an amelioration we cannot ourselves attain. Indeed, the frame of integral human development enables us to see that our progress is not finally about immanent forms of material flourishing, nor even the reestablishment of right relationship (between human beings and between the rest of the created order), but about the reconciliation of the

[113] If it is not obvious, I am alluding here to the story of Cain and Abel. Cain's name is presumably derived from the verb Hebrew *qanah*. While likely alluding to the fact that he is the first progeny of Adam and Eve ("I have produced a man with the help of the LORD," Gen 4.1), it is also possible that he is one who not only *is produced* but also *produces* ("a tiller of the ground," Gen 4.2). While the text itself makes no mention of Cain's tools being used as the weapon in his murder, midrashic and artistic interpretations to this effect abound. See, for instance, Lorenzo Ghiberti's "Cain and Abel" panel on the Gates of Paradise, Florence Baptistery, 1425-1452 (Gwynne Ann Dilbeck, "Opening the Gates of Paradise: Function and the Iconographical Program of Ghiberti's Bronze Door," doctoral thesis, University of Iowa, 2011).

human heart with God—a gift we always only receive, which no amount of nanotech augmentation can engineer.

An insistence on the empyrean aspect of the integral does not diminish the possibility of progress (technological or otherwise) in the mundane, it merely puts it into perspective. It allows us to step back from the claims of our devices, to see them in context. To do so makes it possible to see our devices for what they are, to see ourselves for who we are, with respect to the ultimate reference point: being in relation to God. This does not detract from the possibility of improving the human conditions in the here and now. Quite the contrary, seeing ourselves in relation to God and God's creation necessitates a disposition of gratuitous self-giving and participation in the betterment of self and neighbor. As Meghan J. Clark puts it, "the human person as an isolated, unsituated 'self,' truly detached from society, is an illusion."[114] Positing "*imago dei* as *imago trinitas*," Clark insists on "mutuality and reciprocity as integral to human dignity."[115] Accordingly, the human person "has a profound obligation to belong,"[116] an obligation that transcends a mere recognition of inherent relationality and compels our active involvement in the world, realized in the "virtue of solidarity" that entails "not only political or social conditions but also commitment to the personal flourishing" of one's neighbor according to "the universal common good."[117] To fail in this regard, to participate in the "oppression, scapegoating, and dehumanization," means that we are "sacrificing our own ability, individually and collectively, to more fully and faithfully image God, and, therefore, we stunt our ability to develop and live more fully human lives."[118]

To the extent that technology can facilitate the improvement of our human conditions, it can be an apt artifact possessed and employed to a variety of bettering ends; but to the extent it threatens the impoverishment of our being in relation to God and others, to all of God's creation, it must be refused and resisted. Too readily can technology offer as an illusory mirage of transcendence as an escape from our own humanity. Too easily can we lose sight of ourselves as creatures standing before the God who is all justice, truth, and love. Too quickly can we become monsters. If we are to become something other than monstrous masterpieces amidst a technological ascendancy, we will need to recognize the limits of our devices and ourselves—to see our technology for what it is, to see ourselves for who we are. We must identify and resist the structures of social sin, the violence of the ordinary, which serves as the facilitative backdrop of our given technological

114 Meghan J. Clark, *The Vision of Catholic Social Thought: The Virtue of Solidarity and the Praxis of Human Rights* (Minneapolis: Fortress Press, 2014), 69.

115 Clark, *The Vision of Catholic Social Thought*, 66.

116 Clark, *The Vision of Catholic Social Thought*, 69.

117 Clark, *The Vision of Catholic Social Thought*, 110.

118 Clark, *The Vision of Catholic Social Thought*, 72.

goods. And to do so, we may well need to cultivate an *askesis* with respect to the innumerable tools and toys at our disposal, a voluntary poverty that resists the unbounded exaltation of the possible.

If we are not able to fully escape technology, then perhaps our only option will be to ask not whether but how we use it—what disciplines and practices are necessary to produce people capable of using technology well. An ethics understood as a *techné* of ethos based on reason alone, a rational calculus adjudicating maximized benefit and minimized risk, is inadequate to address the momentousness of that task. We must attend to our technological destiny from principles more comprehensive than its own. Perhaps the place to begin will be to follow in the footsteps of Mary, "first among the disciples of Jesus Christ."[119] Mary, as one "totally dependent upon God and completely directed towards him by the impetus of her faith," serves as "the most perfect image of freedom and of the liberation of humanity and of the universe" and it is her *fiat* ("let it be done") that is always the first step towards "the plan of God's love." In looking to Mary, and most especially to her grace- and faith-filled *fiat*, we find a reckless willingness to offer up oneself in complete dependence—putting all one's goods and one's very being to the service of making tangible God's love. Such humble acquiescence to and bold participation in the will of God is arguably what we need most amidst a technological ontology. The *fiat* of Mary will not be the answer to every particular question about every particular technology, but it is an answer. It is not the resolution to our manifold problems, but it is a start.[120]

---

[119] Pontifical Council for Justice and Peace, *Compendium of the Social Doctrine of the Church* (2004), no. 59, www.vatican.va/roman_curia/pontifical_councils/justpeace/documents/rc_pc_justpeace_doc_20060526_compendio-dott-soc_en.html.

[120] An earlier version of this essay was presented to the Technology Ethics Interest Group at the 2013 meeting of the Society of Christian Ethics. I am grateful to comments and questions received in that forum and especially grateful to Jim Caccamo, Pete Jordan, Matthew Whelan, Liz Costello, and anonymous reviewers who offered helpful comments on successive drafts.

Journal of Moral Theology, Vol. 4, No. 1 (2015): 65-89

Containing a "Pandora's" Box: The Importance of Labor Unions in the Digital Age

Patrick Flanagan

TECHNOLOGICAL CHANGE AND GLOBALIZATION have been identified as contributing factors to the steady decline of labor union membership. This article argues that these two areas in the digital age are, in fact, critically fertile areas for contemporary labor union activity and focuses specifically on technology's impact. The essay uses Pandora, one specific on-demand Internet radio music service, as a case study to illustrate this reality. While generating significant corporate revenue, music artists have argued that Pandora has failed to distribute profits justly. This article appeals to Roman Catholic social teaching on unions to amplify and sustain the work of labor organizations like the American Society of Composers, Authors and Publishers in their efforts to dismantle Pandora's unjust labor practices and ensure "the priority of labor over capital."

Information communication technology has transformed social, economic, political, and healthcare landscapes in revolutionary ways. In just under a generation, the World Wide Web has connected people in ways previously unknown, indeed almost unforeseen save for science fiction and Marshall McLuhan. This technological innovation has certainly increased the amount and, in many instances, enhanced the quality of social, economic, and political engagement. Pope Francis recently acknowledged this in his June 2014 World Communications Day Message, calling the Web "something truly good, a gift from God."[1] Further, Francis added: "Media can help us greatly, especially nowadays, when the networks of human communication have made unprecedented advances. The Internet, in particular, offers immense possibilities for encounter and solidarity."

While the Web has had positive transformative effects on users' lives—in every field from medical research to elementary education, users also contend with criminal activity such as identity theft, assault

[1] Pope Francis, "Communication at the Service of an Authentic Culture of Encounter," Pope Francis's Message for World Communications Day (June 1, 2014), w2.vatican.va/content/francesco/en/messages/communications/documents/papa-francesco_20140124_messaggio-comunicazioni-sociali.html.

(such as cyber-bullying), intrusion such as malware, worms, and viruses, and fraud such as those "419 scam emails" that alert readers to their winning a lottery or being part of an fictitious inheritance.[2] Challenges also surface from user added content and capabilities of the Web itself that many users have found offensive, including a lack of "netiquette." Francis's predecessor, the recently canonized pope St. John Paul II, perhaps because of his station in the early stages of information technology, was more measured than Francis in his appreciation for online activity. In his message for World Communications Day in 1989, St. John Paul II pointed out that "we must learn to *cope* with the computer culture" (emphasis added) and encouraged "wisdom in using the potential of the 'computer age' to serve man's human and transcendent calling, and thus give glory to the Father from whom all good things come."[3] Information technology— both then and now— is not some passing novelty and cannot receive a patronizing disposition or helpless resolve from the Church. Rather, what is needed is a healthy and dynamic appreciation for this age of information—and its concomitant, ever-evolving technology. St. John Paul II, in this same message, was clear that the Church must "rise to the challenge of new discoveries and technologies by bringing to them a moral vision rooted in our religious faith, respect for the human person, and commitment to transform the world in accordance with God's plan."

---

[2] The Federal Bureau of Investigation's Internet Crime Complaint Center's *2013 Internet Crime Report* offers comprehensive statistical information and analysis of fraud in the United States committed over the Internet during 2013. The evidence presented in this report exposes the extent and commonness of Internet fraud in the United States. In 2013, the Center received 262,813 complaints down from the 289,874 complaints received in 2012; fraudulent activity and identity thefts comprised a goodly portion of the cases presented. However, as the Report notes, while the number of filed complaints were lower, there was a 48.8 percent increase in reported losses in 2013 ($781,841,611.) over 2012 ($581,441,110). This now annual document also compiles the number and particular nature of complaints regarding Internet fraud, the complainants' places of origin who have fallen prey, the people or corporations responsible, the median economic loss to victims, and the communications that may have occurred between the two. Identity theft, hacking, spamming, viewing child pornography and marketing scams were the most commonly reported offenses. It is the 14th annual publication of the Internet Crime Complaint Center (IC3), a collaborative venture launched in May 2001 by the National White Collar Crime Center (NWC3) and the Federal Bureau of Investigation (FBI). Originally, the IC3 was established as The Internet Fraud Complaint Center (IFCC). In December 2003, the name was changed to the IC3 to "better reflect the broader character of such matters having a cyber (Internet) nexus." The IC3 has only one goal: sanitizing the Internet of all fraud. This federal agency accomplishes this by expediting the reports to law enforcement or regulatory agencies received from said victims of fraud. (Federal Bureau of Investigation Internet Crime Complaint Center, *2013 Internet Crime Report*, www.ic3.gov/media/annualreport/2013_IC3Report.pdf).

[3] St. John Paul II, "The Church Must Learn to Cope With Computer Culture" (May 27, 1989), www.ewtn.com/library/PAPALDOC/JP2COMPU.HTM.

The sheer number of challenges that the Web poses to users can be overwhelming.[4] For users to resign themselves to a dystopian perspective of the Web would not be faithful to the pope's call to align information technology with the vision God offers. In this essay, I explore the possibility that labor unions, long regarded by the Catholic Church as integral to the cause of labor and the worker, can be a primary resource for resolving one particular type of malicious activity perpetuated on the Web, namely streaming music.[5]

While some have suggested that technological change and globalization are the death knell for labor unions, I contend in this essay that the Web is an opportune platform for extending their reach.[6] This article seeks to contribute to the burgeoning body of literature that acknowledges the invaluable import of information communication technology while conceding the hazardous challenges of the Web's

---

[4] Over two hundred years ago, in response to the introduction of technology into the marketplace, Luddites, who took their name from their fictional leader Ned Ludd, destroyed innovative machinery they believed to have a negative impact on their simple way of life. Kirkpatrick Sale has made perpetuating the Luddite agenda his bailiwick. Unlike his historic predecessors, Sale prefers political and intellectual engagement rather than the historic "hatchet, pike, and gun" to dismantle technology. Neo-Luddism roots its negative posture, at best a cautious position, towards modern technology in the philosophies of Martin Heidegger and Jacques Ellul as well as more contemporary philosophers Albert Borgmann, Hubert Dreyfus, and Don Ihde. A large number of neo-Luddites might consist of those who have chosen intentionally to disengage totally from technology, but there are others who have made it their task advance the Luddite agenda thereby perpetuating challenges like malware, viruses, and worms, to computer users. (Kirkpatrick Sale, *Rebels Against the Future: The Luddites and Their War on the Industrial Revolution, Lessons for the Computer Age* [Cambridge, MA: Perseus Publishing, 1996]).

[5] The long regard the Catholic Church has had for labor justice extends back beyond Leo XIII's 1891 *Rerum Novarum* to the Hebrew Scriptures to where a "preferential option for the poor" can be traced. The Church's concern also finds its footing for regard for the worker and labor in the teachings of Jesus Christ in the New Testament, patristic and medieval scholarship, and in the documentary heritage of modern Catholic social teaching. The *Compendium of the Social Doctrine of the Church* emphasizes the Church's involvement in labor justice is an effort to establish a "civilization of love." (Catholic Scholars for Worker Justice, "Catholic Social Doctrine and Worker Justice: A Call to the Common Good" (July 2008), www.cswj.us/CSWJ%20-%20CATHOLIC%20SOCIAL%20TEACHING%20AND%20WORKER%20JUSTICE-1.pdf.

[6] Daron Acemoglu, "Technical Change, Inequality, and the Labor Market." *Journal of Economic Literature*, 40:1 (2002): 7-72; Andreas Bergh and Therese Nilsson, "Do Liberalization and Globalization Increase Income Inequality?," *European Journal of Political Economy* 26:4 (2010): 488-505; Kjell Erik Lommerud, Frode Meland, and Odd Rune Straume, "Globalisation and Union Opposition to Technological Change," *Journal of International Economics* 68.1 (2006): 1-23; and, Gabriel Nahmias, "Organized Labor in a Globalized World: The Impact of Increasing Economic Integration on the Strategies of Trade Unions" (2013), https://etd.library.emory.edu/view/record/pid/emory:d7bpp.

dark side. The article also seeks to contribute to the cache of scholarship on labor unions by demonstrating their significance in this technology rich time that we find ourselves. The paper is divided into five parts. First, it reviews the foundations of the labor movement in the United States, analyzes recent data on labor union membership, and identifies some of the suggested reasons why union membership is on the decline. This overview is an effort to demonstrate their historical import in resolving disputes between management and labor, sometimes with the help of the government. It is also an endeavor to propose a renewal of interest in labor unions for the pressing concerns labor and management meet in the new work environment of the Web. Second, it introduces readers to Pandora, as an example of one contentious technological platform into which labor unions can make a positive impact on labor in the digital age. Pandora is one specific on-demand Internet radio music service that streams music to subscribers. Music artists whose creative work is streamed on Pandora have claimed in civil courts that Pandora has failed to pay them a just wage. At the same time, Pandora has sought regularly through legal channels to decrease the revenue musicians receive. Third, the article will demonstrate the prominent role which labor unions have held in Roman Catholic social teaching specifically regarding their promotion of human dignity and the battle for a just wage. The essay will then describe wage theft and isolate the cunning methods of wage theft perpetuated by Pandora. It will then introduce the American Society of Composers, Authors, and Publishers (ASCAP) as one labor union pressing for just remuneration vis-à-vis Pandora. Finally, the article will argue that while legislation eventually may resolve this labor dispute, a moral solution is feasible now. Individual computer users can stave off this violation of human dignity in Pandora's wage theft through choosing not to cooperate morally with this music platform until it is resolved rightly.

Labor Unions

The foundational history of unions in the United States reveals the preeminent place of organized labor has had as a social good in the life of the worker since their beginning. Their origin in America can be traced back to post-Civil War economies as increased migration to and rising industrialization in the United States quickly transformed the landscape of labor. Astorga notes that this time "was one of incredible economic and political complexity. It was a time of tumultuous changes resulting from the shift from feudalism to capitalism, which reached its zenith in the Industrial Revolution."[7] As the Industrial Revolution swept across Europe in the eighteenth century and

[7] Christina A. Astorga, *Catholic Moral Theology and Social Ethics: A New Method* (Maryknoll, NY: Orbis Books, 2014), 237.

subsequently penetrated American shores, labor unions emerged.[8] In his commentary on *Rerum Novarum* Shannon commented on the context in which Leo XIII's encyclical was written. Shannon remarked "the availability of jobs lured more and more to the cities. To fill these jobs, family members spent their days outside the home in the factory motivated by the lure of year-round wages as opposed to seasonal farm wages." [9]

With these new workspaces, fresh opportunities seemed to abound for generating revenue, for some, at the expense of the worker. This is not unlike contemporary online economies in cyberspace, including Pandora, which have had their fair share of predatory behavior. Concern for workers' rights in any of these new industrial spaces easily could be compromised in favor of greater production.[10] Organized labor was a natural response then as it could be now vis-à-vis Pandora as workers face a myriad of unanticipated challenges of wages, benefits, working conditions, and relations with dominant management in

---

[8] "While this revolution was most significant for the lower classes, no one escaped its effect. The shift from the land to the city caused massive social dislocation compounded by a lack of housing, and left millions unemployed. The shift from the home to the factory led to miserly wages, deplorable working conditions, particularly for children, and severe strains on families. While the social effects of this revolution were particularly keen in England, few cities in Europe or America escaped [its effects]." (Daniel J. O'Brien and Thomas A. Shannon, *Catholic Social Thought: The Documentary Heritage*, 5th edition [Maryknoll, NY: Orbis Books, 1998], 12).

[9] Thomas A. Shannon, "Commentary on Rerum Novarum (The Condition of Labor)," *Modern Catholic Social Teaching: Commentaries and Interpretations,* Kenneth R. Himes, O.F.M., Lisa Sowle Cahill, Charles E. Curran, David Hollenbach, S.J., and Thomas Shannon, eds., (Washington D.C.: Georgetown University Press, 2005), 129. In relation to *Rerum Novarum,* Astorga argues that "at the heart of the encyclical was a cry of protest against the treatment of workers" (241).

[10] The pleasantries of the family farm, where life tended to be less exacting, gave way to the factory, where work could be grueling, mindless toil. The factory environment tended to lack any formal legal structure. The workplace was run on the "voracious appetite of the marketplace" and the whim of "bosses" whose sole intention was to generate a profit and establish hegemony in a growing competitive culture – all at the expense of the worker. Every employee was replaceable as few skills were needed to function on the demanding assembly labor line. Work days could be painfully exhausting for employees (children included) lasting to ten to twelve hours on the average, sometimes in compromising confines. Employees, though, needed their jobs to live and support their families. For fear of retribution and lack of particular negotiation skills, workers remained silent and endured abuse, particularly women who "had to endure the sexual solicitations of the managers." When labor unions arose, they would serve as the voice of the worker. (Bernard V. Brady, *Essential Catholic Social Thought* [Maryknoll, NY: Orbis Books, 2008]; Shannon, "Commentary on Rerum Novarum [The Condition of Labor)]," 129).

a new workplace. Workers can tackle these issues on their own as individuals, but collective action historically has a more profound effect.[11]

These organized collectives have profoundly impacted the landscape of labor throughout the world both positively and, admittedly, negatively. The trajectory of efforts of labor unions extends to today with the same acute goal to ensure a just quality of living for the laborer in the workplace and in society. Historically, the relationships labor unions have had with management and government have not been always amicable. The struggles contemporary labor unions experience are not new. Tension seems to be an unavoidable reality as labor leaders work with management to achieve what they understand might be the best way of sustaining justice for the worker. Lichtenstein suggests that this is a "power game" by which both sides seek to "rule in the workplace."[12]

To resolve this power differential, labor unions and management have turned to government as a resource. In their own continuing disputes, Pandora and ASCAP have resourced government in an effort to resolve challenges music artists encounter. Government involvement is nothing new. In the history of American labor unions, government has been actively involved in different capacities serving as an arbiter in resolving strikes or closing negotiations. Government has also enacted legislation to protect labor and ensure workers' right to assemble and voice their claims. In 1935, the U.S. government enacted the National Labor Relations Act, also known as the Wagner Act, giving private sector employees the right to form unions, negotiate through collective bargaining, and engage in collective action such as work stoppage (strike). This Act also established the National Labor Relations Board as an independent government agency that conducts elections

---

[11] The history of labor unions is one of fits and starts that soon gained enough momentum to have some sustainability. The initial efforts of the Federal Society of Journeymen Cordwainers in 1794, National Trades' Union in 1834, National Typographic Union in 1852, and National Labor Union in 1866, towards unionizing seemed to disappear as soon as quickly as they assembled. It was not until local Philadelphia labor leader Uriah Stephens formed the "noble and holy order of Knights of Labor" in 1869 that a union truly would become national and enjoy some sustainability. As a collective unit, the Knights, under Stephens' and then Terence Powderly's leadership, provided a powerful base for workers' rights. The Knights wanted to represent the collective concerns of employees to management and government officials in an effort to improve their working conditions. In their negotiating and bargaining efforts, they strove to ensure a better life for workers including, but not limited to, just wages and benefits, job security, restriction of child labor, eight-hour days, and workers' and workplace safety. They also sought to clarify the management-labor power structure. After the downfall of the Knights, other labor organizations, some even greater in membership and influence like the American Federation of Labor-Congress of Industrial Organizations (AFL-CIO)—presently, the leading confederation of US trade unions— stepped in to advance the cause of the worker.

[12] Lichtenstein, *State of the Union: A Century of American Labor,* 240.

and resolves unfair labor practices. This Act shored up the power of labor unions in the U.S. and led to a significant uptick in their membership. From 1935 to 1945, the membership rolls of labor unions grew from 13.2 to 35.5 percent with a slight decrease at the end of the '30s and early '40s. Since 1945, though, membership in American labor unions has steadily declined and hopes of reversing this trend can be suspect given the statistical data.[13] In its 2013 annual summary of unionization, the United States Bureau of Labor Statistics did convey some leveling off, but unions remain in a very vulnerable position. The Bureau reported that the union membership rate of wage and salary workers in one year had remained consistent at 11.3 percent, which amounts to 14.5 million people.[14] While there was little to no difference in the overall total workforce, union membership in the government-sector workforce declined slightly. The reasons for this specific decline are not clear and may very well be connected to a reduction in government-sector jobs overall.

As a social good, labor unions have been the backbone of the middle class—growing and sustaining it—as they expose the hardships and miseries of the working class.[15] Yet, their future appears to be in jeopardy. Responding positively to this concern is vital especially to the music industry in general in which most of the musicians and artists comprise a middle class. While there may have been blips over the past forty-five years, the decline in union membership has paralleled

---

[13] Steven Greenhouse, "Union Membership Drops Despite Job Growth," *The New York Times* (January 23, 2013), www.nytimes.com/2013/01/24/business/union-membership-drops-despite-job-growth.html; James Sherk and Filip Jolevski, "Labor Unions: Stagnant Membership Shows Need for Labor Law Modernization" (January 28, 2014), www.heritage.org/research/reports/2014/01/labor-unions-membership-and-labor-law-modernization.

[14] U.S. Department of Labor Bureau of Labor Statistics, *U.S. Bureau of Labor Statistics' 2013 Union Membership Report* (January 24, 2014), www.bls.gov/news.release/pdf/union2.pdf.

[15] Paula Voos from the Economic Policy Institute argues that unions are critical to the middle class and can help restore them by ensuring a fair wage and just benefit package for workers. She argues "increased union organization would tend to shift the income distribution in favor of the middle class, enhancing the purchasing power of this key group of the nation's consumers and allowing them to once again afford to buy automobiles, homes with 30-year fixed rate mortgages, and all the other goods and services important to American life. Unionization of low-wage service workers similarly would increase purchasing power and help revive the economy. Putting more dollars into the pockets of working families stimulates the American economy – both in the short term and in the long run – because they spend such a high proportion of those dollars here." (Paula B. Voos, "How Unions Can Help Restore the Middle Class" (March 10, 2009), www.epi.org/publication/how_unions_can_help_restore_the_middle_class/). See also: Nicholas Abercrombie and John Urry, *Capital, Labour, and the Middle Classes* (Oxford, UK: Routledge, 2014); Dennis Gilbert, *The American Class Structure in an Age of Growing Inequality* (Thousand Oaks, CA: Sage Publications, 2014); Lawrence R. Samuel, *The American Middle Class: A Cultural History* (Oxford, UK: Routledge, 2013).

the steady decrease in the size of the middle class. Bolstering labor unions' membership role then is critical. In addition to the aforementioned empirical data, scholars have identified several reasons for this steady decline over the past seventy years. They are described here to amplify the tremendous external constraints and self-identity challenges that ASCAP faces in its union efforts to resolve labor disputes with Pandora.

Some have suggested that waning interest in joining labor unions can be traced back to the 1947 Taft-Hartley Act which significantly curtailed labor union activity. Labor leaders called this legislation, also known as the Labor Relations *Management* Act, a "slave labor bill."[16] With the passage of the 1935 National Labor Relations Act, conservative members of the U.S. congress turned their efforts to eclipsing the increasing achievements and burgeoning influence of the labor movement. One of the celebrated achievements of the efforts of this conservative Congress was the Taft-Hartley Act which sought to cripple labor through the thorough reform of the National Labor Relations Act by imposing a considerable amount of restrictions on unions, most notably the prohibition of strikes and the election of rebellious leaders.[17]

The image of labor unions throughout their history also has not been so positive.[18] "Corrupt," "self-serving," "hegemonic," and "bloated" are words that come to unsympathetic people's minds when thinking about labor unions, more specifically vis-à-vis union leadership. Prevost, Rao, and Williams envision labor unions as "shareholder activists," but then question whether labor unions are "champions or detractors" to corporate progress.[19] Labor unions, I would suggest, if left unchecked, can amount to nothing but glorified legal Ponzi schemes that satiate the appetites of the unions' leadership while exacting major annual fees from its members. The classic 1950s movie *On the Waterfront* well depicted such corruption existent within labor organizations and the U.S. government's dogged efforts to purify unions of criminal activity.

Beyond economic factors, there are social factors. For some, labor unions are archaic, inhumane, and inefficient. Contemporary workers,

---

16 "National Affairs: Barrel No. 2," *Time* (June 23, 1947), http://content.time.com/time/magazine/article/0,9171,797962,00.html. See also: Craig Becker, "The Pattern of Union Decline, Economic and Political Consequences, and the Puzzle of a Legislative Response." *Minnesota Law Review* 98 (2014): 1637-1980.

17 Sharon Smith, *Subterranean Fire: A History of Working-Class Radicalism in the United States* (Chicago: Haymarket Books, 2006).

18 James B. Jacobs and Ellen Peters, "Labor Racketeering: The Mafia and the Unions," *Crime and Justice* 30 (2003): 229-282.

19 Andrew K. Prevost, Ramesh P. Rao, and Melissa A. Williams, "Labor Unions as Shareholder Activists: Champions or Detractors?" *Financial Review* 47 (2012): 327–49.

particularly Millennials and younger, are legally intelligent and savvy with social media.[20] This generation is cognizant of their rights as workers and, if need be, know technological and activist platforms to address their concerns. Government is available to them at the click of a mouse and the government has a cache of laws in place that protect the worker in the marketplace to which a laborer can appeal. For these younger workers, there is little need for intermediaries like a labor union.[21] Unions can be nothing more than novel anachronistic relics. Unfortunately, this same younger population fails to recall one of the original motivations for forming unions was their power as a collective force.

For others, there are political impediments. The highly political nature of labor organizations also can be a negative factor that can preclude some from joining. Consider the example of a conservative citizen. While joining a union may be attractive, unions' alliances with the Democratic Party's ideals and agenda may be too contrary to the conservative citizen's own. A recent report on unions in the *Washington Examiner* notes this. The article reported that from 1989 to 2013, unions' political spending amounted to $755 million for Democrats and $64 million for Republicans.[22]

The labor landscape also has changed and is now more richly populated with *new* immigrants.[23] With the decline and movement of America's manufacturing industry and the changing demographics of the nation, these immigrants are not eager to join labor unions. Given the challenges in the workplace with which they have had to contend, they might be wise to do so. However, their participation in a labor union may not be part of their culture or they may choose not to do so for fear of losing their place in the American workforce.

Another reason for the marked decline in union membership is the movement of industry manufacturing jobs in the U.S. to other parts of the world. For all its celebrated positive enhancements to the world's economy, globalization has effected unions, significantly depreciating

---

[20] Ashley Cole, Trenia Napier, and Brad Marcum. "Generation Z: Facts and Fictions" *Not Just Where To Click: Teaching Students How To Think About Information.* Ed. Heather Jagman and Troy Swanson. (Atlanta: Association of College and Research Libraries, 2015); Tamara J. Erickson, *Plugged in: The Generation Y Guide to Thriving at Work* (Harvard: Harvard Business Press, 2010); and, Bruce Tulgan, *Not Everyone Gets A Trophy: How to Manage Generation Y* (San Francisco: Jossey-Bass, 2009).

[21] D. Martin Stanberry, "Youth and Organizing: Why Unions Will Struggle to Organize the Millennials," *Case Western Reserve Journal of Law, Technology, and the Internet* 2:2 (2011): 103-116.

[22] Sean Higgins, "Out of Touch with America: Are Unions Obsolete?," http://washingtonexaminer.com/are-unions-obsolete/unions-and-democratic-party.

[23] Immanuel Ness, *Immigrants, Unions, and the New U.S. Labor Market*, Philadelphia: Temple University Press, 2005.

its membership and influence.[24] Industry leaders can find cheaper labor costs overseas, and with the movement of vehicle and textile factories, jobs have been lost. In addition to this reality, a number of factory plants are situated in right-to-work states and workers either have ignored the call to unionize, perhaps because they do not see its value or they have been dissuaded by management.

Labor, as this paper amplifies, also has moved to cyberspace and consequently technological change is a significant contributing factor to the decrease in union membership.[25] While globalization moves jobs, technology supplants labor. In both instances, companies seek venues to acquire cheaper labor. Where a factory once operated with a cache of workers, now a computer can complete many of the tasks. While increased computerization also may have played a role in emptying labor union rosters, the critical role of labor unions in the digital age cannot be underestimated. Technological change does not have to be the final platform for labor unions; cyberspace can be another venue. Pandora is one example in the world of technology and globalization that demonstrates there is still room for labor unions to exercise their extraordinary regard for worker justice.

The Pandora Problem

In order to introduce the Pandora problem and appreciate its gravity, it would be helpful to begin with a more familiar reality, the famous birthday song. Over the past fifteen years, American restaurants have taken to singing the popular tune "Happy Birthday to You" in a different key and altering the lyrics. The popular Mexican American eatery Chili's is one example of this. Servers at Chili's sing this well-known song, but in a particularly local fashion. Upon hearing it sung in an untraditional fashion, it can be an odd rendition, but other culinary establishments also have turned to singing "Happy Birthday to You" in a different melody and changing the familiar words. Upon further investigation, I discovered that the timeless "Happy Birthday to You" song is under copyright. Whenever eateries use the same musical arrangement with the original precise lyrics, royalties must be paid to the owner of the copyright.[26] Neither Chili's nor many other eateries want to have to dole out regular annual payments so they have adopted a modified version.

Some background would be helpful to understand the origins of this song and its ownership. The copyright for the "Happy Birthday to You" song was purchased by The Summy Company in 1935 on behalf

[24] Gary Chaison, *The Unions' Response to Globalization* (New York: Springer, 2014).
[25] Kjell Erik Lommerud, Frode Meland, and Odd Rune Straume, "Globalisation and Union Opposition to Technological Change."
[26] John Tehranian, *Infringement Nation: Copyright 2.0 and You* (Oxford, UK: Oxford University Press, 2011).

of lyricists Preston Ware Orem and R.R. Forman. Summy successfully acquired the music from the Hill sisters who were the original 1893 creators of the song "Good Morning to All," on which the present birthday song lyrics are arranged. In 1990, Warner Chappell purchased Summy acquiring the birthday song valued at $5 million dollars and annually grossing $2 million dollars in revenue.[27] Given that Summy owned the copyright for "Happy Birthday to You" since 1935, Warner Chappell contends that its copyright expires in 2030.[28] Therefore, any singing of the popular birthday song is subject to copyright restriction.

Paying a royalty each time "Happy Birthday to You" is sung is relatively new or, at least newly enforced. Copyright enforcement seems to have become a concern for eating establishments around 1998 when the Sonny Bono Copyright Term Extension Act, which extended copyright terms for the life of the author plus fifty years or seventy-five if there were corporate authorship, was passed. The 1998 Act subsequently was upheld by the U.S. Supreme Court after a challenge in 2003 in *Eldred v. Ashcroft*.[29]

When the traditional birthday song is not sung, royalties are not paid. Singing the celebratory song in a different tune and wording its lyrics differently is perfectly legal. Restaurants regularly use their own homespun rendition and remain in compliance with intellectual property law. There is something significantly morally disconcerting when a business would rather make up a new song than pay royalties, which is their legal and moral obligation. People are being robbed of their just wages. Pandora, on the other hand, which has its own cache of legal challenges and obligation to pay just royalties, doesn't bother with all that. Pandora amasses a significant revenue stream from its paid subscribers, advertisers, and stock options while compromising

---

[27] "The Economist Explains: Why are the Rights to "Happy Birthday" in Dispute?" (June 16, 2013), www.economist.com/blogs/economist-explains/2013/06/economist-explains-10.

[28] Warner Chappell's ownership still continues to be in question. Robert Brauneis contends that the copyright for "Happy Birthday to You" is no longer under copyright. ("Copyright and the World's Most Popular Song". *GWU Legal Studies Research Paper No. 1111624* (October 10, 2010), http://papers.ssrn.com/sol3/papers.cfm?abstract_id=1111624). See also: Emma Woollacott, "Class Action Suit Aims to Strip Warner of 'Happy Birthday' Copyright" (June 14, 2013), www.forbes.com/sites/emmawoollacott/2013/06/14/class-action-suit-aims-to-strip-warner-of-happy-birthday-copyright/.

[29] TyAnna Herrington, "Copyright, Free Speech, and Democracy: Eldred v. Ashcroft and Its Implications for Technical Communicators," *Technical Communication Quarterly* 20:1 (2010): 47-72.

the royalties of artists whose music is streamed from its service.[30] And, that's the Pandora problem.

As the U.S. legal system seeks to resolve the challenges of copyright violations, information technology has presented new ones. While the well-admired birthday song is protected by a law whereby a royalty must be paid each time it is sung in its original formulation, this is not the case with songs that are streamed on the World Wide Web through music streaming services like Pandora. Laws governing royalties for online streaming music continue to be disputed in American courts. The now-publicly traded Pandora is one streaming music service among a host of other emerging ones like Spotify, iHeart Radio, Last.FM, Slacker, and Apple's recently released iTunes Radio.

Among the competition in music streaming, Pandora is an industry leader and has recognizable brand reputation. It appeals to a new generation of music lovers who are opting not to engage in traditional purchasing and downloading of music, but to stream it. Pandora boasts that it has surpassed 200 million subscribers, about 2.8 million of them paying ones. Up until recently, there was one flat annual fee of $36.00. In May 2014, that annual option was jettisoned. Now, previous subscribers could sign up for month-to-month service for $3.99 while new subscribers would be charged $4.99 per month. Pandora explained that its costs, including royalties, required them to make this fiscal adjustment. While this change was not welcome by subscribers, it was a financial move Pandora had to make given its revenue stream. Pandora's financials filed with the SEC substantiated their claim that despite their steady income, their loss was significant. In the second quarter of 2014, Pandora's revenue rose to 158 million from 122 million the first quarter of 2014. During that same period, Pandora's loss was 5 million, a significant decline from the 20 million dollar loss in the previous quarter.[31]

Despite Pandora's corporate loss, its 2013 annual report revealed some shocking information as to how the generated income was distributed: key executives at the company received exorbitant salaries and compensation benefits. The metrics detailing Pandora's executive pay which included base salary and stock options in the SEC report are staggering.[32] CEO Brian McAndrews earned $29.1 million in 2013. Founder Tim Westergen was paid $11.69 million. The next four

---

[30] This case of Pandora is not an isolated one. Amazon recently has entered a similar fray with its recent "Kindle Unlimited." Publishers and authors are at odds over royalties for online books (George Anders, "Why Amazon Terrifies Publishers: Let's Look At Royalty Statements" (July 21, 2014), www.forbes.com/sites/georgeanders/2014/07/21/why-amazon-terrifies-publishers-lets-look-at-royalty-statements/.

[31] Pandora, "Financial Information" (July 24, 2014), investor.pandora.com/phoenix.zhtml?c=227956&p=quarterlyearnings.

[32] "Pandora Media Inc" (2014), http://insiders.morningstar.com/trading/executive-compensation.action?t=P.

top staff members earned a combined $26.1 million. Unfortunately, musicians featured on Pandora and streamed through their music service are not paid in the same salary bracket for their talent and artistry. Some are compensated, but rarely fairly. Others, particularly emerging music artists, never see any royalties. One musician offered a perspective on Pandora:

> We are big fans of Pandora. That's why we helped give the company a discount on rates for the past decade. Pandora is now enjoying phenomenal success as a Wall Street company. Skyrocketing growth in revenues and users. We celebrate that. At the same time, the music community is just not beginning to gain its footing in this new digital world. Pandora's principal asset is the music. Why is the company asking Congress once again to step in and gut the royalties that thousands of musicians rely upon? That's not fair and that's not how partners work together. Congress has many pressing issues to consider, but this is not one of them. Let's work this out as partners and continue to bring fans the great musical experiences they rightly expect.[33]

Other statements from artists contend that Pandora has made it impossible for songwriters to earn a living.[34] These allegations are repeated over and over again by artists who express their concern for just remuneration for use of their musical work. Such a claim might seem unfounded given our appreciation of whose music is played on Pandora and how much in royalties they are compensated, so some financial data would be helpful.

Forbes has identified the top 25 revenue grossing musicians for 2013. It will come as no surprise to many that leading the list is the pop artist Madonna making $125 million, followed by Lady Gaga with $80 million and Bon Jovi with $79 million. ASCAP protects the interests of these established songwriters and their producers that generate significant revenue.[35] One could suggest that protecting these rich art-

---

[33] Glenn Peoples, "From Alabama to Rihanna, Stars Fight Pandora on Royalties" (November 15, 2012), www.billboard.com/articles/news/474153/from-alabama-to-rihanna-stars-fight-pandora-on-royalties. .

[34] While Bette Midler may not be the best example of the average musician whose median income would classify him or her as middle class, her celebrity status does offer her a bullypulpit for public protesting. She tweeted to her 636K followers: @bettemidler : @Spotify and @Pandora have made it impossible for songwriters to earn a living: three months streaming on Pandora, 4,175,149 plays=$114.11. (The Trichordist: Artists For An Ethical and Sustainable Internet #StopArtistExploitation (April 5, 2014), http://thetrichordist.com/2014/04/05/bettemidler-spotify-and-pandora-have-made-it-impossible-for-songwriters-to-earn-a-living-three-months-streaming-on-pandora-4175149-plays114-11/).

[35] "The World's Highest-Paid Musicians 2013," *Forbes*, November 19, 2013 http://www.forbes.com/sites/zackomalleygreenburg/2013/11/19/the-worlds-highest-paid-musicians-2013/.

ists is a social good, but such a proposition is limited given the exhaustive wealth these individuals enjoy. Protecting millions of not so well-known, not nearly as rich, artists who rely on Pandora for exposure opportunities for their music, is a more obvious social good. ASCAP does that. ASCAP recognizes that musicians contribute to significant components of society enhancing the life of the local community through their talents. They serve as roving music teachers in our schools, act as therapists at care centers, participate in community orchestras, and play at neighborhood events. Through negotiated contracting, marketing strategies, and legislative efforts, ASCAP also seeks to advance the cause of those artists who earn low wages and comprise the middle class of musicians and singers.[36]

I am not making the claim that the aforementioned artists should be given less, but saying that artists who could stand to make less are few and far between. Despite television shows like MTV's "Cribs" that showcase the extraordinary lives of some musical artists, most musicians make very little money. They are not wealthy. Their purported wealth is an assumption that is just not true but unfortunately perpetuated through those affluent music artists more popularly known who enjoy sustained exposure through the media and marketing. The majority of musicians are middle class to low class wage earners. They don't make any charts or appear publicly.[37] Concrete evidence supports this claim in that musicians regularly need other jobs to supplement their salary. Simply put, most musicians do not make or approach anywhere near Forbes top 25 revenue grossing musicians.

At a 2012 South by Southwest conference, an annual festival and conference of film and music artists, Artist Revenue Streams co-directors Kristin Thomson and Jean Cook discussed their Artist Revenue Streams project, "a multi method research project examining changes in musicians' sources of income."[38] Their project destabilizes four common myths regarding musicians and wealth: "musicians are rich; in a post-Napster world, musicians make all their money from shows and live performances; in a post-Napster world, musicians don't make

---

[36] ASCAP's mission is clear: "ASCAP is the leading advocate for the rights of songwriters, composers and music publishers. With over 500,000 music creator members, ASCAP is committed to working together with other stakeholders throughout the music industry to make meaningful changes to our music licensing system so that it works better for everyone—writers, composers, publishers, licensees and music fans," www.ascap.com/.

[37] In January 2014, http://forgotify.com/ went live. It streams the 80% of 20 million songs on Spotify that have had zero plays, equivalent to approximately 4 million songs, (Rebecca J. Rosen, "Forgotify: The Tool for Discovering Spotify's 4 Million Unheard Tracks" January 30, 2014, www.theatlantic.com/technology/archive/2014/01/-forgotify-the-tool-for-discovering-spotifys-4-million-unheard-tracks/283484/.

[38] Kristin Thomson and Jean Cook, "Brass in Pocket: Accessing More Musician Income" (March 15, 2012), http://schedule.sxsw.com/2012/events/event_MP11000.

any money selling music; and, in a post-Napster world, musicians make all of their money from selling t-shirts and other merchandise."[39] Through their research, they confirmed the greater prevalence of the middle class of musicians than those more popularly known and paid better. The findings of this project are disturbing. "Examining the qualitative and quantitative data collected as part of the Artist Revenue Streams project," they found "that the average personal *gross* income for the past twelve months of all survey respondents was $55,561" (emphasis mine). This amount is inclusive of all revenue a musician makes for the craft as well as other employment and fiscal responsibilities. While this gross income was "slightly higher than the U.S. population, Thomson and Cook calculated the "gross estimated music income," the percent of income generated solely from music, at $34,455, "slightly lower than the Bureau of Labor Statistics' per capita personal income estimates for 2010 which was $39,945."[40] Again, here it is important to note that these estimates are gross and not net income. They also do not include expenses that can offset any estimated revenue.

Some might turn to legal remedies for resolving the Pandora problem, and both Pandora and ASCAP continue to engage in litigious actions, but ASCAP as a labor union can make a significant impact on behalf of music artists. Throughout their history, labor unions have sought more just wages to sustain for a viable middle class of which musicians comprise. In doing so, the Roman Catholic Church has been one of labor unions' leading advocates.

Roman Catholic Social Teaching on Unions

Since the time of Leo XIII's approbation of labor unions in *Rerum novarum*, labor unions have enjoyed unprecedented support and consistent buoying from the Roman Catholic Church as evidenced in the history of its social teaching. The Church has been indefatigable in acknowledging the important role that labor unions play in being a "mouthpiece for the struggle for social justice, for the just rights of working people in accordance with their individual professions."[41] Pope Francis confirmed this recently when he remarked "trade unions

---

[39] Kristin Thomson, "Mythbusting: Data Driven Answers to Four Common Assumptions About How Musicians Make Money" (December 2, 2012), http://money.futureofmusic.org/mythbusting.

[40] Berklee College of Music, "Music Careers in Dollars and Sense: 2012 Edition," www.berklee.edu/pdf/pdf/studentlife/Music_Salary_Guide.pdf.

[41] John Paul II, *Laborem exercens*, (May 15, 1991), no. 20, www.vatican.va/holy_father/leo_xiii/encyclicals/documents/hf_l-xiii_enc_15051891_rerum-novarum_-en.html.

have been an essential force for social change, without which a semblance of a decent and humane society is impossible under capitalism."[42]

In its 2004 *Compendium of the Social Doctrine of the Church*, the Catholic Church identifies five key roles unions have in the promotion of labor justice. The first is the role labor unions have in the promotion of the common good through "positive influence for social order and solidarity, and are therefore an indispensible element of social life."[43] Labor unions are responsible for "the whole task of economic and social development and in the attainment of the universal common good."[44] The Pontifical Council for Justice and Peace's 2012 document *The Vocation of the Business Leader* echoed this, affirming, "it is dangerous and misinformed simply to consider business as a 'society of shares', where self-interests, contracts, utility, and financial profit maximization exhaust its meaning."[45] Labor unions must be proactive and must promote just labor as their goal. Any effort towards being "self-referential," to use Pope Francis' language, is destructive to the worker and the cause of justice in the marketplace.[46]

Second, unions have a role to play in protecting worker interests. Stemming from natural law, the Catholic Church argues humanity has "the right to form associations or unions to defend the vital interests of workers employed in the various professions."[47] These groups play a crucial role in negotiating just wages and benefits, particularly in volatile and compromised workplaces. Third, the Catholic Church believes that unions have a role to play in establishing a just wage, which they believe is intimately connected to human dignity. "Remuneration is the most important means for achieving justice in work relationships." The Church defines a fair wage as that by which workers "may be furnished the means to cultivate…material, social, cultural and

---

[42] "Pope Francis is a Rare Christian Leader in that He Espouses and Practices Actual Christian Values" (December 29, 2013), www.ign.com/boards/threads/pope-francis-is-a-rare-christian-leader-in-that-he-espouses-and-practices-actual-christian-values.453653243/.

[43] Pontifical Council for Justice and Peace, *Compendium of Social Doctrine of the Catholic Church* (April 2005), www.vatican.va/roman_curia/pontifical_councils/justpeace/documents/rc_pc_justpeace_doc_20060526_compendio-dott-soc_en.html, no. 305

[44] Pontifical Council for Justice and Peace, *Compendium*, No. 307.

[45] Pontifical Council for Justice and Peace, *The Vocation of the Business Leader* (November 2012), www.stthomas.edu/cathstudies/cst/VocationBusinessLead/VocationTurksonRemar/VocationBk3rdEdition.pdf, no. 58.

[46] Pope Francis, "Homily of Pope Francis: Solemnity of Pentecost, Holy Mass with the Ecclesial Movements" (May 19, 2013), w2.vatican.va/content/francesco/en/homilies/2013/documents/papa-francesco_20130519_omelia-pentecoste.html.

[47] Pontifical Council for Justice and Peace, *Compendium*, no. 305.

spiritual life and that of his dependents," which make up the components of a dignified life.[48]

Fourth, labor unions are to sustain and extend solidarity, "the intrinsic social nature of the human person" and the "bond of interdependence between individuals and peoples."[49] Solidarity acknowledges that all are connected to each other. It breeds greater participation and regard for the common good. Subsidiarity flows from solidarity. "The characteristic implication of subsidiarity is participation…by means of which the citizen, either as an individual or in association with others, whether directly or through representation, contributes to the cultural, economic, political and social life of the civil community to which he belongs."[50] Finally, labor unions must take care to uphold this without political bias, and not "play politics" but foster "relations within the world of work…marked by cooperation; hatred and attempts to eliminate the other are completely unacceptable."[51] Politics in bargaining and negotiations seem unavoidable. Yet, what the Catholic Church promotes is a level playing field where politics are not used in a manipulative self-serving way, but for the good of all parties involved.

WAGE THEFT & ASCAP'S ROLE IN JUST REMUNERATION

Of the many areas in which current labor unions find themselves fighting for the worker, wage theft is a prominent one.[52] A just wage is allied with human dignity; any hedging or withholding of properly due wages is a violation of that dignity. If dignified treatment of workers is to be realized in the digital music industry through just remuneration, allowance for collective intervention and just venues for recourse such as labor unions are required.

Wage theft is much more common and insidious than the average worker would like to believe. After a yearlong study of low-wage industries in Chicago, Los Angeles, and New York City, a group of researchers published "Broken Laws, Unprotected Workers: Violations of Employment and Labor Laws in America's Cities" in 2009.[53] In their landmark report, this group acknowledged the limitations of labor laws in protecting workers throughout the United States. Their findings reported that widespread abuse of American laborers in the

---

48 Pontifical Council for Justice and Peace, *Compendium*, no. 302.

49 Pontifical Council for Justice and Peace, *Compendium*, no. 192.

50 Pontifical Council for Justice and Peace, *Compendium*, no. 189.

51 Pontifical Council for Justice and Peace, *Compendium*, no. 306.

52 John Brueggemann, "The Role of Organized Labor in Civil Society," *Sociology Compass* 8:8 (2014): 1033-1044; C. Melissa Snarr, *All You that Labor: Religion and Ethics in the Living Wage Movement*, New York: NYU Press, 2011.

53 Annette Bernhardt, et al., "Broken Laws, Unprotected Workers," New York: National Employment Law Project (2009), www.leg.wa.gov/JointCommittees/UECI/Documents/112009/Broken%20Laws%20Unprotected%20Workers.pdf .

workplace exists in all sectors, but more evidently in the restaurant and service industries. These are the sectors where workers need their jobs and refrain from speaking out or attempting to organize for fear of retaliation. Music artists are not grouped with either these two cohorts, but easily could be given how the competition in the music industry is significantly high for procuring a job and keeping one. It then tends to keep a musician from raising concerns for fear of retribution. Organized labor, as representative of a collective group of musicians, then is critically important to resolving wage theft.

The U.S. Department of Labor, Wage, and Hour Division has identified six examples of wage theft. The first is overtime abuse.[54] A 40 hour workweek is standard. Any work done beyond that time should be compensated accordingly unless exempt from the Fair Labor Standards Act. In the aforementioned study, "76% of those who worked more than 40 hours were not paid the legally required overtime rate." Next is employee classification. Employees enjoy certain legal rights and protections, but these privileges depend on whether or not the worker is an "employee" or an "independent contractor." The critical survey found that "job and employer characteristics are keys to understanding workplace violations. For example, the industry and occupation of a worker's job was one of the strongest predictors of violations." Third are minimum wage violations whereby employers essentially cheat workers out of the highest federal, state, or city wage. Shockingly, "26% of low-wage workers were paid less than the minimum wage in the week prior to the survey." Fourth is working "off the clock" and not getting paid. Employers sometimes toy with the time as to when work begins, ends, and accordingly paying wages. There are some employers who will pay only for the work time and not for any remote preparation in dressing, assembly, or concluding work, much less breaks or meal time. Fifth are illegal deductions from pay. Some employers compromise minimum wage laws by deducting unauthorized and even illegal amounts from employees' paychecks often for nefarious reasons including bathroom usage, computer browsing, and inattentiveness to time constraints for lunch and breaks, to name a few. And, lastly, wage theft consists in delaying or not paying employees at all. If work is done, an employee should be paid for the time worked. Yet, employees do not receive their paychecks on schedule or an employer fails to pay them for the work that they performed.

There is no regular profile regarding who might fall victim to an employer predator seeking to garnish rightly owed wages. "All workers—regardless of legal status, race, gender and nativity—are at risk of workplace violations, though some groups are more vulnerable than others," predominantly Latino workers who are victimized the most by Black, Asian, and White laborers. Of the six common methods of

---

[54] United States Department of Labor, Wage and Hour Division, www.dol.gov/whd/.

wage theft, minimum wage violations were dominant in the referenced study then overtime followed by "off the clock" ones. Sadly, over two-thirds of 4387 survey experienced at least one pay-related violation in the previous work week which translates into an average of $2634 a year per worker. Pandora, this article argues, is guilty of wage theft. It has failed to pay a just remuneration to the music artists for use of their creative work. Further, it compensates music artists with paltry royalties.

In a recent effort to expose the lack of meaningful royalties online, the music artist David Lowery from the musical group "Cracker" railed against Pandora. Pandora played his song "Low" a little over one million times and he only got $16.89, "less than what I make from a single T-shirt sale."[55] If one were to do the math, that "royalty," if you can call it that, amounted to 1.457 cents for a 1,000 spins of play. However, it is important to remember it is likely that each play was only listened to by one listener. On Sirius, "Low" was played 179 times. Sirius paid Lowery $181.04 or about $1.01 per spin. That amounts to 69,416 more than Pandora. Of note too, music played on Sirius radio, however, is generally broadcast to more than one listener. Lowery notes he was paid $1373.78 or about 7 cents for each play of the 18,797 "Low" spins on terrestrial radio, 5,016 times as much as Pandora and 7.2% of what Sirius paid. Like Sirius, the number of people listening to "Low" on terrestrial radio is inestimable.

Bobo argues that unions are critical to stopping wage theft, in addition to strong corporate and government leadership:

> Unions are still the best and most effective vehicle for stopping wage theft, for the following reasons: Unions train workers about their rights in the workplace...Unions have attorneys available to answer questions and file lawsuits...Unions provide workers a structure for expressing concerns...Unions protect workers who complain...Unions create a counterbalance to management's control in the workplace...Unions maintain relationships with community allies and resources.[56]

ASCAP is the leading performing rights labor union representing over 500,000 songwriters, composers, and music publishers. They have entered the fray. For ASCAP, cyberspace, despite its reach, is a platform that must be faithful to proper royalties. Their efforts have been to

---

[55] "My Song Got Played On Pandora 1 Million Times and All I Got Was $16.89, Less Than What I Make From a Single T-Shirt Sale!" *The Trichordist: Artists For An Ethical and Sustainable Internet #StopArtistExploitation* (June 24, 2013), http://thetrichordist.com/2013/06/24/my-song-got-played-on-pandora-1-million-times-and-all-i-got-was-16-89-less-than-what-i-make-from-a-single-t-shirt-sale/.

[56] Kim Bobo, *Wage Theft in America: Why Millions of Americans are Not Getting Paid and What We Can Do About It* (New York: The New Press, 2011), 88-89.

dismantle the unjust labor practices of Pandora and ensure "the priority of labor over capital." Using the best reliable data they can obtain, ASCAP is dogged in its pursuit of just remuneration for all its music artists and their representatives. In doing so, it challenges the specific claims that technology and globalization are responsible for the decline of unions by demonstrating that, in fact, they are fertile areas for the critical efforts of labor unions.

Since 2011, Pandora and ASCAP have been in an ongoing battle for increased royalties for their particular constituencies. During this period, Pandora has made some public claims that ASCAP has claimed as untrue and, essentially, doublespeak. ASCAP has identified three specific instances where Pandora has demonstrated this assertion.[57] In one case, Pandora hedges on its identity claiming at one point that it is like terrestrial radio and, at another time, that it is nothing like traditional radio stations. Another tension arose when Pandora argued that it could not be subjected to a higher licensing fee for song writers, but then announced its record number of users and significant flow of non- GAAP revenue. Finally, while Pandora indicates that they do support musicians, the evidence proves otherwise. Despite Pandora's claim to be a struggling Internet company, its executives' exorbitant pay does not substantiate that claim. Pandora continues to hold just royalties for musicians hostage. To resolve these ongoing charges of wage theft from music artists, Pandora has attempted to push legislation through Congress that would legalize its unjust payouts.

In an effort to level the radio playing field and have the same opportunity to generate more just revenue like other radio platforms, Pandora forcefully supported the 2012 Internet Radio Fairness Act. It sought to combine digital with satellite and terrestrial radio platforms vis-à-vis royalties. Pandora contested that terrestrial radio is obligated to pay lesser royalties and amasses a bundle of money from advertisements. As one commentator put it, this Act should have been more appropriately entitled the "Internet Radio Rip-Off Act."[58] It would be a "race to the bottom" to see which streaming radio provider could get away with paying the least amount of money to artists.

Pandora eventually realized that their efforts to reduce royalty rates through their support of this Act had created ill will among musicians and supporters. Pandora withdrew its support of this bill in Congress. Tim Westergren in his blog defended the actions of Pandora writing that artists are exaggerating the reality and missing the point of Pandora. Two of Westergen's points are worth noting. First, Westergen

---

57 "Pandora vs. Pandora," www.ascap.com/~/media/files/pdf/playback/2013/pandora_vs_pandora%20092713.pdf.

58 Ray Hair, "Pandora Panders to 'Rip-off' Act" *International Musician* 110:9 (September 2012): 2.

insists that Pandora is not reducing artists' royalties as the Recording Industry Association of America (RIAA) has suggested. In fact, they hope to grow the total payments to artists. Second, Westergen suggested that users need to remember, that one spin of a song is heard generally by one person. A play on terrestrial radio can be heard by millions. Yet, FM radio is required to pay only a fraction of what Pandora pays for any song played. While the argument continues with competing claims, the reality is that musicians are not getting paid justly.

In their most recent 2014 clash played out in American courts, ASCAP demanded that Pandora raise the percentage of royalties which it pays to 3% from the current 1.85%. Pandora claimed that 1.7% of its revenue on a song was sufficient; this is also the rate terrestrial radio pays. However, Pandora was not fully honest. "Although royalties are distributed to songwriters and publishers for public performances for terrestrial radio play, this right does not extend to the performers or the sound recording copyright owner (usually the record label)."[59] The 1.7 percent, therefore, is seen by the songwriters and publishers, but not by the performers and copyright owner. In July 2014, a judge declared that ASCAP's request for 3% was unreasonable and ruled in favor of the present 1.85%, agreeing with "Pandora's position that it is more like terrestrial radio than other music services such as Spotify."[60] The CEO of Sony/ATV Music pointed out the gravity of this ruling: "This rate is a clear defeat for songwriters. This rate is woefully inadequate and further emphasizes the need for reform in the rate court proceedings. Songwriters can't live in a world where streaming services only pay 1.85% of their revenue. This is a loss, and not something we can live with."[61] ASCAP's CEO casts this judicial decision in a broader systemic context of regulatory reform, saying "recent agreements negotiated without the artificial constraints of a consent decree make clear that the market rate for Internet radio is substantially higher than 1.85%, and today's decision further demonstrates the need to review the entire regulatory structure, including the decades-old consent decrees that govern PRO [performance rights organizations] licensing, to ensure they reflect the realities of today's music landscape."[62]

---

[59] "Public Performance Right for Sound Recordings" (November 5, 2013), www.futureofmusic.org/article/fact-sheet/public-performance-right-sound-recordings.

[60] India Thomson, "Collecting from Pandora: A Brief," *Music Business Journal*, www.thembj.org/2014/05/collecting-from-pandora-a-brief/. See also: Karp, Hannah. "Showdown for Pandora." *The Wall Street Journal* (January 20, 2014). See more at: www.thembj.org/2014/05/collecting-from-pandora-a-brief/#sthash.RaimzzAi.dpuf.

[61] "What ASCAP Members Need to Know About the Pandora Rate Court Decision" (March 20, 2014), www.ascap.com/playback/2014/03/action/what-ascap-members-need-to-know-about-the-pandora-rate-court-decision.aspx.

[62] "What ASCAP Members Need to Know."

ASCAP is committed to resolving this labor injustice. Its efforts include dissemination of information and identifying action steps to music industry people and allies so that they can advocate for legal change to the present licensing system. Their primary efforts are aimed at the passage of the Songwriter Equity Act, introduced into Congress in February 2014, that would compensate music artists and writers fair market wages. Until the force of law has any positive impact on streaming music, individual technology users can transform the landscape of Internet music by choosing not to cooperate in the moral evil Pandora is perpetuating.

PANDORA: MORAL COOPERATION IN EVIL

In 1999, Shawn Fanning started Napster, a popular file sharing platform.[63] Users could share documents, music, movies, images, and programs. There was an incredible surge to be a part of Napster primarily for the easy free software and music downloads that one could acquire with the click of a mouse. Computer users exchanged costly popular software programs like Adobe and Microsoft products, as well as the latest movies and entire music libraries. The transfer was always not quick, especially if you were using early telephonic connections. They were "free" though and many ambitious users flocked to Napster – some just to see the miracle of downloading an album or program which one might have to pay for in a store!

Napster was finally shut down in July 2001 and ruled by the courts to be illegal because of copyright infringement.[64] When engaging Napster, some users did not seem to understand that anything was legally wrong, no less morally. For users of Napster and other similar bit torrent software, the Web was an ideal resource. One could find anything on the Web. If it were "free," that was even better. For some consumers, Napster's presence on the Internet was justified and helped users access software and other media that, in their financial calculations, were priced outrageously. Some users became numb to the fact that they had embarked on a "slippery slope." They did not see the imminent practical effects of their actions. Producers, artists, creators, and managers lost revenue. Catholic moral theology categorizes these Napster users' activity as material cooperation in moral evil not unlike the actions in which some Pandora users intentionally engage.

Cooperation is a set of principles in Catholic moral theology that accounts for the fact that there are certain situations, in which a person,

---

[63] Karl Toro Greenfeld, "Meet the Napster" *Time Magazine* 2 (October 2, 2000), http://content.time.com/time/magazine/article/0,9171,998068,00.html. David Spitz and Starling D. Hunter, "Contested Codes: The Social Construction of Napster," *The Information Society* 21.3 (2005): 169-180.

[64] Christopher Mitten, *Shawn Fanning: Napster and the Music Revolution,* New York, NY: Twenty-First Century Books, 2002. Joseph Menn, *All the Rave: The Rise and Fall of Shawn Fanning's Napster*, New York, NY: Crown Business, 2003.

attempting to do good, participates in some evil. Typically, cooperation is resourced in biomedical ethics to resolve precarious situations and determine if a procedure is allowable, but here it will be used in relation to an individual using Pandora.[65] The Catholic Church distinguishes between the types of participation as "formal" and "material" cooperation. These principles serve as a resource for moral discernment about involvement with an action and the degree of sharing in the intention of the principal agent's immoral act. Formal and material cooperation can be further distinguished into its explicit and implicit or mediate or immediate expression, respectively. This distinction can be helpful to understand the gravity of the act and the moral complicity of the cooperator. These principles should never be referenced for the purpose of finding creative ways to bypass proper moral obligations to do the good required.

A computer user who cooperates formally in an immoral action is one who does so freely and shares in the intention of the immoral actor. Such cooperation, whether explicit or implicit, is never morally licit. A Catholic student who regularly uses Pandora as his or her primary platform for streaming music even after learning of Pandora's specious royalty scale is guilty of explicit formal cooperation. Another example would be a Catholic faculty member at a university who knowingly allows the use of illegal, pirated, software in her class such as the popular illegal movie service "LetMeWatchThis" at www.primewire.ag. As for implicit formal cooperation, an example would be if a Catholic professor, in order to enhance a particular class presentation, uses a musical selection, perhaps rationalizing one-time use would not be immoral. We saw otherwise with the "Happy Birthday to You" song. Or, if a Catholic institution, in the interest of saving money, shares WiFi access with another institution whose beliefs and teachings are inconsistent with those of the Catholic Church.

Computer users who are material cooperators are ones who do so freely, but do not share in the intention of the immoral actor, yet they are involved in the performance of an immoral action. Material cooperation may be permissible given the circumstances in which the moral actor is engaged, whether she or he be under some sort of constraint or not.[66] Like formal cooperation, material cooperation may be either

---

[65] More recently, Julie Hanlon Rubio used the category of moral cooperation to explore "the idea that 'less meat' is a justifiable ethical stance that respects the dignity of animal life." Rubio suggests "that everyone has an obligation to lessen cooperation with social evil and increase cooperation with social good by avoiding factory-farmed meat." ("Animals, Evil, and Family Meals," *Journal of Moral Theology* 3:2 [2014]: 35-53).

[66] Cathleen Kaveny, *Law's Virtues: Fostering Autonomy and Solidarity in American Society* (Washington, DC: Georgetown University Press, 2012), 246-48; Gerald Magill, "A Moral Compass for Wrongdoing," *Voting and Holiness*, ed. Nicholas P. Cafardi (New York: Paulist Press, 2012), 135-57.

immediate or mediate. In the instance of immediate material cooperation, a Catholic professor might consider herself virtuous by offering colleagues computer equipment she no longer uses. That very same material then could be used to connect to Pandora to stream music or new Napster like bit torrent websites to download illegal software, music, and books and similar theft of morally questionable goods and services. As for mediate moral cooperation, a Catholic student might sell his or her computer to another only to find out that that computer was used to stream Pandora music at a local business. Or, a Catholic parish manager might donate computer equipment to a promising startup company only to find out that the business involves building a website for dissemination of pornography, clearly engaging in a moral activity contrary to Catholic moral teaching on human dignity. However in this instance of mediate moral cooperation, the immoral action could have occurred without the help of the Catholic parish manager's benevolent action.

To suggest Pandora engages in morally evil policies and practices follows from Pandora's sustained wage theft of music artists. Accordingly, Pandora users then need to examine their intent and action realizing that participation in this streaming music service. The fiscal metrics confirm that Pandora is extending the evil practice of unjust wages. Using this software platform, a user is not promoting the goods, desires, and worries of a section of society. In turn, human dignity is violated. It is unclear, though, how many Pandora users know the extent to which Pandora garnishes the royalties of music artists, despite the efforts of the ASCAP and the boisterous claims of the artists themselves. Yet, it could be conceivable that some Pandora users knowingly intend (formal cooperation) to participate in Pandora's fiscal activity, perhaps claiming the music industry is wealthy already. However, these users fail to account for artists' rights to a just wage, particularly newcomers to the music industry. Realistically, I would argue that the lion's share of Pandora users do not intentionally seek to rob music artists of their just share of royalties (material cooperation). This cache of users may presume that since Pandora is a publicly traded company they are subject to labor laws that protect the music artist and, in turn, pay a just wage. As this paper has demonstrated, this is, unfortunately, not the case.

CONCLUSION

Technology has been associated, with good reason, with the decline of membership in labor unions. Computerization seemingly is supplanting much of what was done by the worker. However, enough dystopia exists on the World Wide Web where people are working in the "new marketplace" that prompts recalling labor unions to "act in new ways, *widening the scope* of their activity of solidarity so that protection is afforded not only to the traditional categories of workers, but also to *workers with non-standard or limited-time contracts*" (emphasis mine).[67] As Pandora streams its music and its corporate leaders enjoy profiting from an ever-growing number of subscribers, just compensation for the worker, the musician, the song artist, and agent also must follow suit.

ASCAP has ventured into a fertile area, virgin territory, which needs the valuable critical efforts of labor unions. Labor unions have a very unique opportunity to collectively bargain for the remuneration and proper treatment of musicians even as the face of labor is experiencing radical computerization and technological change. The venue of cyberspace might be unchartered territory for labor unions, but labor unions are still very relevant in this space. Labor unions could impact online economies significantly as information technology communication continues to evolve and expand. As the "App generation" comes of age, there will be "new frontiers" for labor unions to put their energies.[68]

Until ASCAP is successful in its effort and Pandora jettisons its unfair labor practices, or civil law forces Pandora to do so, computer users can demonstrate their support for just labor activity by refraining from cooperating in perpetuating this moral evil. Such a moral boycott can have incredible effectiveness having lasting detrimental consequences on Pandora, both in terms of public perception and financials.[69] It is morally incumbent upon computer users who support just labor activity to take seriously their obligation not to enable such a disregard for the rights of the laborer. Until such a time that legislative efforts can ensure this, the consumer must exercise moral consciousness by refusing to use Pandora. It would be morally reprehensible for a user to stream music from the Pandora software platform even casually, as if just listening to a few songs would not have any effect on the music artist, composer, or producer. No matter how innocent an act, it only would open "Pandora's box." M

---

[67] Pontifical Council for Justice and Peace, *Compendium*, no. 308.

[68] Anne Foerst, "Signs of the Times: Theology and Technology: A New Frontier?" *New Theology Review* 19.3 (2013); Howard Gardner and Katie Davis, *The App Generation: How Today's Youth Navigate Identity, Intimacy, and Imagination in a Digital World* (New Haven, CT: Yale University Press, 2013).

[69] Monroe Friedman has studied this issue for over forty years and laments the "lack of scholarly attention to ethical issues surrounding these actions." ("Ethical Dilemmas Associated with Boycotts," *Journal of Social Philosophy* 32:2 [2001], 232-240). Mary Lyn Stoll examined a boycott by the American Family Association because of Ford Motor Company's and Proctor & Gamble's advertising directed at cultivating the LGBT community. The boycott compromised these corporations' images, for some, and negatively impacted these company's financials. ("Boycott Basics: Moral Guidelines for Corporate Decision Making," *Journal of Business Ethics* 84:1 [2009], 3-10).

Journal of Moral Theology, Vol. 4, No. 1 (2015): 90-110

We Do Not Know How to Love: Observations on Theology, Technology, and Disability

Jana M. Bennett

DOES TECHNOLOGY ENABLE those who are disabled to be fuller members of society, or does it ultimately seek to eradicate disability and so promote a kind of eugenics against those who are disabled? In the late 1990s and early 2000s, literature and debate on this question ran rampant. A common example is that of cochlear implants, which endured much debate at the time within the Deaf community regarding whether they eradicate an impairment— or whether implants actually do away with entire communities of the Deaf and thus displace an important minority culture.[1] Yet, very little is written today on this question. Is it because the question is settled, or because we have become satisfied with the presumed answers? (Answers which, repeatedly, tend to be: decisions regarding cochlear implants should be left up to patients, focused on their autonomy, and almost entirely avoiding the more troublesome question of whether a culture is being eradicated.[2])

Similarly, in online contexts in the early 2000s, people extolled the internet as a place where those with disabilities would finally find themselves in equal position, authority, and accessibility related to those without disabilities. Relatively early in the development of the internet, scholars regarded digital technologies as ultimately promising and good for people of all disabilities, because of their nature as mitigating disabilities. For example, the internet is often credited with enabling access to texts for those who are visually impaired. Almost since the beginnings of web development, there has been impetus to make the web accessible to all, where "people can collaborate without

---

[1] See, for example, Robert Sparrow, "Defending Deaf Culture: The Case of Cochlear Implants," *The Journal of Political Philosophy* 13, no. 2 (2005): 135-52.

[2] See John B. Christiansen and Irene W. Leigh, "Children with Cochlear Implants: Changing Parent and Deaf Community Perspectives," *Archives of Otolaryngology—Head and Neck Surgery* 130, no. 5 (May 2004): 673-7; Neil Levy, "Reconsidering Cochlear Implants: The Lessons of Martha's Vineyard," *Bioethics* 16, no. 2 (2002): 134-53.

barriers."[3] The rise of social media has seemed to fit into that kind of collaborative worldview. Yet today, very little is written on this point, even and especially in an age of social media, which has largely been presumed to be an equalizer. Those who do write about it are highly suspicious of whether new social media forms have actually engendered the hoped-for social changes relating to disability. One set of scholars observes that the most recent iterations of the internet, sometimes called "web 2.0,"[4] have meant a rejection of web standards that had been set for disability, through which disability is understood and recognized as a serious need in technological development from the very beginnings, rather than an add-on (and afterthought) for every new program that gets developed for the non-disabled. In other words, "web 2.0 has been developed in and by the same social world that routinely disables people with disability."[5]

Our narratives about disability and disease link to narratives about contemporary technology uses, but to my knowledge, few scholars have explored these connections. In this essay, I argue that predominant narratives about technology in combination with predominant descriptions about disability revolve around understanding technology as an asocial tool, which narratively proclaims a kind of neutrality. People using technologies, and the contexts of both the technological users and their technologies, make little or no difference to ways technologies are described or used. My concern and further argument is that this has the effect of making people themselves become defined by tools to the point that some people begin to treat other people as tools rather than as people to be loved.

My attempt at bringing together narratives about disability and technologies warrants a brief discussion about the inherent ambiguities in describing both disability and technology, though I will also articulate further ambiguities throughout this essay. Some disabilities may seem clear and self-evident: perhaps the use of a wheelchair, or a person who is unable to feed himself. Yet a person with a broken arm might also be considered to have a disability, and so might a person with a far less visible condition, like a congenital heart defect. There is, too, as I shall discuss further below, the serious question of whether the term "disability" ever really applies to an individual person, or whether it is a social condition. Likewise, some technologies may seem clear and self-evident: the internet, especially with its variety of social media platforms, comes across in scholarship and literature as

---

[3] Katie Ellis and Mike Kent, *Disability and New Media* (New York: Routledge, 2011), 2.

[4] This term, often used in discussions of digital scholarship, refers primarily to a stage in internet development where the focus is less on content and more on user-generated and facilitated interaction, one example of which might be today's social media platforms.

[5] Ellis and Kent, *Disability and New Media*, 3.

a clear form of technology. Yet what is less evident and obvious is how distinctive the internet as technology is, with its vast array of mechanical, physical, chemical and even social systems that are required to make it function. A pencil is a form of technology too, though with less immediate evidence of the array of systems fostering its production and use, and if we think of it as technology at all, we think of it as an older technology with little thought to the fact that it too inculcates an array of mechanical, physical, chemical and even social systems.

My above discussion of these ambiguities obviously takes pains to note, in a beginning kind of way, how both disabilities and technologies are implicated in human sociality. Yet, in this essay, I shall attempt to display at least two main ways that the sociality of both technologies and disabilities is lost or hidden in our descriptions of them. The narratives I critique as too disconnected from our social world, I name as "asocial" or, sometimes, "disassociated." In particular, I worry that we understand our technologies primarily as tools to be used, picked up and put down at will, but with little sense of their sociality. One of our predominant narratives about technology is to describe it as an "asocial tool," which impacts how we envision and describe disability. In a technology-as-asocial-tool mode, people may be evaluated in terms of their usefulness for the overall culture, or worse still, in terms of their technological know-how. The fusion of narratives about technologies and disabilities negatively impacts people with disabilities, whose usefulness does not compute well in relation to a culture that thrives on efficiency.[6] I proceed in this essay by first discussing some of the prominent views of ethicists who describe technologies in dissociative ways, and I articulate how these views relate to two primary models of disability (a medical model and a social model) that exist in our contemporary discourse. I focus especially on their theological anthropologies and their implications for work in disability.

My concluding section provides some thoughts on what it might mean for theologians and others to narrate technological tools as socially formative rather than as asocial or disinterested. In particular, I turn to discussion of love as communication, technology as communication, and how we might then understand technology socially formative, especially in relation to the person of Jesus Christ. My primary theological interlocutor for this conversation on love and communication is Herbert McCabe, because the ways his work draws together these themes sheds important light on the present concerns about technology. I conclude with some thoughts on how a technological world can, indeed, be a world that shows us how to love.

---

[6] See Hans Reinders, *Receiving the Gift of Friendship: Profound Disability, Theological Anthropology, and Ethics* (Grand Rapids: Eerdmans, 2008).

DISABILITIES AND DISASSOCIATING SOLUTIONS

It is important to begin by noting that when we are dealing with disability and technology together, we are bringing together several disciplines. Scholars often discuss disability in terms of bioethics questions (e.g., cochlear implants) or in terms of socio-political questions (e.g., the Americans with Disabilities Act and the ways that act is carried out). Technology, on the other hand, is often discussed in relation to communications faculties as well as a growing field of sociology of technology. Part of the difficulty in thinking through technology and disability in relation to theological anthropology resides in the fact that very distinctive views of technology and disability emerge from those fields, though as I argue below, both often think in terms of technology-as-disassociative-tool, with different facets of that idea present. Yet because technology is not often identified as being the crux of the question in bioethics, and because disability is often ignored in technology studies, these questions tend to go undiscovered and unanswered. Part of what I will do in this section is attempt to bring together views of disability with views of technology according to, first, bioethics discussions, and second, according to sociological and cultural discussions.

Technology as Tool, Disability as Medical Problem

Bioethicist Adam Briggle describes the current state of bioethics as a "thin," "formal rational," and "instrumentalist" view of a variety of bioethics questions, in which I would include considerations of people with disabilities, to the point that a person with a disability may be overlooked or done an injustice if they do not quite fit the views of personhood emphasized in contemporary discourse.[7] That is, in contrast to former strands of bioethics conversations in which "[s]ubstantive rationality [that] asks whether the means are consistent with ultimate ends or values," the contemporary debate suggests that "formal rationality asks whether the means employed are being maximized to achieve assumed ends," particularly in service of "autonomy, beneficence, and justice."[8] Maximization of autonomy, beneficence and justice in turn emphasizes the "contractual nature of society" in which people are "atomistic rights-bearers" who determine their own good via their own will.[9] Briggle's articulation of contemporary bioethics raises concerns for those with disabilities, especially in its insistence on autonomy, beneficence and justice, exactly because autonomy for a person with disabilities is likely to look very different, if not un-autonomous, compared to a person who is not so disabled. One of the

---

[7] Adam Briggle, *A Rich Bioethics: Public Policy, Biotechnology, and the Kass Council* (Notre Dame: University of Notre Dame Press, 2010), 33-4.

[8] Briggle, *A Rich Bioethics*, 33-4.

[9] Briggle, *A Rich Bioethics*, 62.

chief difficulties with this, as Adam Briggle notes, but also as scholars who think about the nature of human choices discuss, human desires and identities do not come before established human relationships or socio-political, economic, legal and other kinds of systems in which humans are engaged.[10]

Yet the predominant bioethics view of the person that Briggle identifies lends itself very well to visions of technology-as-asocial-tool. In bioethics, especially, we presume that our tools can be picked up and put down at will, especially at the patient's will. The principles of autonomy and rationality act together in such a way to reinforce that the chief person responsible for deciding whether a tool will be used is the patient, or those acting on her behalf, and the chief person wielding the tools is the doctor, or other medical personnel.

As diseases and disabilities are named and identified, so too the fixes are named and identified, precisely in relation to the kinds of technologies that can fix the problem. For example, problems associated with sudden-onset hearing loss include suggestions for how to identify sudden-onset hearing loss as early as possible, followed by specific descriptions of the range of devices that assist in fixing sudden-onset hearing loss.[11] This is a common place understanding of this type of hearing loss and its fix, so it comes as little or no surprise. Indeed, readers may wonder why I lift up such an obvious example (as opposed to, say, more hot button technologically-related questions like contraception or embryonic stem cell research, which perhaps more obviously raise technological questions).

It is important to see, however, the ways in which even so simple a description of condition and its fix intertwines with one predominant way of narrating disability. A medical model of disability emphasizes "disability as primary a medical or biological condition.... It claims that the disabled person's functional ability deviates from that of the normal human body."[12] Medical models of disability presume such a thing as a "normal body" against which disability is measured. From that vantage point, medicine identifies and uses a variety of tools to correct deficiencies. A medical model of disability hence readily fits with a narrative of technology as a tool, which has as its aim correcting the modes of autonomy and rationality so that those with disabilities can fully (as possible) participate in a society that thrives on autonomy

---

[10] On the nature of choice, see, for example, Sheena Iyengar's very interesting set of studies on how people's choices do not either enhance their autonomies or lead to their betterment as people. *The Art of Choosing* (New York: Twelve, 2010).

[11] See, for example, N. Foden, et al., *Australian Family Physician* 42, no. 9 (2013): 641-4.

[12] Deborah Creamer, *Disability and Christian Theology: Embodied Limits and Constructive Possibilities*, Academy Series (New York: Oxford University Press, 2009), 23.

and rationality. At the same time, medical models of disability presume that identifying what counts as a disability is simple and obvious, and especially left to experts.

To see more especially how a tool-based view can operate, especially in relation to questions about medical diagnosis of disability, contemporary ethicist Julian Savulescu has argued, provocatively, that "we have a moral obligation or moral reason to enhance ourselves and our children. Indeed, we have the same kind of obligation as we have to treat and prevent disease."[13] Savulescu's argument presupposes a specific view of disease, which involves the use of technologies to prevent disease. He takes this view further, however, to suggest that we have an obligation to humanity in general to use enhancement technologies as a means of improving ourselves. The limit to such medical fixes and enhancements resides solely in the individuals concerned. Savulescu, who heavily makes use of a utilitarian framework, suggests that while he thinks that "like deafness, intellectual disability [he gives the example of Down's Syndrome] is bad. But my value judgment should not be imposed on couples who must bear and rear the child. Nor should the value judgment of doctors, politicians, or the state be imposed directly."[14] Savulescu's view directly draws upon the horrors of enforced perfection via eugenics programs and he therefore claims that "[as] rational people, we should all form our own ideas about what is the best life. But to know what is the good life and impose this on others is at best overconfidence."[15] Broadly understood, then, technologies exist in this view as tools to be taken up and set down at will, at the behest of people who individually and autonomously determine whether a disease or disability exists, what that disease or disability is, and how it ought to be fixed.

Yet Savulescu's view does not deal with the much trickier questions related to the fact that no person, no one family, acts within a bubble, and that his solution directed at autonomy still does not get around the eugenics problem. That is to say, leaving the question up to individuals or parents or other such tightly constructed tiny communities ignores the impact that these decisions make on others' work and responsibilities. In addition, as Jeffrey Bishop has shown in his work on end-of-life care, the very posing of questions about of quality

---

[13] Julian Savulescu, "Genetic Interventions and the Ethics of Enhancement of Human Beings," in *Oxford Handbook of Bioethics*, ed. Bonnie Steinbock (New York: Oxford University Press, 2007), 516.

[14] Julian Savulescu, "Deaf Lesbians, 'Designer Disability,' and the Future of Medicine," *British Medical Journal* 325, no. 7367 (October 5, 2002): 771-773, at 772.

[15] Savulescu, "Deaf Lesbians, 'Designer Disability,' and the Future of Medicine," 773.

of life shapes the kinds of options people believe they have, in particular with respect to how we view our technologies and machines.[16] Another way to put this is to recognize that the very ways people presume narratives about Down's Syndrome shapes the kinds of choices parents believe they have regarding genetic testing, abortion and bringing a child to full term.[17]

The more minor medical diagnoses I discuss above, with sudden-onset hearing loss signifies the kind of narrative that Briggle describes however: a shift in bioethical thought that focuses on ends in relation to happiness as measured by autonomy and rationality, over against that of a substantive rationality. The "big issues," in other words, only mirror how conversations typically function. Consider the burgeoning issue of artificial contraception. A significant component of recent debates on artificial contraception use regards questions about whether human fertility is, properly speaking, a disease and whether, therefore, it needs to be fixed. When the Institute of Medicine released its recommendations for women's health care coverage under the Affordable Care Act, its rationale for contraceptives included:

> Unintended pregnancy is linked to a host of health problems. Women with unintended pregnancies are more likely to receive delayed or no prenatal care and to smoke, consume alcohol, be depressed, and experience domestic violence during pregnancy. Unintended pregnancy also increases the risk of babies being born preterm or at a low birth weight, both of which increase their chances of health and developmental problems. Family planning services are preventive services that enable women and couples to avoid an unwanted pregnancy and to space their pregnancies to promote optimal birth outcomes. Pregnancy spacing is a priority for women's health because of the increased risk of adverse pregnancy outcomes for pregnancies that are too closely spaced (within 18 months of a prior pregnancy).[18]

The IOM supported these concerns with a variety of studies demonstrating such adverse effects. Opponents of the contraceptives recommendation argued, in part, against the idea of contraception as fixing

---

[16] See Jeffrey Bishop, *The Anticipatory Corpse: Medicine, Power, and the Care of the Dying* (Notre Dame: University of Notre Dame Press, 2011).

[17] For example, Savulescu's knee-jerk reaction to Down's Syndrome babies in his "Deaf Lesbians" article is that Down's Syndrome ought, to rational people, count as a problem best to be done away with.

[18] Linda Rosenstock, "Clinical Preventative Services for Women: Closing the Gaps," Testimony provided by the Institute of Medicine Committee on Preventative Services for Women, www.iom.edu/~/media/Files/Report%20Files/2011/Clinical-Preventive-Services-for-Women-Closing-the-Gaps/Written%20Testimony-House%20Judiciary%20Hearing.pdf. Accessed August 25, 2014.

a medical condition, since on their view, fertility cannot be classified as such.[19]

Disability in relation to digital media similarly looks like technology-as-disassociative-tool, oftentimes where technology appears as a fix for predicaments individuals with disabilities experience. For example, "[d]igital technology allows the manipulation of information in terms of appearance, text size, color, and mode of output including, for example, text-to-sound or Braille. In theory, digital information can be accessed by many users with different needs in different ways."[20] As the authors go on to note, however, in practice, this does not happen, precisely because technology is no longer satisfyingly described (if it ever quite was) as the tools that we use to assist in our daily lives, among other things. That is, "the web becomes more complex and a more ubiquitous part of life" to the point that descriptions of the web, or indeed of many other forms of technology, inadequately use tool imagery. Such descriptions and uses of technology, broadly speaking, inhibit our abilities to reflect on and imagine better possibilities and ways of understanding what it means to be a human that uses technologies.[21]

There are several difficulties with the kinds of descriptions I mention above about disability and technology. Some of these difficulties relate to what I mentioned in the introduction. How does the theological concept of love relate, or not, to the descriptions and visions we have of (disabled) humanity on one hand, and technology use on the other? One point that has arisen again and again in discussions of medical models of disabilities and the technologies that fix them is a focus on rationality and autonomy. This focus privileges only one of many possible aspects of what it means to be human. It is not clear that rationality and autonomy, especially in the Western senses in which these terms typically appear in discourse, are the best ways of thinking about what it means to be a human person. Stanley Hauerwas notes in a 1986 essay: "the very humanity that causes us to cry out against suffering, that motivates us to seek to eliminate retardation, is also the source of our potentially greatest inhumanity."[22] The presence of technology does not abrogate what has always been a difficult negotiation:

---

[19] For two very different discussions of this point, but both raising strong questions about the idea of fertility as medical problem, see: Susan Windley-Daoust, *Theology of the Body, Extended: The Spiritual Signs of Birth, Impairment, and Dying* (Hobe Sound, FL: Lectio Publishing, 2014) and Jennifer Block, *Pushed: The Painful Truth about Childbirth and Modern Maternity Care* (Cambridge, MA: Da Capo Press, 2007).

[20] Ellis and Kent, *Disability and New Media*, 48.

[21] Ellis and Kent, *Disability and New Media*, 48.

[22] Stanley Hauerwas, *Suffering Presence: Theological Reflections on Medicine, the Mentally Handicapped, and the Church* (Notre Dame: University of Notre Dame Press, 1986), 160.

how to live with suffering— our own and others' and what it means to love in the midst of that suffering.

A further concern is the degree to which love and machines intermix. Theologian Deborah Creamer suggests that a medical model tends to identify the human body as "a biological machine that functions to a greater or lesser extent."[23] The "machine" notion of the body makes the body itself out to be a tool as well, a tool that— if it functions well— heightens a person's ability to participate in society, especially a consumer society that takes a dim view to people who are less than useful. If we Christians wish to speak of love of neighbor, one of the questions we need to confront with asocial or dissociative views of technologies is what it means to love a human being who is acted upon largely as a bodily machine. As MIT professor Sherry Turkle has discussed (convincingly on my view) in her book *Alone Together: Why We Expect More from Technology and Less from Each Other*, in our technocratic age, we are developing an inverse ability to relate to human beings and machines.[24] While studies on human behavior and robotics suggest that we develop and demonstrate many forms of sympathy for them, even after knowing the ins and outs of how the robots are programmed to respond to us in certain ways, studies on human treatment of each other, especially when we lurk behind our screens, suggests an increasing inability to respond with sympathy, empathy and compassion. These are changes that Turkle observes with some concern, especially as she observes how we place robotic and internet technologies as presumable appropriate substitutes for human interaction with the most vulnerable among us: the elderly, children, and those with disabilities. The ones who lose out the most from our love affairs with technologies, suggests Turkle, are those whose humanity is often described or viewed at the very marginal edges of human existence. Technologies become asocial, disassociating us from each other, in real and felt ways.

The key difficulty, I suggest, is in the ways this overarching asocial view of technologies limits our abilities to see other possible actions and ways of describing and living out human relationships. Such a view limits our creative thought and action and hence limits our ability to love and respond to love. As Herbert McCabe suggested in his book *Love, Law and Language*: love is a "growing word", a word that we learn to use over a lifetime of experience and encountering exemplary lovers. Yet as McCabe hastens to note in commenting on what it means that love is a "growing word", "this does not in the least imply that it is a vague word, one that might mean almost anything. It is just that a word like 'love' will always have uses that are not constricted

---

[23] Creamer, *Disability and Christian Theology*, 24.

[24] See Sherry Turkle, *Alone Together: Why We Expect More from Technology and Less from Each Other* (New York: Basic Books, 2011).

by such rules for its use as you have managed to formulate any particular time."[25] That is, the word "love" is so spacious and mysterious that it needs great capacity for people learn how to use it, and live it, well. Our technologies, being part of the fabric of our social lives as they are, need to be narrated as capable of such spacious activity as well.

An additional concern with asocial views of technology hinge on how well we name and understand disease, disability and other commonly-thought medical conditions. Our ability, or lack thereof, in identifying diseases and conditions constricts our actions just as do our uses of technology in relation to fixing those conditions. That is, what if the very ways we name diseases is wrong, and what if the very technologies we use already inscribe certain, likely unhelpful, views of disability?

Bioethicist Carl Elliot has written several books calling into question positions like Savulescu's, and exposing the ways communities shape (in sometimes very questionable ways) diagnoses and presumptions about what counts as a medical disease. One of his most often cited examples is a chapter in which he discusses apotemnophiliacs, that is, people who desire to have limbs chopped off.[26] With all their limbs intact, they feel incomplete as themselves. Elliot observes that the number of people in any given human community who desire to have limbs cut off is vanishingly small; the advantages apotemnophiliacs have in an internet age is precisely that a community composed entirely of apotemnophiliacs is possible. Moreover, the existence of groups that now advocate for apotemnophilia means that now there are several people who might approach surgeons with the request to chop off an otherwise healthy limb, and the names of surgeons who acquiesce get traded within these communities.

Part of Elliot's point is to note that what apotemnophiliacs desire— to be more themselves— is the same kind of argument that others with more identifiable "diseases" make in advocating for treatment: for example, anxiety disorders across the spectrum, or a desire for breast enhancement surgery. Elliot seeks to blur lines between medical diagnosis and a person's identity, especially in relation to how communities shape and form both diagnoses and identities, and even the very notion that medical diagnosis is largely a cut-and-dried task that has very few grey areas or wiggle room (despite the fact that many physicians are quick to say that diagnosis is far more an art than a craft). A medical model of disability seeks the problem to be fixed, as compared with all the "normal" people in the crowd, and then seeks the tool to

---

[25] Herbert McCabe, *Love, Law and Language* (London: Continuum, 2003), 18.

[26] See Carl Elliot, *Better than Well: American Medicine Meets the American Dream* (New York: Norton, 2003), especially chapter nine.

be used; it also depends on a universal norm against which disability gets measured.

Elliot develops the technology point far less well but it is important nonetheless. The question of communities and identities is surely part of the whole question, but the specific ways that technology enables creation of communities, indeed could even perhaps be considered the community (in a certain way) of apotemnophiliacs, is indispensable. Without the logic of technologies and their particular ways of fostering communication, there is no coming-into-being of apotemnophilia, and no community of apotemnophiliacs or sympathizers that presume its normalcy. Carl Elliot's point in this chapter is not that he necessarily thinks apotemnophilia or other such diagnoses are good or healthy or beneficial, but the interconnectedness between the diseases and problems we humans identify in each other, and the many facets of human life, including technologies, that form and shape our thinking about what counts as a problem as well as a solution to it.

Thus, focusing on a medical model enables almost complete focus on each individual person and directs the "problem" of disability and its technological fix toward the disabled person, rather than examining the communities of which they are part, and the ways even our tools act on us and shape us all. These concerns about medical models have led, however, to a different vision of disability, one that at the outset looks more promising in its understanding of both disability and technology.

Disability as Socially Embedded, Technology as Formative of the Social

Elliot's concerns about medical diagnosis, and the attendant critiques about technology use relates to what disability scholars increasingly name as the "social model" of disability. Social models of disability are often regarded in stark contrast to medical models, since social models tend to understand disability as a marker of societal prejudice and lack of accommodation to peoples' various impairments. As theologian Deborah Creamer notes, social models understand disability as "social constructed and results from society not being organized according to the needs of disabled people. The 'problem' is no longer identified as the physical, cognitive, or psychological characteristics of the individual, but rather is identified as prejudicial, exclusive, and oppressive attitudes and barriers."[27] Mitigating against socially constructed disability means becoming engaged in social activism against unjust barriers and exclusion of the disabled. Creamer further notes that examples of social models of disability include the passage of the

---

[27] Creamer, *Disability and Christian Theology*, 25.

Americans with Disabilities Act and a focus on giving all people "equal opportunity and full participation."[28]

On a social model of disability, scholars make distinctions between impairment, which is the physical attribute a person has, over against disability, which is the social construct. Impairment, on this view, is analogous to whether a person is left-handed or right-handed, than it is a question of how well a particular person matches up with the concept of "normal." Left- and right-handedness provides a strong analogy here in the sense that many of the tools humans create have been with the right-handed person in mind, such that left-handedness becomes a problem and a "disability" in the face of a majority culture where door knobs and kitchen utensils (among many, many other things) are decisively right-handed. The social construction model of disability is the most-often used model in contemporary disability scholarship, though some theologians have begun to explore still other ways of articulating disability.[29]

Identifying that the problem is chiefly about society's response (or lack thereof) rather than with the person who has impairment affects peoples' engagement with and assumptions about technologies. Rather than thinking in terms of technologies as tools for individuals with individual problems, technologies instead become communally focused, known as universal accessible design. One of the benefits of thinking about technology in this way is that, while technologies developed particularly for disabilities end up seeming weak, technologies developed for broad use do not carry these negative connotations. For example, an architectural design of a ramp can be accessible to wheelchairs and walkers alike, seamlessly woven into building design in such a way that there need be no sign indicating "Wheelchair Ramp" any than there need be a sign indicating "Walker Stairs." Other examples include curb cuts that assist wheelchairs, but also strollers, skateboards, and walkers, and family restrooms that are large and spacious, and can be used across gender, age and ability. One example in current design is the SMS system, developed for those are hearing impaired and Deaf, but used by nearly everyone with a cell phone for texting.

The internet has often been seen as a special site for universal accessible design. It lacks many of the physical barriers, particularly with respect to building barriers, that may prevent those with disabilities from even entering through the doors to attend meetings, classes,

---

[28] Creamer, *Disability and Christian Theology*, 26.

[29] Deborah Creamer's book, cited above, is a prime example of someone exploring other ways of articulating disability, as is the work of John Swinton, Brian Brock, and their collaborators, in *Disability in the Christian Tradition: A Reader* (Grand Rapids: Eerdmans, 2013).

movies and so forth. Additionally, internet avatars provide great flexibility in terms of peoples' representations of themselves, so that females can present as males, those without legs can present as having legs, and so forth. Such an experience of an avatar can be liberating simply because the disabled aspects that often cause knee-jerk and prejudiced reactions to persons with disabilities can disappear.

Just as claims that the web is gender or race neutral are specious, so too arguments that the web is disability neutral are problematic. Digital documents may claim to be accessible for those with visual impairments, but the documents themselves do not interface well with screen readers. Those with hearing impairments frequently encounter barriers regarding sound and video, especially in relation to inaccurate or non-visible captioning, but also whether those who speak sign language can use that language to sign in to various online platforms. While the ability to surpass such barriers exists in many cases, the attention to details regarding technologies required to surpass those barriers is not present.

I suggest that part of the difficulty is that some of the prevailing presumptions about digital technology and impairment presume asocial views of technologies, even as they explicitly advocate social models of disability. Though there is a key and significant shift from individual to society in narratives about disability, there is no similar shift in narratives about technologies as embedded in social life as well. Technologies are often understood, broadly, as tools for eliminating social discrimination, with no special attention to the nature of the technological "tool" itself. Universal accessible design sounds so terrific, that it is easy to make very generalized statements about its benefits, especially online. Yet, as Katie Ellis and Mike Kent note, universal designs end up not being as universal as sometimes hoped, since some groups may be helped and others not.[30] Universal ramps, for example, could be exceedingly dangerous for walkers in inclement weather, and websites that are made accessible for visual impairments are not necessarily accessible for other kinds of impairments, or for use by people with no impairment. The social media site Facebook has become known as particularly inaccessible to those with disabilities, in contrast to the now defunct MySpace. Much of the reason is in the design of the sites themselves, and associated philosophies driving the designs. MySpace, with its fewer guidelines and greater options for individual collaboration with the program itself was recognized for its greater accessibility.[31]

Shifting the focus from individual to society, then, does not necessarily mitigate against an asocial view of technologies, and less still

---

30 Ellis and Kent, *Disability and New Media*, 93.

31 Ellis and Kent, *Disability and New Media*, 111.

toward reflecting on technologies themselves in use relating to disabilities. Indeed, the Facebook versus MySpace example indicates how dissociative views of technology mitigate against accessibility. Facebook's emphasis on controlling its medium and interface has become the standard, perhaps most evidently relating to privacy controls, though I suggest that Facebook's control over all aspects of its design and functionality affects questions about accessibility as well.

What is especially interesting in the case of Facebook's privacy concerns is that, while certain descriptions of Facebook involve insistence about the new world or new era that Facebook ushers in, most of our conversations about Facebook do not reflect such change. A 2010 *Time Magazine* article notes: "Facebook has changed our social DNA, making us more accustomed to openness. But the site is premised on a contradiction: Facebook is rich in intimate opportunities — you can celebrate your niece's first steps there and mourn the death of a close friend — but the company is making money because you are, on some level, broadcasting those moments online."[32] Yet while we speak about Facebook doing something distinctive, changing our social DNA, our speech about Facebook and its privacy controls remains at the level of tool. How do we fix our concerns about Facebook privacy controls? There is a list: turn off certain Facebook functions, avoid posting baby pictures, go to these websites and click on these links. Yet if it is true that Facebook really does change our very way of relating to each other and to it, it cannot be the case that a simple tool view suffices as a fix.

I note here that Savulescu's argument for enhancement technologies articulated above relates equally well in a social disability model. For someone who thinks that society is to blame for holding back those with impairments, technologies, broadly defined, provide ways forward toward incorporating bodies into a fully-functioning society precisely by enhancing their bodies. What now count as "normal" impediments to human imaginings also become enhanced through technology so that in effect, each body no longer needs to exist according to "normal" versus "disabled" labels, but rather "enhanced" and "unenhanced." Such views of both technology and disability hint at both an idyllic present and future, one in which differences wrought by disability are made relative by the fact that all humans seek enhancements of one kind or other. We are all imperfect bodies seeking perfection, or as close as we can come, via technology use.

One of the primary difficulties in these descriptions of disability and the attendant technological concerns is that we humans still want to name ourselves as masters of our technologies, including and espe-

[32] Dan Fletcher, "How Facebook is Redefining Privacy," *Time Magazine* (May 20, 2010), http://content.time.com/time/magazine/article/0,9171,1990798,00.html.

cially masters of the social media websites we use, without quite realizing the ways that technology masters us, and particularly masters, and even hides, those who are disabled when we presume too much about our technological tools. If we really can master technologies, then we really can use them as tools to pick up and put down at will, to fix individual and social affects wrought by disabilities, and more besides. If we cannot master technologies, then… what about disability and pain and suffering? In a world where *not* leaving people suffering is one of the highest goods we presume we can achieve, perhaps even equivalent to loving that person, asocial descriptions of technology reinforces certain views about hope and love (or lack thereof).

It should be said, as well, that the presumption that technology fixes things in a way that requires little or no imagination about technology's or disability's connections to our social world also tends to neglect or silence the fact that for many people with impairments who experience disabilities, technologies never thoroughly erase pain and suffering or the sense that one is "not normal." Indeed, to return to the question of cochlear implants that I raised at the beginning, lay people often presume that cochlear implants will operate somewhat akin to glasses in the sense that they will restore hearing to something like 20/20 vision, which we accept as normal eyesight. Yet, in fact, cochlear implants do not achieve this feat; for the user hearing still often sounds mechanical. Add to this the surrounding questions of Deaf culture and the degree to which cochlear implants raise questions about eugenicizing whole communities, then obtaining a cochlear implant can potentially increase suffering on two fronts. Hearing is both not "normalized" and a person may experience doubts and concerns about the degree to which one belongs to a community should an implant be attempted.

Thinking technologically about human beings and enhancements can mean that disability becomes simply one among many things to be eradicated, such that disability as a specific part of some human beings disappears. As well, a focus on enhancements can make it look like everyone is disabled, in a sense, everyone in need of technological enhancement, but with all the technological enhancements directed toward individuals rather than their social and cultural contexts.

Thus, while a social view is in some ways more positive with respect to people with disabilities, in the sense that the "blame" for disability is not placed solely on the disabled themselves, such a view also puts certain constraints on our abilities to learn to love. Love is not boundless in the sense that just any activity, any use of technology, counts as love, even when directed at the social problems we identify. Nor is any sense of having "fixed" a problem the likely boundary of what it means to love. To the contrary, learning to love people in our uses of technologies and even with a sense that it is the social that creates disability, removes none of the burden that a call to love places on our interactions with individuals.

All that said, I think a social model of disability has good potential, especially if we likewise can understand and articulate technologies in relation to social formation. Perhaps one of the benefits of disabilities is that they offer spaces where we can see some of our technologies' workings and also failures. While I do think that we humans generally take technologies both far too seriously than we ought (but in the wrong ways), and far less seriously than we ought (but in the wrong ways), I am not an advocate of technological rejection. Indeed, the insistence of those who are disabled pressing constantly against the inaccessibility that they encounter in a range of technologies affords some hope for thinking through what it means to need technologies but also how to grapple with the various problems technologies present, some of which I have represented above.

How Do We Learn to Love in a Technological Era?

Thus far, I have broadly discussed what I see as two majority ways technologies, especially in relation to disabilities, get discussed and interpreted. Whether the focus is on the individual with a disability, or on society that creates a disability where only impairment existed beforehand, I suggest that a nearly automatic response is to consider what can fix the problem so described, and in primarily asocial ways. In this final section, I briefly and very broadly discuss a potential theological way forward, one that perhaps permits us judiciously to use some technologies as tools, but also helps us articulate a far more complex narrative that may not, on its own, solve questions about disability as such, but may at least allow us to think more proactively about what it means to use our technologies in the service of love. My brief exploration of themes about Christ, technology, communication and love here will not be wholly satisfying; this work will need further development. Yet as I suggested at the beginning of this essay, I do not wish simply to describe the problems I see regarding technology and disability without also suggesting possible different way forward.

A first step is to think about technology not merely as a tool, but as constituting a social world, naming ways that we relate to other humans, even and especially when people do not quite realize or articulate that relationship, particularly when the sociality of technologies has been disrupted. Brian Brock's work on technology and theology articulates such an assessment in his descriptions of historical developments of a range of technologies. He discusses how the development of the Psalter and practices of this "textually formed performance of collective worship" in which peoples' very bodies and also relationships to other bodies are shaped and formed.[33] By contrast, he finds that the increasing use of books, as such, in the Scholastic period and later, makes use of bookish technologies in such a way that the focus becomes the individual reading that book, and memory becomes "a carefully constructed archive of wisdom contained in the individual's mind."[34] Brock then carries his discussion to a consideration of present-day Christian worship online, where he suggests, "[when] the consumption of people's everyday lives has become entertainment, and surveillance an everyday fact of life, a new humanity is born… the public and publicity become all-encompassing."[35] How, then, does this social world born of internet relationships impinge on Christian life in particular? Brock suspects that the mode of constant self-publication in internet life turns us away from other, more gospel ways of relating to people.

My main point in bringing up Brock here is to attempt to show, in brief, how examinations of technologies require a view toward the social. A utilitarian technological focus on "fixes" tends to focus on one individual, or individual part of social fabric, assuming that once fixed, that individual can then more fully participate in social fabric—whether that "fix" involves a person with hearing loss, a privacy control setting, or as in Brock's examples, an individual church hoping to fix declining membership simply by generating a web presence. Such a view is asocial, not requiring attention to particularities.

For Christians, recognizing the kinds of social formation that technology engenders can have several possible responses, including the well-known approach of Christian societies themselves rejecting various forms of technology. Many contemporary theologians writing about technologies have been hesitant to make quite so drastic a move, since in most cases rejection of certain technologies merely postpones inevitable further conversations as technologies continue to develop. In relation to particular questions about disability, moreover, rejection of technologies in whole or in part stand, in whole or in part, to ignore peoples' pain and suffering and the effects of their impairments/ disabilities. That is, such a response to technology is as potentially eugenicizing as a medical model's overemphasis of cochlear implants may be.

Attempting to discuss technologies in terms of social formation is difficult, however. Even in this essay where I am attempting to narrate the ways we often describe technologies as asocial, and turn toward

33 Brian Brock, *Christian Ethics in a Technological Age* (Grand Rapids: Eerdmans, 2010), 274.
34 Brock, *Christian Ethics in a Technological Age*, 275.
35 Brock, *Christian Ethics in a Technological Age*, 280.

social narratives in contrast, I have at times failed. I suspect that creating the kind of community that pays attention to technology for its sociability, or lack thereof, requires embodied practices that help shape peoples' responses to technology in ways different from our unreflective approaches.

My concern and proposed remedy takes a cue from problems in Christology. Too often, the meaning of the incarnation is reduced to asocial usefulness, too. Jesus's life is reduced to a set of teachings, a useful person on the sidelines who could be consulted for making difficult decisions, or again, a useful emblem to display at will. This problem is a main concern of Wittgensteinian Thomist Herbert McCabe, who articulates again and again how God Incarnate cannot be so easily used and discharged, in ways similar to the technological tools I have described above. In one of his later Christological essays called "He Was Crucified, Suffered Death, and Was Buried," McCabe writes, "[Jesus'] alternative was not a philosophy or a theology or a social theory or a political programme. It was simply himself. Believe in *me*, he says."[36] McCabe continues by maintaining the crucial point that what it means to believe in Jesus is to enter into a relationship with Jesus, and the only way to do so is to make a response to Jesus with one's whole life.

Elsewhere, McCabe observes: "Jesus is not offering a blueprint for a new kind of society, an ideal which men [*sic*] may or may not choose to realize, he is offering *himself* as the centre of this new society."[37] McCabe strongly rejects motifs that describe Jesus primarily in terms of useful tools that lead to a better society, as in the blueprint, but rather *as* the new society itself. What McCabe does here is place all focus, all emphasis, on the whole of who Jesus is, rather than making any hint whatsoever that Jesus might be a step on the road toward the solution or ideal we seek.

Technology is often defined in terms of mere usefulness because sociality, too often, is defined in utilitarian terms (i.e., social contract theory), where humans exist as apparent independent beings who come together at stated times for stated purposes, and especially to "fix" problems requiring, say, the use of an army, or taxation and so forth.[38] In the revelation to which McCabe refers, the incarnation constitutes a set of social relations, which are not a means to an end but a sacrament— a making present— of the end of reconciliation and love. Consider the praise Jesus gives to a woman who wastes an entire jar of expensive perfume by breaking the jar and pouring the contents on

---

36 Herbert McCabe, *God Still Matters* (New York: Continuum, 2002), 98 (emphasis original).

37 McCabe, *God Still Matters*, 130 (emphasis original).

38 This is certainly how I interpret Robert Nozick's account of justice and society. See *Anarchy, State and Utopia* (New York: Basic Books, 2013).

his feet. Both jar and perfume are ancient forms of technology that have an obvious use. But that "use" is spoiled. The jar is broken. Wasted in terms of use, the broken jar of perfume becomes a sign of the woman's self-giving love—which itself serves as a sign of God's self-giving love poured out, regardless of expense.

McCabe sees love embodied especially in the particular community of Christian church and its practices, and so do others whose work borrows from his ideas.[39] In these terms, technologies can be seen not merely as useful, but as "making present" sociability— sociability that conveys wholeness, reconciliation, and redemption in itself, in just the way that Jesus cannot be a mere blueprint, but is himself what we seek.

In relation to disability and technology, then, what it means to think of technology as sociable formation is for whole communities to put on the technologies that are so often used as fixes for disabilities. For Christians, this means particularly to think about, and allow formation from, technologies in relation to making present reconciliation and love, especially to those who suffer. At times, this kind of sociable technological formation may look similar to a social model of disability because I think it requires us all to be formed by the technologies that currently mostly disabled people use. The ramps mentioned above that are for the use of all, not only those in wheelchairs, are a key example. What might it mean, too, to allow hearing and vision technologies to form and shape communities, architecture, structure and all? This view also makes use of medical models of disability and technology, especially in helping articulate ways in which medical solutions can be sociable.

Yet, as I described my concerns with these various models of disability in the previous section, I do not think this kind of communal life focused on the ways technologies (including older forms of technologies that we no longer consider even as technologies) entirely enables this sacramental making present of reconciliation and love. Part of the reason is that the social model of disability, as with technology itself, often aims to fix something that cannot be fixed, and that is human suffering. An emphasis on technology and its sociality does not hold with a sense of utopia, at least not when understood in Christological view. Technology does not eradicate suffering and death, not even in the presumed halcyon fields of (relatively) disembodied life online.

---

[39] Of course, the concern with this view is that we all know of Christian communities that operate precisely not in these ways, and which do not make present reconciliation and love. But I think McCabe here is not trying to presume, or recover, any sense of ideal "church" just in the same way that he rejects Jesus as a blueprint. We are given the gifts of Jesus, and other humans, to whom we can respond in love and reconciliation—or not. That our various responses to these gifts do not measure up is not, on Christian terms, a reason to reject Jesus as a way of life.

Such a view of technology linked to suffering and death accords with a new understanding of disability that has emerged as an alternative to the medical and social models. Deborah Creamer has advocated for a theology of disability that focuses on and embraces limits. "The limits model highlights the fact that human limits need not (and perhaps ought not) be seen as negative or as something that is not or that cannot be done, and instead claims that limits are an important part of being human—a fact that is overlooked when we reflect on the human body as generic."[40] For Creamer, one of the advantages of her argument is that it enables some of the best parts of both the medical and social models, but also allows for the fact that those models do not, in fact, "cure" disability. A medical model of disability has an important place, just as a social model does, with their attempts to enable those with disabilities/impairments as full access to social participation as possible. Still, both models leave a gap, which is that despite the diagnoses and the fixes, impairment and disability is still felt in various ways. To talk of eradicating impairments or disabilities, as in the cochlear implant debate, is indeed to speak of eradicating people, even a culture, because eradicating disability cannot be done via technology, except insofar as those tools enable death.

By contrast, Creamer's theology of embodiedness accepts that we have limits, despite, and sometimes because of, our technologies. Acknowledging those limits in relation to disability and technology enables people state and reflect on those limits in particular ways. This deep reflection on limits can and should be part of peoples' lives, irrespective of disability and impairment. For example, instead of envisioning the internet as a broadly open and accepting space for those with disabilities, a view to embodiedness acknowledges that humans access the internet bodily and in only limited ways; there is no other way to access it (not even Google Glass enables full disembodiment). The more we recognize our own limits when we use our technologies, the more able we are to understand others' limits in relation to technology and see that our technologies, however good, are not absolute fixes.

Thus, our best attempts to be formed by sociable technologies also requires us to walk with (and hear with, and see with, and think with, and so forth) people in the full ranges of their impairments, suffering, and disabilities. It means acknowledging the limits of both bodies and technologies, seeking ways, instead, to articulate clearly the times when technologies fail to form us well. Jesus' own life, suffering, and death offer a strong strand of Christian tradition in this regard, one that Christians have articulated and embodied in numerous ways, including the sacrament of the sick, the sacrament of reconciliation, healing

---

[40] Creamer, *Disability and Christian Theology*, 116.

services, foot washing, the Eucharist, peace and reconciliation commissions, prayers and meditations on Jesus' suffering, and so forth. These, too, need reflectively to be a strong part of any Christian community's desire to be responsive in a technological and able-bodied way. The most technologically-savvy and apparently welcoming church misses the point if pain and death are not also routinely part of that community's social formation, especially with attention to the sufferings of particular people in those communities.

In conclusion, it is all too easy to slip into a dominant mode of technology-as-asocial, and from thence, to unhelpful and even harmful ways of thinking about people with disabilities. Solutions to the dominant thoughts about dissociative technologies cannot come from thinking about rules we might put in place for using our technologies, as we and our technologies are far too diverse for such simplicity. Rather, as McCabe has suggested, Christians have a whole way of life, a life that, if oriented and practiced (at least in part) toward our technologies and their use because of Jesus, we may have better hope of learning, ourselves, how to love.

Journal of Moral Theology, Vol. 4, No. 1 (2015): 111-130

Unmanned: Autonomous Drones as a Problem of Theological Anthropology

Kara N. Slade

> As for the rest of this life's experiences, the more tears are shed over them the less are they worth weeping over, and the more truly worth lamenting the less do we bewail them while mired in them. You love the truth because anyone who does truth comes to the light. Truth it is that I want to do, in my heart by confession in your presence, and with my pen before many witnesses.
>
> Augustine of Hippo, Confessions[1]

> I think it's certainly a problem when our government cannot assess whether or not technology is decent.
>
> Mary Cummings, former fighter pilot
> and current Duke University engineering professor[2]

IN 2001, I WAS A NEWLY-MINTED PH.D. GRADUATE in mechanical engineering interviewing for a tenure-track position at a large public research university. During my tour of the department and its facilities, I was shown a Department of Defense funded research project involving what can best be described as robotic hummingbirds or bees, each slightly larger than a human hand. I remember thinking at the time that this was a technically interesting, if ultimately impractical effort, although I made suitably polite noises about how my own work might be of use. I wasn't hired for that position, but a year later I landed in a federal laboratory whose research portfolio also included unmanned vehicles (UxV) of another sort. Throughout my career as an engineer, the figure of the drone—whether autonomous or not—was a constant presence in the background, if not the foreground of those corners of the aerospace world where I traveled. Now, as a doctoral student in theology and ethics, I have been invited by the editors of this journal to revisit the topic from the perspective of moral theology. I do so knowing that I cannot approach it *de novo*, as an abstract problem in either the ethics of warfare or of technology. The

---

[1] Augustine, *Confessions,* trans. Maria Boulding, OSB (New York: Vintage Books, 1997), 197.

[2] Megan Garber, "Brain Drain Is Threatening the Future of U.S. Robotics," Defense One, June 30, 2014, www.defenseone.com/technology/2014/06/brain-drain-threatening-future-robotics/87562/.

reader who hopes to find in these pages a casuistic analysis of whether or not the use of autonomous drones is permissible under just war theory, or of what legal structures might helpfully govern their responsible use, will likely be disappointed.

This paper does not answer the question, "What are we to do about autonomous drones?" Instead, it attempts to excavate the multiple levels of "we" at work within that question, "What are we to do?," as well as the forms of doing it seems to presuppose. In so doing, I hope to bring to light the underlying problem of anthropology shared by both the construction of autonomous UxV's and their discussion as an ethical issue. Using the work of two theologians, Karl Barth and Søren Kierkegaard, I hope to trouble the understanding of the human being that shapes our conversations about the development and use of autonomous unmanned vehicles.

The World Target in the Age of Austerity

The first "we" at issue is the American we, and the first approach to the question of autonomous UxV's begins with their role in the discourses of the American military-industrial bureaucracy. How do those in decision-making positions talk about this technology when they talk amongst themselves? More specifically, how does it function as a means of what the Department of Defense and related agencies refer to as "global power projection"?[3] The drive to develop more, more effective, and more autonomous unmanned weapons systems arises out of a very particular context of national anxiety. One very typical analysis of the future of U.S. defense technology states the problem in near-catastrophic terms:

> The military foundations of the United States' global dominance are eroding. For the past several decades, an overwhelming advantage in technology and resources has given the U.S. military an unmatched ability to project power worldwide. This has allowed it to guarantee U.S. access to the global commons, assure the safety of the homeland, and underwrite security commitments around the globe. U.S. grand strategy assumes that such advantages will continue indefinitely. In fact, they are already starting to disappear.
>
> Several events in recent years have demonstrated that traditional means and methods of projecting power and accessing the global commons are growing increasingly obsolete becoming "wasting assets," in the language of defense strategists. The diffusion of advanced military technologies, combined with the continued rise of new powers,

---

[3] Cortney Konner and Ronald Pope, "Integration of Space-Based Combat Systems," *Air and Space Power Journal* (Fall 2006), www.au.af.mil/au/afri/aspj/airchronicles/-apj/apj06/fal06/konner.html.

> such as China, and hostile states, such as Iran, will make it progressively more expensive in blood and treasure—perhaps prohibitively expensive—for U.S. forces to carry out their missions in areas of vital interest, including East Asia and the Persian Gulf. Military forces that do deploy successfully will find it increasingly difficult to defend what they have been sent to protect. Meanwhile, the U.S. military's long-unfettered access to the global commons—including space and cyberspace—is being increasingly challenged.[4]

The default response to this perceived need to do more with less is not to question the need itself or, indeed, the accuracy of the perception. Instead, the sheer inertia of organizational logic demands a technological solution that leaves its grounding assumptions and latent ideologies unexamined.

Given this framework of anxiety, the primary Department of Defense planning document for unmanned systems reads in a very real sense as the invocation of a *deus ex machina*. The opening pages of the 2011 Unmanned Systems Roadmap present unmanned systems as the inevitable, ideal solution to the problem of global power in an age of fiscal austerity:

> The DoD, along with industry, understands the effect that innovation and technology in unmanned systems can have on the future of warfare and the ability of the United States to adapt to an ever-changing global environment. DoD and industry are working to advance operational concepts with unmanned systems to achieve the capabilities and desired effects on missions and operations worldwide. In building a common vision, DoD's goals for unmanned systems are to enhance mission effectiveness, improve operational speed and efficiency, and affordably close warfighting gaps.... By prudently developing, procuring, integrating, and fielding unmanned systems, DoD and industry will ensure skillful use of limited resources and access to emerging warfighting capabilities. Pursuing this approach with unmanned systems will help DoD sustain its dominant global military power and provide the tools required by national decision-makers to influence foreign and domestic activities while adapting to an ever-changing global environment.[5]

The extensive discussion of autonomous UxV's that follows in both the 2011 and 2013 versions is thus framed by an expansive vision of the scope of American military power. Nations such as China or Iran

---

[4] Andrew F. Krepinevich, Jr., "The Pentagon's Wasting Assets," *Foreign* Affairs (July 1, 2009), www.foreignaffairs.com/articles/65150/andrew-f-krepinevich-jr/the-pentagons-wasting-assets.

[5] Department of Defense, *Unmanned Systems Integrated Roadmap FY 2011-2036,* www.acq.osd.mil/sts/docs/Unmanned%20Systems%20Integrated%20Roadmap%20FY2011-2036.pdf, 5.

may be mentioned in passing, but only insofar as they function as signifiers of the category of the global, not as particular threats to national security.

Before turning in earnest to this notion of the global, however, a word of clarification is in order. The category of autonomous unmanned systems encompasses vehicles intended to operate on land, sea, and air, only some of which may have lethal capabilities. Furthermore, autonomous robotic systems function along a continuum of independence from human control. Skynet (in the *Terminator* series) is an autonomous system but, strictly speaking, so is a Roomba. An aerial vehicle with autonomous control over firing a weapon is a limit case, but even so it deserves sustained attention. First, as the second section will examine in greater detail, enough research in this direction has been funded that it represents at least a desired outcome if not a realistic technological possibility. Second, it occupies a pre-eminent place in the cultural imagination, at least partially due to the current use of remotely-piloted UAV's in active conflicts.

More broadly, the autonomous lethal unmanned aerial vehicle represents the most obvious instantiation of a particular logic that ties vision to destruction on a global scale. In her essay "The Age of the World Target," literary theorist Rey Chow argues that the development and subsequent use of the atomic bomb by the United States occasioned a shift in the perception of the world—the global—from the American perspective:

> [W]e may say that in the age of bombing, the world has also been transformed into—is essentially conceived and grasped as—a target. To conceive of the world as a target is to conceive of it as an object to be destroyed. As W. J. Perry, a former United States Under Secretary of State for Defense, said: "If I had to sum up current thinking on precision missiles and saturation weaponry in a single sentence, I'd put it like this: once you can see the target, you can expect to destroy it." Increasingly, war would mean the production of maximal visibility and illumination for the purpose of maximal destruction.[6]

In light of this notion of the world as target, the ubiquity of the autonomous unmanned aerial vehicle in the cultural imaginary becomes intelligible. It is a technology of absolute vision and destruction, both fantasy and nightmare of a globalized perspective beyond the limitations of human embodiment.

At the same time, it also continues a trajectory that increasingly separates those who see from those who are seen (and bombed):

---

[6] Rey Chow's essay "The Age of the World Target: Atomic Bombs, Alterity, and Area Studies" in in her *The Age of the World Target: Self-Referentiality in War, Theory, and Comparative Work* (Durham: Duke University Press, 2006), 25-44, quotation at 31.

> For the U.S. men and women of combat, the elitism and aggressiveness of panoramic vision went hand in hand with distant control and the instant destruction of others; for the ordinary men, women, and children of Iraq (as for the ordinary people of Korea and Vietnam in the 1950s and 1960s), life became more and more precarious—immaterial in the sense of a readiness for total demolition at any moment. Even as we speak, the Pentagon is reported to be building its own Internet for the wars of the future, with the goal "to give all American commanders and troops [including those on the ground] a moving picture of all foreign enemies and threats—a 'God's eye view' of battle."[7]

To conceive of the world as a target is thus to divide it into categories of "above" and "below," where those categories represent more than just a physical separation between the air and the ground.

As the convergence of the targeting of the world and the ubiquity of information, the autonomous drone is symptomatic of a much broader change not only in the technology of war but also in the meaning of "war" itself. Using Paul Virilo's concept of "pure war," Chow explains that war after Hiroshima and Nagasaki would be qualitatively different from the wars of the past:

> The dropping of the atomic bombs effected what Michel Foucault would call a major shift in epistemes, a fundamental change in the organization, production, and circulation of knowledge. War after the atomic bomb would no longer be the physical, mechanical struggles between combative oppositional groups, but would increasingly come to resemble collaborations in the logistics of perception between partners who occupy relative, but always mutually implicated, positions.... Moreover, war would exist from now on as an agenda that is infinitely self-referential: war represents not other types of struggles and conflicts—what in history classes are studied as "causes"—but war itself. From its previous conventional, negative signification as a blockade, an inevitable but regretted interruption of the continuity that is "normal life," war shifts to a new level of force. It has become not the cessation of normality, but rather, the very definition of normality itself. The space and time of war are no longer segregated in the form of an other; instead, they operate from within the here and now, as the internal logic of the here and now. From being negative blockage to being normal routine, war becomes the positive mechanism, momentum, and condition of possibility of society, creating a hegemonic space of global communication through powers of visibility and control.[8]

---

[7] Chow, *The Age of the World Target*, 35.

[8] Chow, *The Age of the World Target*, 31-2.

In this new logic of war, the distinction between foreign and domestic, and between the technology of war and its domestication, ceases to exist in any appreciable sense.

At the same time, these seemingly opposite spheres have been already more blurred than they might seem. Writing about women's literature of the 19th century, historian Amy Kaplan argues that domesticity and the notion of "the foreign" have always existed in relationship to each other:

> The notion of domestic policy makes sense only in opposition to foreign policy, and uncoupled from the foreign, national issues are never labeled domestic. The idea of foreign policy depends on the sense of the nation as a domestic space imbued with a sense of at-homeness, in contrast to an external world perceived as alien and threatening. Reciprocally, a sense of the foreign is necessary to erect the boundaries that enclose the nation as home.[9]

Amy Laura Hall uses this concept of "manifest domesticity" to describe the domestication of atomic energy immediately subsequent to the bombing of Hiroshima and Nagasaki at the close of World War II.[10] For Hall, the "Atomic Age" was the reaction to the use of the bomb, the wholesale re-packaging of a deadly military technology into the fabric of American domestic life. Subsequently, however, it can be argued that the development of a military technology and its domestication would take place simultaneously, rather than sequentially.

As a result, the development and deployment of drones by the military cannot be thought of apart from their use in even the most banal of domestic applications. It is not a digression from an otherwise serious argument to note the use of remote-controlled drones in American wedding photography to capture "one of a kind images" that "brides absolutely love,"[11] even as "foreign" weddings have been erroneously targeted by the lethal version.[12] Nor is it beside the point to note that military technical expertise in the development of autonomous drones has been limited by the much more lucrative compensation offered to engineers from the likes of Amazon and Apple.[13] Rather, the presence

---

[9] Amy Kaplan, "Manifest Domesticity," *American Literature* 70.3 (1998), 581-582.

[10] Amy Laura Hall, *Conceiving Parenthood: American Protestantism and the Spirit of Reproduction* (Grand Rapids: Eerdmans, 2008), 292.

[11] CBS Interactive, "Couples Taking Wedding Photography to New Heights with Drones," *CBS News* (August 5, 2014), www.cbsnews.com/news/drone-for-hire-as-wedding-photographer/.

[12] Greg Miller, "Yemeni victims of U.S. military drone strike get more than $1 million in compensation," *Washington Post* (August 18, 2014), www.washingtonpost.com/-world/national-security/yemeni-victims-of-us-military-drone-strike-get-more-than-1million-in-compensation/2014/08/18/670926f0-26e4-11e4-8593-da634b334390_story.html.

[13] Garber, "Brain Drain is Threatening the Future of U.S. Robotics."

of the domesticated drone is an indicator of the extent to which all of us are enmeshed in, and implicated by, the disembodied global vision of the American "we."

Strong (and Limiting) Simplifying Assumptions

The second "we" at issue is the technological we, for whom autonomous drones may function more as a vehicle for intellectual curiosity or careerism and less as a tool of national policy. While the previous section addressed the ways in which the American body politic as a whole is implicated in this project, this section turns to a smaller, and easily overlooked constituency. Indeed, it can sometimes seem as if those tasked with turning drones from the previously described object of political desire into a technological reality are the least visible participants in the process from the standpoint of moral discourse. And yet, close attention to the technological end of this conversation reveals not only the limitations of current technical competence to produce such vehicles but also the problematic nature of "engineering ethics" as a discipline within the broader process of engineering education. Given the potential of autonomous lethal drones to replace the moral agency of a pilot-operator in favor of a pre-programmed algorithm, I believe that attention is especially warranted.

As a technological project, the development of autonomous military vehicles began in earnest with the National Defense Authorization Act of 2000, which introduced a congressional mandate for the development and use of unmanned deep-strike aircraft and ground vehicles and created "increasing pressure to develop and deploy robotics, including autonomous vehicles."[14] Along with the "compelling military utility" of the use of robots for "dull, dirty, and dangerous" tasks, some researchers have named the misconduct of soldiers in Iraq and Afghanistan as an additional reason to pursue autonomous robotic weapons as an alternative.[15] Ronald Arkin, a computer scientist at the Georgia Institute of Technology, has argued that "an unmanned system can perform more ethically than human soldiers," although he admits that it would not be possible to create a "perfectly ethical" system.[16] He advocates the implementation a deontic logic based on the adaptation of the categorical imperative to "a set of more direct and relevant assertions regarding acceptable actions towards noncombatants and their

---

[14] Patrick Lin, George Bekey, and Keith Abney, *Autonomous Military Robots: Risk, Ethics, and Design*, California Polytechnic State University San Luis Obispo, Ethics + Emerging Sciences Group, Report for Office of Naval Research (December 20, 2008), 6.

[15] Lin et al., *Autonomous Military Robots*, 7.

[16] R. C. Arkin, "Governing Lethal Behavior: Embedding Ethics in a Hybrid Deliberative/Reactive Robot Architecture—Part I: Motivation and Philosophy," Proc. Human-Robot Interaction 2008 (Amsterdam: March 2008), 124.

underlying rights."[17] Tellingly, he selects this strategy based not on its suitability as an ethical system but on "computational tractability."[18] From the technological perspective, the ease of achieving technical goals trumps the moral advisability of the resulting product. As Arkin admits, he has made "strong (and limiting) simplifying assumptions" about the actual functioning of the algorithm.[19]

At the same time, there is no consensus about even the technical feasibility of such a system. Another analysis, conducted for the Office of Naval Research, argues that it would require "an impossible computational load due to the requirements for knowledge... and the difficulty of estimating the sufficiency of initial information."[20] The authors recommend a virtue ethics approach that would enable the robot to "embody the right tendencies in their reactions to the world and other agents in the world."[21] Leaving aside the question of whether or not a machine can embody anything at all, the admission that "morally intelligent behaviour may require much more than being rational" would seem to obviate any chance that a computing device could be programmed for moral intelligence.[22] However, the authors recommend continued work towards that end, "before irrational public fears or accidents arising from military robotics derail research progress and national security interests."[23] In doing so, they ask that engineers conduct "extensive pre-deployment testing" and "think carefully about how the subsystem they are working on could interact with other subsystems... in potentially harmful ways," while simultaneously ensuring that they can confidently certify safety.[24]

Given the lethal consequences of these technologies, it might be expected that significant attention would be given to ethics in the course of engineering education and in professional practice. However, what passes for "engineering ethics" is often marked by a combination of epistemological overconfidence, sheer naiveté, and a profoundly isolating rhetoric that assumes near-heroic individual action instead of communal moral discernment. This, then, is the second level at which the technology of drones points towards an anthropological problem, detaching that technology from ethics through a pro-

---

[17] R. C. Arkin, "Governing Lethal Behavior: Embedding Ethics in a Hybrid Deliberative/Reactive Robot Architecture—Part III: Representational and Architectural Considerations," Proceedings of Technology in Wartime Conference (Palo Alto: January 2008), 4.

[18] Arkin, "Governing Lethal Behavior Part III," 4.

[19] Arkin, "Governing Lethal Behavior Part III," 9.

[20] Lin et al., *Autonomous Military Robots,* 34.

[21] Lin et al., *Autonomous Military Robots,* 38.

[22] Lin et al., *Autonomous Military Robots,* 37.

[23] Lin et al., *Autonomous Military Robots*, 91.

[24] Lin et al., *Autonomous Military Robots*, 69.

cess of cognitive abstraction. For example, one popular textbook instructs each student to "choose their personal engineering ethics threshold," methodically evaluate their crises of conscience with a handy "Ethics Dilemma Scorecard," and then "determine a suitable course of action once this threshold is reached."[25] But in a meta-analysis of 42 engineering ethics courses, civil engineering professor and engineering education researcher David Haws deems almost all of these approaches inadequate to the hard work of moral formation, and he finds most engineering faculty ambivalent at best towards that work:

> Most of us, as engineers, feel that the computational aspects of engineering… are the most important topics for our students to learn. We feel that… ethics should be taught in other departments (or in the home, or other "institutions of faith"). We feel that as engineers we should concentrate on developing a good product and then let the rest of the world worry about how, where and when that product is used…. This, of course, is the problem. And by the time we realize that this is an ethical problem (like the weapon designers of Los Alamos), it's usually too late.[26]

The root of the problem, according to Haws, is that "engineering attracts convergent thinkers who tend to become oblivious" to the "wider ramifications of their work."[27] And as the state of research on fully autonomous, lethal unmanned aerial vehicles plainly reveals, moral considerations still tend to lag far behind the ongoing design process.

While engineering may indeed attract students who tend to focus on a problem in isolation from its context, the work of design itself contributes to a sense of abstract detachment from the particularity of existence. As a system-building activity that proceeds by its own internal logic, the practice of engineering design already exists in a default frame of movement "from function to form" through a "process of synthesis" that "emanates from Hegel's philosophy," in the words of one design textbook.[28] Meanwhile, the overarching narratives of aerospace engineering in particular—inevitable progress, national necessity, and the "offensive-defensive" dialectic—do even more work to place engineering within a necessary world-historical process.[29] But

---

[25] Gail D. Baura, *Engineering Ethics: An Industrial Perspective* (Burlington, MA: Elsevier, 2006), xviii, 194.

[26] David R. Haws, "Ethics Instruction in Engineering Education: A (Mini) Meta Analysis," *Journal of Engineering Education* 90.2 (April 2001), 223.

[27] Haws, "Ethics Instruction in Engineering Education," 223.

[28] Amaresh Chakrabarti, ed., *Engineering Design Synthesis: Understanding, Approaches, and Tools* (London: Springer-Verlag, 2002), 9.

[29] Robert M. Cassidy, *Counterinsurgency and the Global War on Terror* (Westport, CT: Praeger, 2006), 46.

as Julia Watkin argues in her commentary on Kierke-gaard's *Concluding Unscientific Postscript*, a thinker within such a system loses contact with ethics—and with oneself as well:

> Loss of contact with ethics occurs firstly through the thinker's make-believe standpoint in which he or she takes some fantastical God's-eye position outside the universe, that is, outside existence. Since objective thinking, in that it concerns description of the world, has no relation to the individual thinker's personal life, daily life becomes an inconvenient appendage to the great work of System-building (CUP, 1:119, 122-23). Secondly, there is a loss of ethics in the Hegelian-style System because it contains ethics and morality as a necessary process. Yet in a necessary process there can be no freedom and hence no ethics.[30]

As moral conversations around autonomous drones continue, it is crucial to take into account the ways in which the process of technological development itself can at least hinder—if not actively work against—thoughtful discourse. At the same time as the technological "we" assumes more responsibility for lethal technologies, it remains unable to reflect on that responsibility in a coherent way.

Some writers within the engineering profession have become disillusioned with this status quo, both in terms of its idealization of progress for its own sake as well as the failure of the discipline to incorporate more robust ethical standards. Samuel Florman, a civil engineer with experience in the construction industry, traces out a technological declension narrative in his book, *The Existential Pleasures of Engineering*, laying much of the blame for the profession's "dark night of the spirit" firmly at the feet of the education process:

> Part of the problem is surely the stultifying influence of engineering schools. In too many of these institutions, the least bit of imagination, social concern, or cultural interest is snuffed out under a crushing load of purely technical subjects. This situation appears to be improving, although a whole generation of engineers has already been disfigured.[31]

Florman proposes a solution through his reading of Goethe's Faust, who, "jaded with every conceivable worldly experience," found "in a land-reclamation project" the "contentment that had eluded him all his life."

---

[30] Julia Watkin, "Boom! The Earth Is Round! – On the Impossibility of an Existential System," *International Kierkegaard Commentary: Concluding Unscientific Postscript* (Macon,GA: Mercer University Press, 1997), 101.

[31] Samuel Florman, *The Existential Pleasures of Engineering* (New York: St. Martin's Press, 1976), 92.

> Faust's soul was saved, not because he reclaimed land, but because, in Goethe's words, "whoever aspiring, struggles on, for him there is salvation." In this sense – in the knowledge that we are engaged in the struggle to improve the lot of Everyman – we can still share Goethe's enthusiasm, and a taste of Faust's salvation.[32]

This secular narrative of salvation hinges on embracing the concreteness of existence by "turning away from abstract religion and philosophy and returning to a less intellectualized brick-and-mortar existence," in which we "arrive closer to God through leading a normal life," and "enjoying the blessings of bourgeois society."[33] But this is a particularity that still lies within a trajectory of human progress, and it is still in thrall to a poetic idealization of the work of a heroic individual. It is a call to work out one's salvation, but crucially it neglects the fear and trembling that must accompany such work.

Søren Kierkegaard, too, engages with Faust, through his pseudonym Johannes de Silentio, but what emerges is a cautionary tale more than a model to be emulated. This Faust is "too ideal a figure to go around in bedroom slippers," a "doubter" who "wants to save the universal" by "being hidden and by remaining silent."[34] Yet even this Faust may be saved, "if the doubter can become the single individual who as the single individual stands in an absolute relation to the absolute," if his "doubt" is turned into "guilt," shifting from the register of the intellectual to that of the existential.[35] As Louise Carroll Keeley has suggested, this pivotal move is narrated through another story, that of Tobias and Sarah from the book of Tobit, and it is one that hinges on reception rather than heroic action.[36]

> If a poet read this story and were to use it, I wager a hundred to one that he would make everything center on the young Tobias... Tobias behaves gallantly and resolutely and chivalrously, but any man who does not have the courage for that... has not even grasped the little mystery that it is better to give than to receive and has no intimation of the great mystery that it is far more difficult to receive than to give.[37]

---

[32] Florman, *The Existential Pleasures of Engineering,* 145.

[33] Florman, *The Existential Pleasures of Engineering,* 148.

[34] Søren Kierkegaard, *Fear and Trembling*, trans. Howard V. Hong and Edna H. Hong (Princeton: Princeton University Press, 1983), 107, 110.

[35] Kierkegaard, *Fear and Trembling*, 111.

[36] Louise Carroll Keeley, "The Parables of Problem III in Kierkegaard's Fear and Trembling," *International Kierkegaard Commentary: Fear and Trembling/Repetition* (Macon: Mercer University Press, 1993), 127-54.

[37] Kierkegaard, *Fear and Trembling*, 102.

The hero in this story is not Tobias, but Sarah, who receives the loving work of another in a parable that Kierkegaard uses as an analogy for the work of Christ:

> Sarah is the heroic character. She is the one I want to approach as I have never approached any girl or been tempted in thought to approach anyone of whom I have read. For what love for God it takes to be willing to let oneself be healed when from the very beginning one in all innocence has been botched, from the very beginning has been a damaged specimen of a human being! What ethical maturity to take upon oneself the responsibility of letting the loved one do something so hazardous! What faith in God that she would not in the very next moment hate the man to whom she owed everything![38]

If, as J. Robert Oppenheimer said in the wake of the Manhattan Project, the builders of military technology "have known sin," it stands as an indictment of an inability to grasp the reality and the totality of sin beforehand. And yet this seems to be a mistake we as engineers are bent on repeating.

The End of Everything We Had Respected and Honored

Beyond the consideration of drones as a technology or as an instrument of state policy lies a further level of discourse that operates on the level of moral conversation. The question noted at the outset of the paper, "What are we to do about autonomous drones?", also contains the "we" that functions at the level of ethical speculation. A recurrent temptation in such discussions is to take recourse to a form of nostalgia for an idealized prior human "natural" state, for a purer or more chivalrous form of warfare that leaves the deeper problems of modern war untouched. One example of this confusion in current moral discourse may be seen by drawing analogies from Sebastian Junger's 1957 novel, *The Glass Bees*, to contemporary autonomous drones. *The Glass Bees* tells the story of a former military man, Captain Richard, as he interviews for a position with the mysterious Zapparoni Works. Zapparoni's miniature robots, the "glass bees" of the title, are intended to perform precisely the sorts of "dull, dirty and dangerous" tasks envisioned by the Unmanned Technology Roadmap:

> They could count, weigh, sort gems or paper money and, while doing so, eliminate counterfeits. They worked in dangerous locations, handling explosives, dangerous viruses, and even radio-active materials. Swarms of selectors could not only detect the faintest smell of smoke

[38] Kierkegaard, *Fear and Trembling*, 104.

> but could also extinguish a fire at an early stage; others repaired defective wiring, and still others fed upon filth and became indispensable in all jobs where cleanliness was essential.[39]

Captain Richard, like many contemporary students and practitioners of technology, falls "under the spell" of the robots before him.[40]

> All this was a spectacle which both enthralled and mesmerized. It put one's mind to sleep. I cannot say what astonished me more—the ingenious invention of each single unit or the interplay among them. Perhaps it was essentially the dancelike force of the spectacle that delighted me—power concentrated within a superior order.[41]

This spectacle of power, as Captain Richard would discover, can become simultaneously alluring and repulsive, and in the novel it leads him eventually to a reactionary impulse grounded in disgust.

To his horror, Captain Richard learns that the products of the Zapparoni Works, unsubtly located in a former Cistercian monastery where "they worked, of course, on Sundays" may be far from harmless.[42] Near the end of the novel, which switches between the world of the glass bees and memories of his former military life, he laments the loss of a martial ideal heralded by the triumph of technique:

> I knew with certainty this was the end of everything we had respected and honored. Words like honor and dignity became ludicrous. Again the word "alone" loomed up out of the night. An outrage has an isolating effect, as though our planet were threatened with extinction.[43]

One tendency in moral reasoning on the subject of autonomous drones (and pilot-controlled drones, for that matter) is to echo Captain Richard in this longing for a reliably stable notion of honor and chivalry upon which the warrior's identity is grounded. Writing on drones in the context of a study of military virtue, Christian Enemark traces a shift from a "heroic" to a "post-heroic" era in "the American way of war."[44]

> The notion of honour within the warrior ethos further distinguishes the military profession from civilian ones, and it is important from an ethical perspective as a potential source of restraint in the conduct of

[39] Ernst Jünger, *The Glass Bees,* trans. Louise Bogan and Elisabeth Mayer (New York: The New York Review of Books, 2000), 8.
[40] Jünger, *The Glass Bees,* 143.
[41] Jünger, *The Glass Bees,* 133.
[42] Jünger, *The Glass Bees,* 35.
[43] Jünger, *The Glass Bees,* 181.
[44] Book Description, *Armed Drones and the Ethics of War*, www.routledge.com/books/details/9780415540520/.

> war. Historically, a code of honour—be it the Christian code of chivalry or the Japanese Bushido—is what has given warriors a sense of belonging to their profession, and this sense has been bound up with an ethic of responsibility to those within and beyond it. Critically, "honour" has been the main point of reference by which warriors have sought to distinguish themselves from mere butchers.[45]

In Enemark's account, and in similar ethical arguments grounded in traditional military ethics, it is the mutuality of risk that distinguishes the warrior from the butcher, the soldier from the hangman. Without maintaining the "vital distinction" between "risk reduction" and "risk elimination" that is threatened by drones, he argues, "warfare is not war at all" and thus "any pre-meditated, organized killing that is risk-free must be called something else."[46]

Perhaps it is this disturbance, this disruption in the generally agreed upon understanding of what it means to be human beings who kill each other in war, that is the most perplexing aspect of drone warfare. Confronted with a technology that points toward the ways that war is too closely related to other forms of "premeditated, organized killing," the default moral response is to repristinate certain forms of conduct in war. The reactions of unease and the provocation of the uncanny that Jünger describes can drive moral discourse toward circumscribing a zone of innocent, chivalrous war and idealizing the figure of the warrior. Chivalry may be part of the cultural baggage of Christendom, but in itself it is a thin basis for Christian thought. Certainly, there is an element of truth in the argument from chivalry. Mutual exposure to risk also entails mutual exposure to the possibility of seeing, and recognizing, the enemy as also a neighbor to be loved. However, the technologies of seeing involved in drone warfare precludes this possibility. The globalized remote vision described in the first section makes it impossible to see the enemy as anything other than a target to be identified and destroyed. Rather than attempt to naturalize certain forms of killing and exclude others, or to create an idealized figure of the honorable warrior, moral discourse may be more fruitfully turned in other directions.

Unmanned Vehicles and the Pride of Man

Writing in a recent essay in *Ethics and International Affairs*, Roger Berkowitz has also pointed toward the intersections of drone technology and contemporary understandings of "the human." Berkowitz reads Jünger's novel as a warning of the dehumanizing effects of tech-

---

45 Christian Enemark, *Armed Drones and the Ethics of War: Military Virtue in a Post-Heroic Age* (New York: Routledge, 2014), 79.

46 Enemark, *Armed Drones and the Ethics of War,* 81.

nology, and especially of the dangers entailed by replacing the fragility and contingency of human existence with idealized technical perfection. He explains,

> The danger posed by Zapparoni's bees is the one we face today: that we allow our fascination with technology to dull our humanity. We have become infatuated by perfection and intolerant of human error; we worship data-driven reliability and disdain untested human intuition; and we value efficiency over beauty and chance. "Technical perfection," Junger [sic] writes, "strives toward the calculable, human perfection toward the incalculable. Perfect mechanisms—around which, therefore, stands an uncanny but fascinating halo of brilliance—evoke both fear and a titanic pride which will be humbled not by insight but only by catastrophe." As we humans interact more regularly with drones and machines and computers, we may come to expect ourselves, our friends, our colleagues, and our lovers to act with the same efficiency—and inhumanity—of drones.[47]

This re-configuring of human expectations and human relationships is, to be sure, part of the anthropological problem posed by the proliferation of drones, both in warfare and elsewhere in more mundane, domestic life. However, I contend that autonomous drones pose a problem not only through the expectation of inhuman perfection, but also through the failure to recognize the totality of human imperfection consequent to the Fall. The "titanic pride" lamented by Jünger points towards the reality of sin and the necessity of recognizing that sin in the debate occasioned by the development and deployment of this technology. For Christian moral theology, the ways in which drones press against the problem of "the human" acknowledged by Berkowitz suggest the need to recall, as Karl Barth memorably wrote the in *The Epistle to the Romans*, that the first step in ethical reflection must be that of repentance.[48] It is to Barth's work that this paper now turns.

The matter of human pride, especially in its "titanic" form, is the focus of one of the key sections in Volume IV.1 of the *Church Dogmatics*. Barth's turn from Christology to anthropology within this volume takes place through an account of the sinfulness of pride as it is revealed in the person and work of Jesus Christ. The rhetoric of §60 ("The Pride of Man") reflects the postwar context in which it was written, with the German version appearing in 1953 and the English translation following in 1956. The tumultuous years between the publication of Volumes I and IV had seen Europe become the ground of Cold

---

[47] Roger Berkowitz, "Drones and the Question of 'The Human,'" Ethics and International Affairs 28.2 (2014), 162.

[48] Karl Barth, *The Epistle to the Romans,* trans. E. C. Hoskins (London: Oxford University Press, 1968), 432-35.

War confrontation, as the United States emerged as a military and economic superpower. The idealized, Aryan version of the Übermensch who served as Barth's primary Christological foil in *Church Dogmatics* I.2 has been replaced by a representation of sinful humanity that reflects his critique of an emerging American hegemony, based in a faith in individual self-sufficiency and collective progress. As such, this section of Barth's text has much to recommend it as Christian moral theology reflects on the particularly American form of weaponized technological progress that autonomous drones represent.

One of the most crucial, and most helpful, insights in this section is the connection between errors in anthropology and errors in the doctrine of God caused by projecting the former into the latter. Barth opens §60.2 by defining sin in terms of the disobedience arising from unbelief, and the man of disobedience as one who "only wants to exalt himself and to be as God" (*sicut deus*) and to "pass his limits" as a creature. In doing so, however, he "places himself in a self-contradiction which can result only in his destruction."[49] Barth then explains that the man who tries to put himself in the place of God in self-sufficient independence makes two profound errors: one about himself and one about who God is. The first assumes that the highest form of human existence is self-sufficient, self-centered, atomized individualism:

> The error of man concerning himself, his self-alienation, is that he thinks he can love and choose and will and assert and maintain and exalt himself in his being in himself, his self-hood, and that in so doing he will be truly man.... Neither as an individual nor in society was he created to be placed alone, to be self-controlling and self-sufficient, to be self-centred, to rotate around himself.

The second imagines that God in actuality is as utterly self-sufficient, self-contained, and self-centered as the man, *sicut deus*, believes he would be if he were God. In actuality, of course, God cannot be who God is without being in relationship:

> The error of man concerning God is that the God he wants to be like is obviously only a self-sufficient, self-affirming, self-desiring supreme being, self-centered and rotating about himself. Such a being is not God. God is for Himself, but He is not only for Himself. He is in a supreme self-hood, but not a self-contained self-hood, not in a mere divinity which is obviously presented to man in the mere humanity intended for man. God is a *se* and *per se*, but as the love which is grounded in itself from all eternity. Because He is the triune God, who

[49] Karl Barth, *Church Dogmatics* IV.1, trans. G. T. Thomson and Harold Knight (Peabody, MA: Hendrickson, 2010), 419.

> from the first has loved us as the Father in the Son and turned to us by the Holy Spirit, He is God *pro nobis*.[50]

Here, Barth challenges any attempt to assume a "God's eye view" beyond human limitations. In so doing, his account of anthropological error provides a helpful way of thinking through the problems of vision and destructive potential named in the first section of this paper. It is also, however, a cautionary word against any attempt to elude those problems through recourse to a naturalized, nostalgic vision of humanity apart from the reconciling work of Christ.

For Barth, the Cross is the unavoidable ground of God's confrontation with the "titanic man" who "tries to be his own helper" and "the subject of his own redemptive history."[51] The story of man's "great and fantastic attempt to help himself," he argues, is one of ongoing dissatisfaction and restless acquisitiveness:

> Throughout his life he rushes and grasps at this thing and that thing, striving and fighting in a dissatisfaction and longing which cannot be explained by the fact that this thing or that thing is useful and necessary and noble and satisfying, which does not stand in any relation to the extrinsic or intrinsic value of the things to which he can help himself if all goes well. In this longing and dissatisfaction he can never be satisfied with the attainable once he has attained it, but he must immediately demand and reach out after something more and different.[52]

While the individual "titanic man" strives to find an illusory "salvation which he can prepare and make for himself," titanism *en masse* relies on similarly illusory narratives of human progress and improvement:

> What a misunderstanding when we think it is all a matter of what we value and seek as the "progress" necessary and possible to us, of our inventions and discoveries, of the establishment of our pious and impious philosophies and ethical or unethical principles, of our wars and treaties and new wars, of the movements in which we think we are caught up, of the reactions which they provoke to the things and ideas and persons which are from time to time in the foreground: the extension of our knowledge; the improvement of our techniques; the deepening of our understanding and the corresponding dissemination of instruction; love and hate; power and possession and desire; the sway of this or that individual or people or position in itself and as such.[53]

Despite these ostensible markers of progress, humanity remains "strikingly the same in spite of all the changes in costume and scenery

[50] Barth, *Church Dogmatics* IV.1, 422.
[51] Barth, *Church Dogmatics* IV.1, 460.
[52] Barth, *Church Dogmatics* IV.1, 460.
[53] Barth, *Church Dogmatics* IV.1, 467.

throughout the centuries." Despite every human attempt to supplant, ignore, or avoid God, the Word still brings alienated man "back to a true knowledge of what God is in truth."

An Outward Air of the Most Serious Responsibility

At the same time as Barth critiques this misplaced faith in human progress, he also highlights the dubious nature of ethical reflection upon it. The figure of the serpent in the Garden makes several appearances in §60, each time with a new way to tempt humanity into being *sicut deus*. We have already seen the result of his first temptation, to become like God by choosing a "false and destructive" path of "aseity and independence" rather than sociality. Later, however, the serpent brings an even more dangerous and compelling argument: the knowledge of good and evil would be "a rise to genuine morality, to the freedom of a knowledge which distinguishes and an activity which elects, and therefore to the freedom of genuine commitment, of a final and true unity with God."[54] This fatal moment marks "the establishment of ethics" as a separate discipline from dogmatics.

As Barth reminds his readers (especially those readers who happen to be ethicists), this is a profoundly dangerous turn:

> In Gen. 3 the desire of man for a knowledge of good and evil is represented as an evil desire, indeed the one evil desire which is so characteristic and fatal for the whole race. The consequences for the theory and practice of Christian ethics—and not only that—would be incalculable if only we were to see this and accept it instead of regarding this very questionable knowledge—whether sought in the Bible or the rational nature of man or conscience—as the most basic of all the gifts of God. The armour behind which the real evil of the pride of man conceals itself is obviously thicker and more impenetrable at this point than at any other.[55]

In his desire to know good and evil, man *sicut deus* is unable to comprehend his inability to do this as God does, to "affirm and accept the cosmos and deny and reject chaos."[56] He envisions himself as a knight, fighting for the cause of God and man against the forces of disorder, and he deems this good:

> Of course he does not believe that he is doing that which is evil but that which is good, that which is commanded and necessary, and therefore the best of all. In this form of sin there can be no question of any indolence or frivolity or negligence. On the contrary, there is a pathetic earnestness, an outward air of the most serious responsibility, the most stringent sense of duty, the most militant virtue. As judge of

54 Barth, *Church Dogmatics* IV.1, 448.
55 Barth, *Church Dogmatics* IV.1, 449.
56 Barth, *Church Dogmatics* IV.1, 450.

> good and evil, man wants to stand at God's side in defense of the cosmos great and small against the invasion of chaos and disorder and wrong—himself a cherub with drawn sword at the gate of paradise, or at the very least a watchman on the walls of Jerusalem. He wants to spring into the breach, safeguarding the right with his own affirmation and negation, with his own building up and tearing down, successfully maintaining the *causa Dei* and the cause of man.[57]

Barth's caustic evocation of an ethics meant to circumscribe the conduct of righteous Crusades and responsible swordplay immediately brings to mind his ongoing public dispute with Reinhold Niebuhr. As such, it calls into question any attempt to theologize around drones from the standpoint of Niebuhrian realism, just as it originally questioned Niebuhr's efforts to theologize around the atomic bomb. Beyond that, however, it also points to the constant temptation of moral theology, that of the desire to provide those in power with respectably serviceable answers to ethical dilemmas.

What, then, are *we* to do about autonomous drones? If the "we" in this question is the ecclesial "we," then a faithful response may look very different from either an attempt to regulate their use by legislation, regulation, or treaties, or to repristinate a chivalrous martial ideal. Instead, it may have more in common with T. S. Eliot's critique of technological modernity in "Choruses from the Rock."

> O weariness of men who turn from God
> To the grandeur of your mind and the glory of your action,
> To arts and inventions and daring enterprises,
> To schemes of human greatness thoroughly discredited,
> Binding the earth and water to your service,
> Exploiting the seas and developing the mountains,
> Dividing the stars into common and preferred,
> Engaged in devising the perfect refrigerator,
> Engaged in working out a rational morality,
> Engaged in printing as many books as possible,
> Plotting of happiness and flinging empty bottles,
> Turning from your vacancy to fevered enthusiasm
> For nation or race or what you call humanity;
> Though you forget the way to the Temple,
> There is one who remembers the way to your door:
> Life you may evade, but Death you shall not.
> You shall not deny the Stranger.
>
> Why should men love the Church? Why should they love her laws?
> She tells them of Life and Death, and of all that they would forget.
> She is tender where they would be hard, and hard where they would be soft.

[57] Barth, *Church Dogmatics* IV.1, 450.

She tells them of Evil and Sin, and other unpleasant facts.
They constantly try to escape
From the darkness outside and within
By dreaming of systems so perfect that no one will need to be good.
But the man that is will shadow
The man that pretends to be.[58]

In the end, the best we can do may be to turn, and return, to the proclamation of these "unpleasant facts," and to the Word who reminds us of the dubiousness of all our words—including the words in this paper. At the very least, it is a place from which to begin. M

[58] T. S. Eliot, *The Complete Poems and Plays 1909-1950* (New York: Harcourt, Brace, and World, 1962), 104, 106.

Journal of Moral Theology, Vol. 4, No. 1 (2015): 131-150

Learning With Digital Technologies: Privileging Persons Over Machines

Mary E. Hess

IN 1989 THE FILM, *DEAD POETS SOCIETY*, was released, eventually garnering four Academy Award nominations, winning one for best original screenplay by Tom Schulman as well as several other international awards for best film that year. The film centered on the unorthodox ways in which an English teacher at an elite private all-male high school inspired his students to think for themselves and to develop authentic forms of self-expression. The film climaxed with the suicide of one of the young men whose passion for and achievement in acting ran afoul of his wealthy father's ambition for his son to study at Harvard and become a doctor.

Echoes of the film emerged again this year, with the release of Apple computer's iPad campaign, "What will your verse be?", which was narrated by Robin Williams using lines his character had recited in that movie. Images of the film reverberated even more with the death of Robin Williams himself.

Why raise memories of this film, the Apple commercial, and the difficult echoes of suicide in an exploration of the ethics of technology and teaching? Precisely because at the heart of that movie is this question: What is the end of education, to what purpose is learning directed? In our contemporary, thoroughly digitally-infused world, the commercial makes a specific claim in response. Yet the movie also reminds us that this question is neither abstract nor without lethal implications. For me, the tragic death of the movie's star, who is also the narrator of the commercial, only makes the recognition that humans are both creative and death-dealing all the more tangible as a prompt for moral reflection.

Long before 1989 the United States was caught up in a decades-long argument over the question of the *telos* of education, but it has taken a particularly pressing turn in the last several years.[1] The advent of digital technologies—and the enormous economic forces arrayed within the industries that build them—has produced a battle to control how we understand education. Much of the effort, and millions upon

[1] One of the more provocative entries in the long discussion about the *telos* of education is Neil Postman's *The End of Education: Redefining the Value of School* (New York: Vintage Books, 1986).

millions of dollars, has gone into producing public support for education oriented toward producing qualified workers for an ever expanding economy.[2] Students are being held accountable for their ability to read, to write, to perform mathematical tasks, and at least in some states, to have a rudimentary grasp of science. They are generally not asked to demonstrate abilities in music, art, civic engagement, collaborative advocacy, and so on. Entering vibrantly into this public debate comes Apple's iPad commercial, which has been viewed more than two million times on YouTube alone.

The commercial depicts all kinds of learning, and subtly asserts a much more open and creative response to the question of the end of education than is otherwise dominant right now. Implied in the commercial is the response that the *telos* of learning is to be more fully human, and to be human is to participate in creative activity. This is a profoundly theological claim, although Williams' narration is not explicitly theological:

> We don't read and write poetry because it is cute, we read and write poetry because we are members of the human race, and the human race is filled with passion. Medicine, law, business, engineering… these are noble pursuits and necessary to sustain life, but poetry, beauty, romance, love—these are what we stay alive for…. The powerful play goes on, and you may contribute a verse.[3]

The commercial is a direct invitation to creation, which requires (of course) the purchase of a digital tool, the iPad. The images in the commercial are beautiful, inspiring, uplifting, but both the music of the commercial and the echoes from the film (for those who are aware of it) provide an ominous counterpoint. Apple is joining a battle here, puting itself clearly on the side of the creative, participatory forces. Like any battle, however, death is not far off; or perhaps it would be less tendentious simply to note that human creation inevitably comes intermingled with human sinfulness.

To ask, What are the ethics of teaching with technology?, is first then, in this time period and in the U.S. context,[4] to ask a deeper question: What does it mean "to know," and how do answers to that question shape how we think about teaching and learning? I will begin there in this essay, and then go on to explore briefly the shape of digital mediatization in learning environments, with particular attention to classrooms in the higher education sphere. I will conclude by lifting

---

[2] For a cogent and ongoing exploration of this public contestation, see Julian Vasquez Heilig, *Cloaking Inequity* (available online: http://cloakinginequity.com/).

[3] The commercial can be seen here: www.youtube.com/watch?v=jiyIcz7wUH0.

[4] I have been raised in the U.S., educated in the U.S. system, and am employed by a U.S. seminary. Thus I will speak from that specific location. My intention is that my exploration be from a situated perspective, and thus evocative rather than definitive.

up specific questions to which moral theologians could direct their attention.

Epistemological Musings

What does it mean to "educate"? What does it mean to "learn"? What about words like "teaching" "schooling" "instructing" or "indoctrinating"? In order to consider the ethics of teaching in cultures which are thoroughly shaped by various technologies, we have to begin by considering what we mean by "knowing," how knowing shapes learning, and what role teaching might have in designing and nurturing learning.

We are living in a period in the United States in which the dominant narratives around education are narrowly focused on its instrumental good—that is, narratives which privilege education as a means to an end and where this end is often articulated as "getting a job" or "being a good worker." We are also living in a period in which digital technologies are introducing massive and rapid changes into the contexts in which we learn and the practices by which we learn. These two trends—an ever increasing focus on education as an instrument by which to achieve the specific end of employment, and processes of mediatization—are converging into a very challenging and difficult set of conundrums.

For many reasons now is a good time to return to some very ancient understandings of what it means to know, which is the foundation upon which what it means to teach and to learn is built. Parker Palmer writes that:

> [I]f we regard truth as something handed down from authorities on high, the classroom will look like a dictatorship. If we regard truth as a fiction determined by personal whim, the classroom will look like anarchy. If we regard truth as emerging from a complex process of mutual inquiry, the classroom will look like a resourceful and interdependent community. Our assumptions about knowing can open up, or shut down, the capacity for connectedness on which good teaching depends.[5]

In a Christian context, an understanding of truth is rooted deeply in our conviction that we know as we are known by God. This is a deeply relational and communal model for knowing, one which draws many implications from a biblical imagination.

Rolf Jacobsen notes, for example, that "the people that formed the Bible did not differentiate between different types of knowledge in the same ways that we moderns do…. [B]iblical concern for the corporate

---

[5] Parker Palmer, *The Courage to Teach* (San Francisco: John Wiley & Sons, 1998), 51-2.

good must crowd in on us when we are thinking about education. Education must be about the common good."[6] This concern for the common good is not simply pragmatic however, it is an essential consequence of the deep recognition of relationality that pervades the biblical witness, the felt sense that our Bible tells us of God's ongoing relationship with God's people. Charles Melchert writes that:

> Congruence between the *what* and the *how* (content and method) is pedagogically striking in Jesus' teaching and in the Gospel texts. Jesus talked of the kingdom, the compassionate and just rule of God, what it was like to be a subject, and he enacted that in his interactions with people. The texts not only portray Jesus' sending apprentice-disciples to do as he did but effectively invite later reader-learners to find themselves sent as well.[7]

Parker Palmer has drawn a diagram of what we might term the "competing paradigms" of knowing which are circulating in our culture:

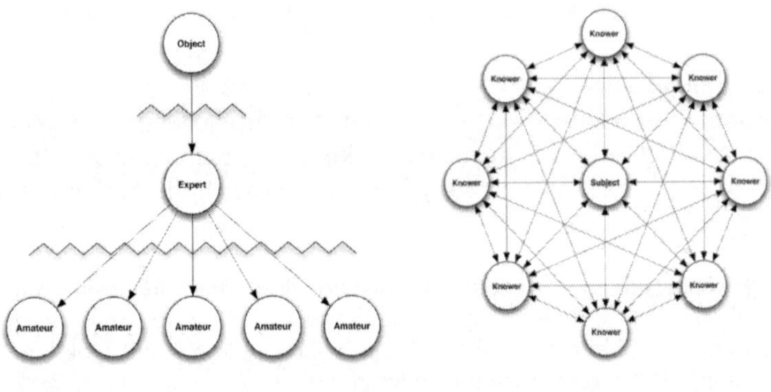

The image on the left he labels the "objectivist myth of knowing" and the one on the right, a "community of truth" model.[8] While any two dimensional visualization of necessity can only flatten the richness of lived experience, this diagram is useful for highlighting how epistemological assumptions underlie learning.

Consider the diagram on the left, in which Palmer labels that which is to be known as the object. The object is observed by an expert, who then passes on that information to amateurs. In this paradigm there is

---

[6] Rolf Jacobson, "Biblical Perspectives on Education," *Journal of Lutheran Ethics,* 4:7 (July 2004).

[7] Charles Melchert, *Wise Teaching: Biblical Wisdom and Educational Ministry* (Harrisburg: Trinity Press International, 1998), 264.

[8] Palmer, *The Courage to Teach*, 103, 105.

no connection amongst the amateurs, and no direct relationship between the amateurs and the object. Most of us will assume that the expert is the teacher in this paradigm, with the students as passive learners.

The diagram on the right, by way of contrast, labels that which is to be known as "subject," and depicts relationships as existing directly between each knower and the subject, and between each knower and every other knower. In this diagram it is difficult to identify the "teacher" and the "learner," although perhaps a case can be made that each knower is at once teacher and learner. In Palmer's work, however, the teacher actually does not appear in that diagram, but rather creates and holds the entire space, because "to teach is to create a space in which obedience to truth can be practiced."[9] In other words, the teacher designs the space in which the knowers engage the subject, doing so in ways that ensure that each knower develops a relationship with the subject, and each knower's contributions are held in appropriate balance with other knowers. Here the focus of inquiry is a subject, both in the sense of a topic to be studied, but also, even more importantly, in the sense of an entity who has agency, an entity with whom we can be in relationship. This is a profoundly theological claim, made explicit in Palmer's argument that "we know as we are known"—the primary knower being God.

In Palmer's depiction both the pedagogical methods of lecture as well as that of small group collaboration could be described by either model, but his argument would be that lectures and small groups which embody the epistemology on the left lead to learning that realizes only an imposition of flat information rather than interdependent wisdom, while lectures and small groups which embody the epistemology on the right will make evident how a lecturer or facilitator can "disappear" behind the subject, with the subject becoming so compelling that students are drawn into direct relationship with it. Here Palmer is emphasizing an understanding of human persons which is deeply relational, without being relativistic. That is, knowing emerges in a "community of truth" which is by definition made up of interdependent persons who all participate in the larger Truth from their own finite locations and vantage points. Thus the more diverse the knowers, the more robust the knowing.

We face a difficult dilemma in our current moment, where the model on the left is most often associated with technical forms of knowing, with skills understood to be directly connected to educational outcomes. In other words, there is a dominant conviction that learning must lead to marketable skill, and marketable skill, in turn,

---

[9] Parker Palmer, *To Know As We Are Known* (San Francisco: Harper & Row, 1993), 69.

remains the sole province of experts to dispense. Further, in that paradigm, digital tools become mere channels through which content flows, and learners are merely receptacles of information.

Yet that dominant conviction is everywhere contradicted by true experts, those who function at the center of various knowledge domains. These people speak of the need to exercise deep creativity and wise judgment, to develop penetrating insight and sophisticated narratives, to invent illuminating interpretations and insightful analysis, all the while being sufficiently self-differentiated to maintain appropriate forms of empathy and self-critical awareness. Such forms of understanding are neither routinely taught nor instrumentally produced. They are, in contrast, deeply relational in character.[10]

Human Persons in Interdependent Community Involved in a Shared Search for Truth

The biblical understanding of education and Palmer's "community of truth" model are both ways of understanding knowing, and then teaching and learning, that not only privilege relationality, but are actually constituted by it. Yet what kind of relationality? At this point in our exploration, newer work in the arena of Trinitarian thought becomes immediately relevant. At the risk of oversimplifying a vast corpus, I believe that this theological research has brought fresh focus to the social elements of engaging God through a Trinitarian lens.[11]

We can go all the way back to Augustine for an explanation of the Trinity as "Lover, Beloved, and Love," an analogy for this mystery which uses the dynamism of relational love for its power. And we can flow all the way forward into very recent descriptions of the Trinity as a perichoretic dance of relationship. Matthias Scharer and Jochen Hilberath, for instance, speak of God's communication within God's very self and God's self-communication to the creature:

> This is what the communicative-participatory understanding of revelation and faith events is all about. God invites people into a communion with God. God takes the initiative. God moves toward people and gives them the Spirit, who enables them to live in and from this com-

---

[10] For an extensive discussion of these issues, see Grant Wiggins and Jay McTighe, *Understanding by Design* (Alexandria, VA: ASCD, 2005).

[11] There is more work in this field than I can cite here, beginning with Karl Rahner, Catherine Mowry LaCugna, Elizabeth Johnson, Jürgen Moltmann, and so on, but I would note that Gary Simpson's work has been particularly helpful to me. See, for instance, Gary Simpson, "No Trinity, No Mission: The Apostolic Difference of Revisioning the Trinity" in *Word and World*, 18:3 (Summer 1998).

> munication. This is what is meant by *mysterion/mysterium* and by *sacramentum.* Through the communion of people with one another, communion with God comes into existence. [12]

This profound dance of communication flows throughout our knowing, and thus must also be deeply a part of our teaching and learning. Any descriptions of teaching and learning that refuse to acknowledge this relational mystery of our transcendent God risk distortion if not outright deception.

In the U.S. context we are inundated by claims of "community," of "social networking," of "friend spaces" and "crowd knowing" as auspicious signs of digital spaces.[13] Yet we are also increasingly challenged by descriptions of such spaces that argue that we are "alone together" in them, or that we are swimming only in "the shallows."[14] Which of these assertions are descriptive? Both? Neither? How might we truly place communication "at the service of an authentic culture of encounter,"[15] to use Pope Francis' words? And what are the criteria we might use for answering these questions? To return to Palmer's earlier quotation, a strictly hierarchical classroom might be described as a dictatorship, but one based entirely on individual personal whim would be anarchy. His third metaphor for the classroom is of a "resourceful and interdependent community," and that is the goal to which we ought to be oriented, and the criteria to which we should be holding ourselves accountable.[16]

Robin Williams' character in *Dead Poets Society* sought to invite his students into full self-expression, reflective engagement with core philosophical ideas, and collaborative learning in a community of peers. In some ways the film seeks to describe this kind of "resourceful and interdependent community." But it, too, exists in the middle of flawed and at times destructive systems. Torn between his own creative impulses and the stifling dictates of his highly competitive and

---

[12] Matthias Scharer and Jochen Hilberath, *The Practice of Communicative Theology: Introduction to a New Theological Culture* (New York: Crossroad Publishing Company, 2008), 78.

[13] See for example, James Surowiecki, *The Wisdom of Crowds* (New York: Anchor Books, 2004); Clay Shirky, *Here Comes Everybody: The Power of Organizing Without Organizations* (New York: Penguin Books, 2008); and David Weinberger, *Small Pieces, Loosely Joined: A Unified Theory of the Web* (New York: Basic Books, 2002).

[14] See, for example, Sherry Turkle, *Alone Together: Why We Expect More from Technology and Less From Each Other* (New York: Basic Books, 2011) and Andrew Carr, *The Shallows: What the Internet is Doing to Our Brains* (W. W. Norton & Company, 2010).

[15] Pope Francis, 48th World Communications message, http://w2.vatican.va/content/francesco/en/messages/communications/documents/papa-francesco_20140124-_messaggio-comunicazioni-sociali.html.

[16] Palmer, *The Courage to Teach*, 51-52.

narcissistic parent, the character of Neil killed himself in the film. Universally acknowledged for his creativity and self-expression, Robin Williams, the actor, nevertheless succumbed to depression and killed himself during the time I sat writing this essay. This paradox of humanity, in which we are both made in the image of God, and at the same time are deeply wounded and broken, plays itself out in digital contexts as well. There is no utopia to be found there, but God continues to reveal Godself in our midst.

If during the time in which the film was set the student characters were driven by parental pressures and societal norms to perceive their education as oriented only towards narrow, mechanistic, purely employment-focused goals, then how much more restricting are our current contexts? We must ask how practices of relational knowing, knowing that is deeply conscious of God's revelation in the midst of community, could and should drive educational practice in a world permeated by digital technologies. We must continue to strive for learning which is deeply interdependent, which centers on persons in community, and which fosters authentic self-expression and creativity.

Such educational foci, however, are becoming ever more rare. Decades of experimentation with ways to improve public education, instead of leading to more accountable, civically-engaged systems have instead led to increasingly privatized frameworks which resist real accountability and are counterproductive of learning. Diane Ravitch, renowned scholar of education, and formerly an avid advocate of various experiments in privatization, has documented this destructive process in significant detail in much of her current writing.[17] For the purposes of this essay it is worth noting that the speed of this engine of privatization has been greatly increased by a push to get digital tools into classrooms, and indeed to create classrooms that are primarily, or solely, digital. Yet simply placing technologies in a classroom in no way ensures that they will be used with thoughtful pedagogical intent. Far too many classrooms have become graveyards for abandoned technologies, technologies which were installed with great fanfare but then not engaged in any pedagogically useful way.

Further, in many settings digital technologies have become the latest way to control and constrain students' thought rather than to empower and challenge students to greater connection to the common good, and to personal excellence.[18] Here again we have the paradox of the "good" and the "bad" together.

---

[17] See in particular, Diane Ravitch, *The Reign of Error and the Hoax of the Privatization Movement and the Danger to America's Public Schools* (New York: Alfred A. Knopf, 2013).

[18] Given the many challenges to free speech for students, the ACLU of Minnesota has put together a special site focused on helping youth know what their rights are in

Lest readers of this article perceive the challenges as existing only in elementary and secondary school contexts, there is substantial research pointing to ways in which large infusions of capital from tech companies are reshaping the higher education context as well. Clayton Christenson and Henry Eyring's recent book *The Innovative University* argues at some length that the shifts catalyzed by online technologies are already causing massive disruption in higher education.[19]

Here the work of scholars of mediatization such as Knut Lundby becomes particularly pertinent. Sonia Livingstone describes the theory as follows:[20]

> Distinct from, through overlapping with, the notion of "mediation," which exists in most languages to refer to processes of conciliation, intervention, or negotiation among separate, often conflicted, parties, in the Germanic and Scandinavian languages, "mediatization" refers to the meta process by which everyday practices and social relations are historically shaped by mediating technologies and media organizations…. [T]he argument here is that the media do more than mediate in the sense of "getting in between" whether to generate mutual understanding by reconciling adversaries or whether to promote (and naturalise the effects of) powerful interests…. Rather they alter the historical possibilities for human communication by reshaping relations not just among media organizations and their publics but among all social institutions—government, commerce, family, church, and so forth.

What we are seeing, in the pervasive spread of digital technologies, is massive reshaping of our daily practices, of our ways of knowing and being in the world. On the one hand this reshaping is opening up space for participation at a level and of a diversity never before possible.[21] Over and over again scholars point to the enormous creativity and collaboration which digital tools unleash. On the other hand, at the same

---

relation to speech (www.aclu-mn.org/resources/forstudents/youthrights), and Journalism 360 (a project based at the University of St. Thomas in St. Paul, MN) has a site devoted to helping youth understand the consequences of speech in social media (http://protectmyrep.org/).

[19] Clayton Christenson and Henry Eyring, *The Innovative University: Changing the DNA of Higher Education From the Inside Out* (San Francisco: Jossey-Bass, 2011).

[20] Sonia Livingston, "Foreword," in *Mediatization: Concept, Changes, Consequences*, ed. by Knut Lundby (New York: Peter Lang, 2009), x.

[21] See, for example, Clay Shirky, *Cognitive Surplus: Creativity and Generosity in a Connected Age* (New York: Penguin Press, 2010); Yochai Benkler, *The Wealth of Networks: How Social Production Transforms Markets and Freedom* (New Haven: Yale University Press, 2006); Douglas Thomas and John Seely Brown, *A New Culture of Learning: Cultivating the Imagination for a World of Constant Change* (CreateSpace, 2011); and Howard Rheingold, *Net Smart: How to Thrive Online* (Cambridge, MA: MIT Press, 2012).

time, this reshaping is disrupting every element of our relationships with each other and by implication, with God.

There is no going back. Digital technologies have become too pervasive and too thoroughly entangled in our lives. We must strive to hold onto the heart of our convictions about God, and God's good creation, and engage all of our culture-creating abilities as human persons in relation in the midst of these technologies. We have to learn to "see" what is happening within our communities, to explore the problematic elements of digital tech, and to strengthen and share the most beneficial elements of these new media. We can, as scholars note, learn how to play, perform, simulate, appropriate, multi-task, distribute our cognition, promote collective intelligence, learn authentic judgment, navigate across various media, network, and negotiate. These are the characteristics of digital literacy, and scholars of what is rapidly becoming known as a "new culture of learning" place their emphasis there.[22]Widespread and substantial research into the ways in which digital mediatization is reshaping learning has been funded by the MacArthur Foundation.[23] Douglas Thomas and John Seely Brown have summarized that research in thoughtful ways, pointing to three key elements: (1) a shift to learning-centered (as contrasted with teaching-centered) pedagogies, (2) a focus on the "personal and collective" rather than the "public and private," and (3) a renewed emphasis on exploring tacit forms of knowing.[24]

Each of these elements resonates well with the second model Palmer is describing when he contrasts "objectivist" forms of knowing with "community of truth" models. Each of these elements emphasizes human persons in interdependent community. Perhaps, then, there is a new opening here for expression of deep relationality in learning, and at the same time, learning which is oriented toward wisdom, not simply information transfer.

What does this kind of learning look like in the higher education classroom? In particular, what are the questions teachers ought to be asking—and moral theologians could help us work through—when we engage with technologies, either in a typical classroom (geographically placed, synchronously framed, "in person" classroom), or in an "online" classroom? Working with these three elements articulated by Thomas and Seely Brown, let us consider some of the implications of

[22] See in particular Henry Jenkins, et al., *Confronting the Challenges of Participatory Media Culture*, (Cambridge: MIT Press, 2009), available online: https://mitpress.mit.edu/sites/default/files/titles/free_download/9780262513623_Confronting_the_Challenges.pdf.

[23] For bibliography and other resources, start at the Digital Media Learning Hub: http://dmlhub.net/about.

[24] Thomas and Seely Brown, *A New Culture of Learning*, 37ff.

their work for our classrooms.[25]

FROM TEACHING CENTERED TO LEARNING CENTERED

Three of the most pertinent learning dynamics that are changing in the midst of mediatization have to do with how we understand authority, how in turn that authority is shaped by changing definitions of authenticity, and then, how both authority and authenticity shape our grasp of agency, both our own and that of the material under study.[26] Authority, authenticity, agency—these dynamics require a shift from an emphasis on a teacher's content expertise, to that teacher's ability to support student learning. Content is clearly still important, but the questions differ. Rather than asking whether content has moved from the object through the expert to the amateur, we are asking in what ways our students are already knowers, and in what ways their previous knowledge enhances—or creates obstacles to—their learning. We are not only interested in their ability to grasp, explain and interpret a specific "piece" of content, we are at least equally interested in discerning whether they have considered the authority of that content, recognized their specific situatedness relative to it, developed some degree of empathy for the subject at hand, and placed that piece of content appropriately into the midst of an overarching framework or ecology of knowledge.

In a typical classroom many of these questions about student learning are asked and answered intuitively. Experienced teachers have gained, through extensive practice, the ability to sense ways in which their students are engaging material, and the standardization of a higher education classroom—structured by credits, a defined number of meeting hours a week, and standardized syllabi—gives faculty a framework for assessing student learning.

In an online classroom, by way of contrast, standards are still evolving alongside of emerging technologies, and many classes in the same school and the same curriculum will differ quite widely in process from one teacher to the next. Whereas in a typical classroom many teachers presume that they can "read" the body language of their students, in an online classroom—most of which are still asynchronous and text-based—teachers often feel blinded by lack of access to nonverbal gestural language.

---

[25] For further exploration of these elements, see Mary Hess, "A New Culture of Learning: What Are the Implications for Theological Educators," in *Teaching Theology and Religion*, 17:3 (July 2014): 227-32.

[26] For a lengthier exploration of "authority, authenticity and agency" in theological classrooms, see Mary Hess, "Loving the Questions: Finding Food for the Future of Theological Education in the Lexington Seminar," in *Theological Education*, 48: 1 (2013): 69-89.

This is one powerful reason why teachers who shape learning environments in wholly online spaces often find themselves experimenting with pedagogical strategies they had never previously explored. Suddenly carefully designed small group collaborations become a means by which to ascertain what students are actually thinking about a particular chunk of content. Indeed, teachers who "lurk" in such small groups (something which is much more possible in an online asynchronous environment than in typical classrooms) can find themselves "overhearing" student thought in process, making interventions in ill-considered interpretations easier and more direct.

When teachers who have enlarged their palette of teaching materials through online courses return to typical classrooms, it is often with a transformed perspective on the possibilities of learning. It is ironic that whereas two decades worth of education literature supporting learning-centered classrooms has had little impact, the head long rush into online environments is transforming teachers' imagination as they struggle—at both the K12 and higher levels—to articulate what really matters to them in education.

We must ask: How do we know our students are learning? What are they learning? How do they know they are learning? From those questions develop fruitful pedagogical strategies, strategies of necessity focused on student learning, rather than teacher performance. This is a very different focus than the predominant one which tracks a teacher's performance as publisher of research content and links the outcome assessment of programs only to popularity contests managed through magazine rankings of colleges and universities. Unfortunately it is these latter forms of evaluation, both of which are highly instrumental, which are increasingly given voice in our public debates.

Here again, we need to recognize how the way in which we understand knowing inevitably shapes how we embody teaching and learning. If the narratives driving our imagination are centered on transfer of content, on "covering the field," on perpetuating a certain kind of technical mastery, then evaluations narrowly focused on teacher publication and student job attainment are inescapable. If, on the other hand, we can retrieve a "community of truth" paradigm for knowing, a model which is deeply learning-centered rather than teaching-centered, and if we can begin to explore and live into the implications of such a model for education, we might find ourselves with both renewed relevance and enlivened energy for engaging digitally mediated environments well.

From the Public/Private to the Personal/Collective

The second element of a new culture of learning which Thomas and Seely Brown articulate is a focus on the "personal and collective" rather than the "public and private." This is already a focus that is more promising for community of truth models, because it privileges the relational elements of the movements between the individual and the community. Much like Catholic social teaching articulates a distinction between the personal and the communal to strengthen recognition of a community of knowing, this specific articulation of the personal and the collective focuses on the dynamic relationship between these two poles. Neither makes sense apart from the other.

This element is quite visibly different between the two models we have been considering. In Palmer's "objectivist myth of knowing" diagram, knowledge remains quite private. Content moves in linear ways from the object through the expert to the amateur. It is travelling into each amateur, with no lines of connection between learners. This is a very private form of learning, one that is highly individualized. Success in learning rests or falls on the shoulders of the individual student, unsupported by her or his colleagues; or perhaps on the shoulders of the teacher, who remains solely accountable for whether the information moves from the object to the amateur. This model is by no means confined to digital spaces. Indeed in some ways, as I noted earlier, it is more often embodied in typical classrooms.

In the "community of truth" diagram, by way of contrast, there is a "personal" focus on learning—there are distinct knowers, each has a self—but that knowing is intimately connected both to the subject at heart of the study and to every other knower. Thus there is the "personal" as well as the "collective." To shape a context for learning, the teacher must create a space in which there is both personal and collective engagements with the subject. Online classrooms, if learning is to take place, most often must function in this paradigm.

In many digital contexts the shift from focusing on the "public and private" to the "personal and collective" emerges first in discussions of what constitutes privacy in online spaces. Vivid debates over privacy in Facebook, for instance, have resulted in a recognition that one's agency over one's information is of great importance and interest to users of those environments. In environments in which trust is the operative currency, the ability to choose when and how one makes personal information available is highly relevant,[27] much more relevant, it seems, than whether there are any sharp lines between "public" and "private" spaces. Users indeed choose to share certain kinds of personal information precisely because they want to be able to participate in certain kinds of spaces. Social media, in general, function best when massive numbers of people choose to participate in them. Such functional mechanics raise keen questions about the degree of personal information that is appropriately shared in order to participate in

[27] For an extensive discussion of the ways in which trust is a new currency in digital environments, see Rachel Botsman, *What's Mine is Yours: The Rise of Collaborative Consumption* (San Francisco: HarperBusiness, 2010).

a collective space, but the fact that personal information will be shared is *sine qua non.*

Such pressing questions include, for instance: To what extent can personal information be commodified and sold in the context of online spaces? Is there any kind of boundary to personal information that ought not to be broached? Are there any essential rights to such information? For example, it is clear that sharing one's social security number can lead to increased vulnerability to data breaches and identity theft. But what if the only way to participate in an online learning environment is to certify one's identity by use of one's social security number?[28]

Or consider the recent controversies over national security access to individual email accounts and cell phone calls. To what extent should personal privacy be trumped by collective security concerns? These are the kinds of questions which ethicists and moral theologians ought to be addressing—and not simply in research settings, but with our students in our classrooms. These are also the kinds of questions which are going to be answered not simply by what Lessig terms "east coast code" (that is, federal and state regulatory structures), but also—and perhaps more insidiously—by "west coast code" (the software and hardware architectures which create the space in which we function, which afford or do not afford specific abilities in specific settings).[29]

As another example of the challenges we can see when we consider how the personal and the collective are entwined, consider the question of access to learning. A community of truth model presumes that the more diverse the knowers, the more robust the knowing. So in what ways can we create a "community of truth" in our classrooms if only a limited number of students can even enter those classrooms?

There is an increasingly vigorous argument taking place right now over the accessibility of higher education classrooms to students who have few financial resources, or who may be the first persons in their families to attend college. I teach in a free-standing seminary based in one particular denomination. We are working hard to figure out how to make theological education more accessible and affordable to a broader diversity of students. To date, however, we have not had much

---

28 Concerns about fraud in online education were heightened in 2011 when the federal Office of the Inspector General issued a report which identified "serious vulnerabilities" in distance education programs (www2.ed.gov/about/offices/list/oig/invtreports/l4210001.pdf). Enrollment of students whose identities could not be confirmed was linked to student loan fraud.

29 Lawrence Lessig, *Code and Other Laws of Cyberspace* (New York: Basic Books, 1999). New work on the issue of how technology "affords" certain capacities, or offers "affordances" for meaning-making is pervasive in media studies. A good introduction to its use in learning can be found in Henry Jenkins, et al., *Confronting the Challenges of Participatory Culture: Media Education for the 21st Century* (The John D. and Catherine T. MacArthur Foundation Reports on Digital Media and Learning), www.macfound.org/media/article_pdfs/JENKINS_WHITE_PAPER.PDF.

success. To the extent that we have, most of it can be traced to creating hybrid educational programs in which students can remain in their own communities, taking classes online, and only venture onto our campus for limited periods of time for residential intensives. In that case digital tools are an important means of providing access, enlarging the collective community in which learning is occurring.

Yet even while these hybrid programs have opened up some room, created some additional student access, the online classrooms themselves contain structural obstacles. My school, like most others, uses a content management system as the space in which our online classes occur. These are proprietary systems which not only cost schools tens of thousands of dollars to operate, they require of students that they have up-to-date computers with high speed broadband access.[30] We are creating new access and at the same time, building structural obstacles to participation. In a world in which mobile technologies are allowing countries such as Liberia, Ghana and Brazil to jump directly to wireless tech, sidestepping wired frameworks, too many U.S. schools are recreating the worst of typical classrooms online, rather than seeking to embody the community of truth model by embedding it in more open technologies.[31]

What would it look like to step into mobile tech environments with a community of truth model? That question is being explored in a limited number of schools and settings around the world, but these bold experiments are demonstrating that it is indeed not only possible, but potentially liberating to create spaces which are "inquiry-driven, project-based, and portfolio-assessed."[32] Spaces, that is, which put the subjects (both the persons and the topics) at the heart of the model, and then resource learners with a community around them which both challenges and supports learning. Thomas and Seely Brown tell many stories of places in which this kind of learning is taking place right now. They conclude that:

> Each of these stories is about a bridge between two worlds—one that is largely public and information-based (a software program, a uni-

---

[30] These are systems such as Jenzabar, Moodle, Blackboard, Sakai, etc. A thoughtful survey of the ways in which content management systems constrain pedagogies is Lisa Lane, "Insidious Pedagogy: How Course Management Systems Impact Teaching," in *FirstMonday*, 14:10 (5 October 2009), available online: http://first- monday.org/ojs/index.php/fm/article/view/2530/2303.

[31] See for example Randy Bass, "Disrupting Ourselves: The Problem of Learning in Higher Education," in *Educause Review* (March/April 2012) 23-33; and Ethan Zuckerman, *Rewire: Digital Cosmopolitans in the Age of Connection* (New York: W. W. Norton & Company, 2013).

[32] For specific exploration of this pedagogical frame, see Mary Hess, "A New Culture of Learning: Digital Storytelling and Faith Formation," in *Dialog*, 53:1 (Spring 2014): 12-22.

> versity, a search engine, a game, a website) and another that is intensely personal and structured (colleagues, a classroom, a business, family, the daily challenges of living with a chronic disease). The bridge between them—and what makes the concept of the new culture of learning so potent—is how the imagination was cultivated to harness the power of almost unlimited informational resources and create something personally meaningful. In each case, fusing a vast informational resource with a deeply personal motivation led to an unexpected, unplanned, or innovative use of the space. In short, the connection between resources and personal motivation led people to cultivate their imaginations and recreate the space in a new way. [33]

This shift to a focus on "the personal and the collective" brings us to the third element of a new culture of learning which Thomas and Seely Brown identify, an element which takes seriously Michael Polyani's understanding of the tacit characteristics of knowing.

From Explicit to Tacit Forms of Knowing

Thomas and Seely Brown argue specifically that digital spaces make tangible how tacit knowing functions in learning. Further, they highlight the ways in which explicit knowledge tends to be stable, while tacit forms of knowing often highlight the unstable, ever-changing, fluid nature of knowledge. There have been many evocative explanations of what it means to attend to tacit knowing in learning settings, but I would point to two that arise in wholly digital contexts. The first is Diana Laufenberg's TEDx 2010 talk in which she makes the overall points that students need to make mistakes in order to learn and that learning takes place in making explicit what was previously only sensed tacitly. She also vividly describes how project-based learning unfolds. Another oft-shared TED talk is the 2009 presentation of Liz Coleman, president of Bennington College, who called for a radically cross-disciplinary approach to undergraduate education, an approach that brings tacit knowing into full and explicit meta-reflection.[34]

Why reach to TED talks to illustrate this point rather than the vast educational literature? Quite honestly because readers of this essay are more likely to glance at these talks than to track down the specialized literature from the citations found in my footnotes.[35] They are excellent examples of making explicit what the speakers have learned from their own experiences, from the tacit forms of knowing which have

---

[33] Thomas and Seely Brown, *A New Culture of Learning*, 31.

[34] Laufenberg TEDx, www.ted.com/talks/diana_laufenberg_3_ways_to_teach; Liz Coleman TED, www.ted.com/talks/liz_coleman_s_call_to_reinvent_liberal_arts_education.

[35] For entry into this discussion in the educational literature, a good place to start is Maryellen Weimer, *Learner-centered Teaching: Five Key Changes to Practice* (San Francisco: Jossey-Bass, 2013).

lived in their experiential encounters with teaching and learning. Further, they are examples of scholars seeking to address the challenges that digital technologies pose in typical classrooms. That is perhaps the larger point I want to make by raising the issue of focusing on how to make explicit, tacit forms of knowing. Such a shift has huge implications not simply or solely for teaching in online spaces, or even more generally to teaching with technology, but to all of the ways in which we think about teaching and learning.

Here again, I want to return to the Palmer diagrams from the beginning of this essay, and note that exploring tacit knowing is particularly pertinent to a discussion of learning from and with a subject when that subject has agency. That is, I want to call attention to the distinction between the two diagrams that is exemplified in the labeling of the topic at hand—tacit and explicit forms of knowing. Is the "object" of knowing, something that is stable, susceptible only to linear forms of change, the focus of a well understood discipline? Or does the very idea of an "object" miss the mark? Is it more adequately descriptive to speak of a "subject" which is dynamically changing (or even subject to "dynamical" change?[36]), and in relationship with a knower? Certainly "to know as we are known," if we posit that it is God who first knows us, is a process which we cannot name in relation to anything so deadened as a finite object. Nor can we allow ourselves to be drawn into metaphors for teaching and learning that instrumentalize such processes and turn them into mere mechanisms for transferring content, or routinizing specific skill bases—processes which erase persons and communities in all of their diversity and specificity.[37] Here is where I am yet again hungry for the resources which moral theologians bring to the table, because ethicists have both the experience and the investment necessary for lifting up, for making explicit, what is generally implicit in our practices around relationality.

Digital technologies are contributing dramatically to the mediatization of our environments, and that process demands careful attention to the ways that we help our students bring their tacit knowing, bring their implicit socialization processes, into explicit reflection. There are more and more examples emerging of faculty in quite disparate disciplines finding ways to do this work with their students. One of my

---

[36] Glenda Eoyang and Royce Holladay define "dynamical change" as "complex change that results from unknown forces acting unpredictably to bring about surprising outcomes." Glenda Eoyang and Royce Holladay, *Adaptive Action: Leveraging Uncertainty in Your Organization* (Palo Alto: Stanford University Press, 2013) 62.

[37] It is perhaps worth clarifying at this point that I am not arguing that practice isn't a useful process by which something can be learned. It's simply that I do not believe mechanistic processes of content transfer, reminiscent of computer data downloads, are educational. I would point to the ways in which artists practice an art form, breaking it down into manageable pieces and then integrating it all back together over time, as more descriptive of a "live" practice.

favorites is that of communications professor David Levy who asks his students to log their engagement with their digital devices for a day, and then also invites them into a practice of contemplation at the beginning of his large lecture courses.[38] Another is professor of economics Daniel Barbezat who works with contemplative practices to help his students grasp complicated mathematical models.[39] Both of these professors are working in fields in which there is significant content which needs to be engaged, and both have found that focusing on, and thus expanding students' repertoire of practices of attention and reflection have dramatically contributed to student learning, while deeply engaging personhood in community.

There is an entire field emerging around the use of contemplative practices in higher education, with most of that exploration happening outside of religious studies or theological environments.[40] Somehow "mindfulness" has become a practice that is recognized for its powerful impact on student learning, without being linked to the religious communities in which such practices were originally developed and circulated. Here again we face a dilemma: is mindfulness simply a practice by which individuals better grasp specific topics, or is it a practice which reunites the personal with the collective, which draws learners more deeply into a community of truth in which engagement with an agential subject is possible?

Perhaps one final example will be pertinent here. There has been a veritable "gold rush land grab" in recent years around the implementation of MOOCs ("massively open online courses"). Large corporate entities such as Coursera, Udacity, EdX and Khan have entered into agreements with a variety of universities, placing millions of dollars on the "bet" that these university agreements will lead to massive new opportunities for learning, and massive new—and thus profitable—enrollments.[41] MOOCs began, years ago, as an intentional effort to make learning accessible to people who otherwise could not get access to it, particularly to higher education. Thoughtful scholars such as Stephen Downes were involved in exploring how to support this kind of access, and what kinds of communities of learning might be built.[42]

That kind of exploration is still ongoing, but it has been nearly drowned out by the publicity attached to the major elite institutions

---

[38] Marc Perry, "You're distracted. This professor can help," in *the Chronicle of Higher Education*, (24 March 2013), http://chronicle.com/article/Youre-Distracted-This/138079/.

[39] Daniel Barbezat and Mirabai Bush, *Contemplative Practices in Higher Education: Powerful Methods to Transform Teaching and Learning* (San Francisco: Jossey-Bass, 2014), 51.

[40] Barbezat and Bush, *Contemplative Practices*, 105.

[41] These are the major players cited in a *Chronicle of Higher Education*, http://chronicle.com/article/The-Major-Players-in-the-MOOC/138817/.

[42] You can find Stephen Downes' work online at www.downes.ca/.

who are entering this arena. What has been learned thus far? For the most part MOOCs are not demonstrating anything near the potential claimed, if the criteria considered is student learning. Empirical observation of the impact of MOOCs has barely begun, but already it is clear that the majority of people who enroll in MOOCs do not go on to complete a course. Of the few who do, most claim their success grew out of the learning community in which they engaged the course. Perhaps they put together a local learning group, gathering to work on course content together. Perhaps the teacher of the MOOC required such a gathering. Perhaps the school realized that they needed to put in place supports that invited people to connect with each other around content. In each of these cases, learning community was necessary for the MOOC to be effective.[43]

Both the ancient paradigm of which Palmer writes and the "new culture of learning" to which Thomas and Seely Brown draw our attention are best described and evaluated by attending to the underlying epistemological assumptions we hold. Basing our efforts on drawing students into a community of truth which recognizes that "we know as we are known," and which demands accountability for that knowledge, holds the potential for radically transforming our current educational environments and reclaiming narratives for education which privilege civic engagement, the common good, wholeness of Creation, and so on.

Rather than being the "end of education," with all the connotations that phrase implies when we "trawl in the shallows" and function "alone together," we could retrieve an end to education which emphasizes a *telos* of relationality and, in doing so, draws upon the digital tools which best afford such relationality. When Robin Williams asks, "What will your verse be?", in the Apple iPad commercial, we could claim the richest, deepest and most liberating resonance for that question. We could see in that question an invitation into God's loving co-creation, rather than a prompt for crass commercialism. We could choose specific digital tools by which to offer our students the best supports we are capable of sharing with them, for being known by God and by each other. We could, to turn again to Pope Francis, recognize that:

> It is not enough to be passersby on the digital highways, simply "connected"; connections need to grow into true encounters. We cannot live apart, closed in on ourselves. We need to love and to be loved. We need tenderness. Media strategies do not ensure beauty,

---

[43] A focused collection of data and research reports on MOOCs is available at *EDUCAUSE*, www.educause.edu/search/apachesolr_search/MOOC; the journal *Hybrid Pedagogy* (www.hybridpedagogy.com/) and the *International Review of Research in Open and Distance Learning* (www.irrodl.org/index.php/irrodl).

> goodness and truth in communication. The world of media also has to be concerned with humanity, it too is called to show tenderness. The digital world can be an environment rich in humanity; a network not of wires but of people. The impartiality of media is merely an appearance; only those who go out of themselves in their communication can become a true point of reference for others. Personal engagement is the basis of the trustworthiness of a communicator. Christian witness, thanks to the internet, can thereby reach the peripheries of human existence.[44]

It is my profound hope that together we might indeed transform education to once again embody a community of truth, a space in which there is authentic encounter with the One who knows us fully. Digital tools are disrupting our "taken-for-granted" understandings in ways that may well make this hope newly plausible.[45] M

[44] Pope Francis, 48th World Communications Day message, /w2.vatican.va/content/-francesco/en/messages/communications/documents/papa-francesco_20140124-_messaggio-comunicazioni-sociali.html.

[45] For more on how our "taken for granted" perceptions are disrupted by digital environments, see Cathy Davidson, *Now You See It: How Brain Science Will Transform Schools and Business for the 21st Century* (New York: Penguin Group, 2012).

Journal of Moral Theology, Vol. 4, No. 1 (2015): 151-180

What's in a Tech? Factors in Evaluating the Morality of Our Information and Communication Practices

James F. Caccamo

THERE ARE CERTAINLY MANY INTRIGUING and enlightening stories within the gospels. One that I have found particularly interesting over the years is the Transfiguration, in particular Saint Luke's account of it (Luke 9: 28-36). A portion of my fascination certainly comes from the sheer drama of the events that are recounted. Up on the mountain, in the midst of his very sleepy friends, Jesus is revealed as the Son of God in spectacularly dramatic fashion. "[H]is face changed in appearance and his clothes became dazzling white" (v. 29). The prophets Moses and Elijah appear and talk with him. A voice from the clouds identifies Jesus as the Son and instructs Peter, James, and John—and presumably the reader—to "listen to him." There is no question that this is an important revelation, and the events measure up to the enormity of the message. Moreover, conditioned by a century of film and television depictions of divine appearances, the miraculous scene is exactly the kind of thing that we would imagine would happen when God makes God's self manifest. Indeed, it is a story worthy of a big budget film by the likes of Michael Bay or Ridley Scott, minus the explosions, of course. It all makes for an engaging story to reflect on and imaginatively enter into in prayer.

Yet, as interesting as the large-scale drama is, I find equally fascinating the hints of how challenging this experience was for Jesus' disciples. In particular, we get a glimpse of Peter struggling to respond well to this unexpected situation. Instead of doing what we might hope we would do—namely falling on our knees to adore the divine presence—Peter responds by offering hospitality to these travelers. Given the importance of hospitality in ancient near eastern cultures, this makes sense: Strangers need to places to stay, and Moses and Elijah are strangers, so it must be time to build some lodging. Yet, laudable as it is, Peter's action ultimately falls short of living up to the reality that he witnesses. It's almost as if he simply can't process this world-changing event. Luke goes so far as to say that Peter offers his idea, "not knowing what he said." Perhaps the words of the paraphrase in *The Message* Bible gets closer, though, when it says that Peter "blurted this out without thinking." Here is Peter—the rock, the foundation of the church—at wit's end, defaulting to his community's typical script. It is a drama writ small, a portrait in human limitation more typical of Sofia Coppola or Woody Allen than Bay or Scott. The Transfiguration marked a new world, and it went beyond what he could even begin to process.

While some of Peter's experiences are certainly more dramatic than our own, we struggle with the same underlying dynamics that challenged Peter. We work hard to cultivate virtues of thought and action that enable us to act well within the contexts that we find ourselves. These virtues serve us well most of the time, for the moral wisdom of our ancestors and the Christian tradition has grown, in large part, through encounters with many of the very same struggles we experience today. At the same time, we are living in an age of significant change. While we have not seen a new transfiguration, we have seen our world radically reconfigured over the past thirty years by digital information and communication technologies, transforming the way that human beings work, learn, socialize, and engage in spiritual pursuits. As a result, all of us have had to reassess the particular practices we take up as we aim to live out lives of discipleship and devotion.

On one hand, there is no shortage of voices to assist us as we consider the role of new information and communication technologies. Pastors and bloggers, journalists and PR professionals alike offer their assessments of how technology can alternately enhance or compromise our lives.[1] Yet, on the other hand, scholars in moral theology play a very small part in this conversation. Reflection on the theological and moral implications of communication and information technologies—reflection that would assist churches and broader society—is still relatively unusual in the disciplines of theology in general and moral theology in particular. We have not been able to bring the wisdom of the tradition to bear on the public discourse aimed at revising our image of how we are to live lives worth living.

One place where this can be seen most clearly is in the absence of a robust method that can be used in assessing the morality of technological practices. While there are exceptions to the rule, conversations around the ethics of technology frequently involve what we might call a "comparative morphology" approach, where technologies are evaluated by comparing their shapes with their non-technological counterparts. Are relationships that we engage in using online communication "real" in the same way that face-to-face friendships are? Is reading the Bible on a screen as transformative as reading it from a book or a

---

[1] This article will use the concise term "technology" to refer to the broad range of digital technologies (i.e., cell phones, tablets, computers, and gaming devices) that generally fall under the more unwieldy rubric of "information and communication technology." It will use "new media" to refer to media (i.e., email, texting, video conferencing, social media, podcasting, blogging, and microblogging) that have emerged on these technologies. Relevant distinctions will be noted where necessary.

cyber-ritual as meaningful as physical participation? Is being a parent or child in the digital age as authentic as it was "back in the good old days"? This sort of comparative approach suffers, in part, because it often sets up artificial binary oppositions (e.g., online and offline, mediated and unmediated, real and virtual) that do not exist in practice. But, more problematically, it presumes that we are describing these realities accurately and in sufficient depth. To assess the morality of any action, one needs to understand that action fully. Yet, by starting with a particular comparison drawn from previous life experiences, it becomes easy to overlook critical factors that lie beneath the surface, factors that distinguish the new from what has come before. Without a deep methodological well to draw upon, we can end up like Peter, with the best of intentions, but misreading the signs we see.

This article will offer a framework for considering the morality of contemporary information and communication technologies and new media. The proposed framework moves beyond the one-dimensional approach of comparative morphology. It will begin by considering the three primary models that are most frequently used to conceptualize technology's influence on human life—instrumentalism, determinism, and cultural materialism—identifying their limitations as well as their central insights. While these approaches originated and developed primarily within the fields of philosophy and history of technology, they serve as the methodological underpinnings of a great deal of scholarly and popular work on technology ethics, including the eighty year body of work of Catholic social teaching on social communication.

Using the traditional notion of the three fonts of moral wisdom as a guide, this essay will argue that alone, none of these approaches is adequate to the task of understanding the moral implications of contemporary information and communication technologies and digital media, but that together, they function to provide sufficient information to assess the central elements necessary for a moral evaluation of action. The essay will close with some examples of how utilizing the approach recommended by the three fonts frame can help us include a much broader range of considerations in a determination of digital media's effects on moral and theological reflection, and thus increase our ability to understand the new realities before us, offer a more insightful witness into civic society, and more effectively meet the moral and pastoral needs of people living in today's hyper-mediated, connected world.

Approaches to the Influence of Technology in Human Life

Instrumentalism

As I suggested, scholars in moral theology have, to this point, played a small role in the scholarly and cultural conversation on the ethics of new digital technologies. That being said, over the past eighty years, the Roman Catholic magisterium has produced a significant body of work on theological, moral, and pragmatic aspects of communication and information technology that was particularly influential during the emergence of moving image technologies. In the early part of the twentieth century, especially in the United States, there was a widespread mistrust of the new medium of film, including a broad-based movement in the 1920's to establish government censorship of the motion picture industry.[2] As early as Pope Pius XI's 1936 encyclical Vigilanti cura, Catholic social teaching on Social Communication (a.k.a. "mass media") offered to this debate the particular insight that no communication technology is innately good or bad; rather, media receive their theological significance and moral species from the messages that they are used to convey.[3] By emphasizing the instrumental character of communication technologies, Catholic social teaching on social communication stood firmly against those—even within the Church—who believed that film, as well as radio and television, were inherently evil. In doing so, the Vatican played a part in opening up space for the development of new and powerful forms of art, information, and expression.

Broadly speaking, as it applies to technology, instrumentalism will be familiar to many readers, either through knowledge of Catholic social thought on communication or as a result of living in a cultural context in which instrumentalism provides the primary mode of understanding the use of material objects. When used both within the discipline of philosophy of technology and in daily discourse, instrumentalism is the view that technologies are human creations that have the primary characteristic of extending existing human powers. Like any object, a common technology can be used for a variety purposes, thus the character of their influence is dependent upon the person who uses them and the way in which they are used. Because it coheres strongly with our daily experience of tools, this is a popular approach to technologies across the board, not just communication and information technologies. As we often here people say in the U.S., "guns don't kill people, people kill people."

This approach can be seen in Catholic social teaching on social communication when documents like Pope Pius XII's 1957 encyclical *Miranda prorsus* suggest that the means of social communication are

---

[2] On the censorship climate, as well as the history of Vatican writing on social communication, see James F. Caccamo, "The Message on the Media: Seventy Years of Catholic Social Teaching on Social Communication," *Josephenum Journal of Theology,* 15 no. 2 (2008); 394.

[3] Pope Pius XI, *Vigilanti cura*, (1936), www.vatican.va/holy_father/ pius_xi/encyclicals/documents/hf_p-xi_enc_29061936_vigilanti-cura_en.html.

morally neutral gifts of God.[4] One of the classic statements from this perspective can be found in the 1973 Pastoral Instruction *Communio et progression. Communio* presents the means of social communication as human creations—born of God's creative power—that enable human beings to reach for communion with one another and with God. As such, media have an "allotted place in the history of Creation, in the Incarnation and Redemption" through increasing the common good in accord with truth.[5] This role, however, is not guaranteed. "If… men's minds and hearts are ill disposed, if good will is not there, this outpouring of technology may produce an opposite effect so that… evils are multiplied."[6] Any harm done cannot be ascribed to the means of social communication themselves, for the TV is just a TV and a cellphone is just a cellphone. Rather, harm is ascribed to the particular intention and act of the communicator. The Pontifical Council on Social Communications put it a bit more directly in 1997's *Ethics in Advertising* when it stated:

> There is nothing intrinsically good or intrinsically evil about advertising. It is a tool, and instrument: it can be used well, and it can be used badly. If it can have, and sometimes does have, beneficial results…, it can, and often does, have a negative, harmful impact on individuals and society.[7]

While this statement is specifically focused on advertising, it is a fair representation of the general approach to social communication across the Roman Catholic tradition, as well as other parts of the Christian community. Where media goes wrong—be it in sexual, violent, or degrading programs, news that makes private matters public or invites scandal, or new media that foment discord—it goes wrong because those who use technologies of communication seek to carry out evil.[8]

---

[4] Pope Pius XII, *Miranda prorsus* (1957), www.vatican.va/holy_father/pius_xii/encyclicals/documents/hf_p-xii_enc_08091957_miranda-prorsus_en.html.

[5] Pontifical Council for Social Communications, *Communio et progressio,* (1971), nos. 15-17, www.vatican.va/roman_curia/pontifical_councils/pccs/documents/rc_pc-_pccs_doc_23051971_communio_en.html.

[6] Pontifical Council for Social Communications, *Communio et progressio,* no. 9.

[7] Pontifical Council for Social Communications, *Ethics in Advertising* (1997), no. 9, www.vatican.va/roman_curia/pontifical_councils/pccs/documents/rc_pc_pccs_doc_-22021997_ethics-in-ad_en.html.

[8] Notably, this instrumental approach is not unique to Catholicism. As James Gustafson notes, the story of the Protestant approach to the Industrial Revolution is the story of instrumentalists as well. Factory owners and those who reshaped the land understood themselves not as the destroyers of nature that England's Romantic poets called them. Rather, they saw themselves as instruments of God's creative impulse to tame nature, to recreate a fallen world in the image of God's original design. See James Gustafson, "Christian Attitudes Toward a Technological Society," *Theology Today* 16 (July 1959): 173-189.

At its core, then, instrumentalism understands technology as a powerful force that is fundamentally shaped and controlled by human beings. The flip-side of this emphasis is that instrumentalists are resistant to the notion that technologies have an interior formative function. A person uses a gun, but the gun does not change the person who uses it. The gun—or the media, or a cell phone—expresses the intentions, meanings, and views of the actor, but does not shape the actor in the process of expression. Our messages clearly affect receivers. *Ethics in Advertising*, for instance, recognizes that advertising "helps shape the reality it reflects."[9] But the meaning here is clear: The messages in advertisements do not change the advertisers as much as they transform those who see or hear them. Communicators need to be formed separately in order to use the means of communication well. The danger for the formation of society is that media will be used effectively, in the technical sense of communicating a message clearly, but that the message will be aimed at the wrong goal.

Determinism

While instrumentalism has won the day in the philosophical, popular, and broader theological understanding of communication and information technology and the media, it is not the only way of thinking about the power of our gadgets. Two other approaches are particularly important.

The first alternate approach picks up from this question of formation, but moves in the opposite direction, understanding technology not as a tool for shaping the world, but as a powerful force that forms its users. Referred to as technological determinism, this approach is probably most strongly identified with Marshall McLuhan. Well known for his pithy and often misunderstood comment, "the medium is the message," McLuhan's sense was that the material conditions of our existence as human beings shapes our experience, often in unknown ways, and beyond our control, regardless of our stance toward the influence. Consider, for instance, his notion that the real power of any communication medium lies not in content of the communication, but rather in the way that it "shapes and controls the scale and form of human association and action."[10] While originally predicated of the changes in media that McLuhan saw in the 1950's, with the widespread adoption of television, it is easy to see the wisdom of his claim in the Internet age. Blogging and tweeting, for instance, have reshaped the reach of the individual, effectively eliminating the relevance of space as a separator between individuals, regardless of the message we wish to communicate.

---

[9] Pontifical Council for Social Communications, *Ethics in Advertising*, no. 3.

[10] Marshall McLuhan, *Understanding Media,* ed. by W. Terrence Gordon (Corte Madera, CA: Ginko Press, 1964, 2003), 20.

New media have also reconfigured the entire system of metrics by which the American media landscape is governed. Using the Internet, citizen journalists have wrested power from big media. Even if you have never read a blog or tweet, the news you consume—and your perception of what you can know—has been transformed by the new communication realities. The case of the shooting of an unarmed teenager, Michael Brown, by police officers in Ferguson, Missouri in August, 2014 is a dramatic example of this: It was a minor local news item that was catapulted onto the national and international stage only after the news of protests spread on Twitter. As the *Financial Times* noted, there were "almost 1m tweets sent before CNN had spent a single minute reporting."[11] By enabling anyone with a cell phone to report and share news instantly, Twitter brought new information into the national "public square." Critically, this largely happened without our explicit intent or informed consent, or even our awareness. Little messages, meant simply to share information, reshaped national news and the American conversation on race and policing in the process.

Of course, McLuhan is not the only thinker or critic to take this approach. Preceding McLuhan, Martin Heidegger fundamentally challenged the presumed radical autonomy of the human subject, which undergirds the instrumentalist approach. Albert Borgmann has written a substantial body of work on technology that is nuanced and varied, evincing shifts, development, and a good deal of wrestling back and forth with a wide variety of issues, yet his general orientation over the decades has been a determinist one. A central theme in his work has been that the technologies that we use shape the basic patterns of our daily living. Borgman's influential early work centered on the disruptive influence of technological devices on our focal practices.[12] Focal practices are daily practices that human beings do to accomplish particular goals, but that have value not solely for the good produced as the end, but also for the goods internal to the practices as

---

[11] Hannah Kuchler, "TV Networks Play Catch-up to Twitter in Ferguson's Rolling Story," *Financial Times*, August 22, 2014, www.ft.com/intl/cms/s/0/3b9243ce-2984-11e4-8b81-00144feabdc0.html#axzz3IVq2Snkr. See also David Carr, "View of #Ferguson Thrust Michael Brown Shooting to National Attention," *The New York Times*, August 17, 2014, http://www.nytimes.com/2014/08/18/business/media/view-of-ferguson-thrust-michael-brown-shooting-to-national-attention.html?_r=1.

[12] Albert Borgmann, *Technology and the Character of Contemporary Life* (Chicago: University of Chicago Press, 1984). Neo-naturalists like John Dyer, *From the Garden to the City* (Grand Rapids: Kregel Publications, 2011), follow in Borgmann's footsteps. For an interesting application of Borgmann's work to the ecclesial and liturgical experience, see Richard Gaillardetz, *Transforming Our Days* (New York: Crossroad Publishing Company, 2000).

they are carried out and to the network of relationships that they require.[13] The introduction of technologies (like central heating) interrupt focal practices, destroying the associated goods and networks of relationships as they are adopted. Technologies, by their simple existence and use change users, whether or not they agree to be changed, even if they are unaware of the changes.

More recently, the determinist approach has come into full force in the popular press. While no one wants to admit to taking McLuhan's kitchy-sounding and often hyperbolic claims particularly seriously, an array of contemporary technology critics have received much more notice espousing this approach. We see, for instance, journalist Nicholas Carr's approach to the inherently destructive power of digital technology on reading and intellectual culture in popular book *The Shallows.*[14] In the other direction, we see media scholar Clay Shirkey's optimism that the cognitive surplus created by networked populations will enhance, even liberate, society.[15] Also consider the work of Kevin Kelly, whose book title really says it all: *What Technology Wants.*[16] Indeed, we see determinism across the board in the rhetoric surrounding the detrimental effects of violent video games, a rhetoric that persists in spite of an absence of empirical evidence supporting intuitions about their destructive influence.

Cultural Materialism

In addition to the instrumentalist and determinist perspectives on the influence of technology, there is a third approach worth noting. Referred to as cultural materialism (with variations like political materialism and social materialism), this approach picks up the determinist's suspicion of our power over technology and the instrumentalists' recognition that technologies have multiple uses, but triangulates them through a belief in the profound role that social structures play in shaping the life, desires, and actions of the person. Cultural materialism notes that, strictly speaking, technologies are never the product of an individual. Even when we name an inventor, every single technology is built on the work of others, from experimenters who came before, contemporaries who collaborate and compete, and even material suppliers and social systems that make the creation and development process possible. More importantly, perhaps, technologies are only adopted broadly when they meet the preexisting interests, rationality schemes, and broader social practices of the cultures in which they are

---

13 There are significant resonances here with the approach to practices taken in Alasdair MacIntyre, *After Virtue* (Notre Dame: University of Notre Dame Press, 1981).

14 Nicholas Carr, *The Shallows* (New York: W. W. Norton, 2010).

15 Clay Shirkey, *Cognitive Surplus: Creativity and Generosity in a Connected Age* (New York: Penguin Press, 2008).

16 Kevin Kelly, *What Technology Wants* (New York, N.Y.: Penguin Books, 2011).

introduced. Thus, despite how they are used, technologies never solely serve the ends of the individual user. Rather, they always serve multiple layers of ends that are intertwined with the structures and ends of society. It should not be surprising, then, that the Internet—championed at its birth as an empowering technology where "information wants to be free"[17]—has grown into a massive marketing and commerce machine over the course of a thirty year development in the American capitalist context. Insofar as technologies shape the actions of persons or groups, they do not do so in isolation, but in concert with the larger forces of the culture in which they are adopted.

Cultural materialism is a popular approach among historians of technology. Exploring diverse technologies like farming and nuclear power, Langdon Winner and Jared Diamond explore the role of social valuation in adoption and deployment of technologies, noting the "auto-catalyzing" nature of technological adoption—the systems we use build upon one another, recapitulating and reinforcing the power structures and social practices that led to their adoption in the first place.[18] Cultural materialism is also a popular approach among philosophers. Perhaps the most well known cultural materialist writing on technology from philosophy is Jacques Ellul, whose writing on the technological society predicted a whole swath of changes that happened in industrialized societies over the course of the late twentieth century. Perhaps the most significant change that Ellul described was the eclipse of all appreciation of good that is not expressed as a factor of instrumental value as the result of the technologization of all modes of labor.[19] In *The Homeless Mind*, sociologist of religion Peter Berger and co-authors Brigitte Berger and Hansfried Kellner trace some of the same lines as Ellul, but—interestingly enough—emphasize the increasing role that social self-differentiation will play as human beings increasingly see themselves as just another interchangeable technological device in the economic system.[20] The self-orientation at the core of social media is not blatant narcissism, but rather the necessary outlet for identity formation in the nameless and faceless technological society.

---

[17] The notion originated in the 1970s, but this particular language is generally attributed to Stewart Brand, "Discussions from the Hacker's Conference, November 1984," *Whole Earth Review* (May 1985): 48-9. Notably, this formulation misrepresents Brand's position. His whole quote read: "On the one hand, information wants to be expensive, because it's so valuable. The right information in the right places changes your life. On the other hand, information wants to be free, because the cost of getting it out is getting lower and lower all the time. So you have these two fighting against each other."

[18] Langdon Winner, *The Wale and the Reactor* (Chicago: University of Chicago Press, 1986); Jared Diamond, *Guns, Germs, and Steel* (New York: W. W. Norton, 1998).

[19] Jacques Ellul, *The Technological Society* (New York: Knopf, 1964).

[20] Peter Berger, Brigitte Berger, and Hansfried Kellner, *The Homeless Mind* (New York: Random House, 1973).

In the popular press, cultural materialists are much rarer than instrumentalists or determinists. Among the most well known and influential of them is Jaron Lanier. An influential programmer and early virtual reality pioneer, Lanier has been outspoken about the way in which Internet technologies have been subsumed into the capitalist framework to the point that the freedom and generativity of the early Internet have given way to a gadgetization of the user.[21] We may use social media software to communicate, but its primary reason for existing today is to gather information about you that can be sold to third parties. You are, it turns out, a natural resource. Perhaps the people most strongly in the materialist camp are security specialists and reporters like Laura Poitras and Glenn Greenwald, who broke the story on the NSA's collection of phone metadata and PRISM system.[22] You can use your phone to reach your family, but ultimately it is also a tool for surveillance at the service of national security. While we as individuals have illusion of control over our devices, technologies are made available for use in limited ways—ways that support the economic, political, and social interests within social groups. What is important, then, and morally significant about technologies are not the technologies themselves, but the larger systems in which we participate and the ways in which those systems condition, enable, or block certain kinds of actions.

The Approaches to Technology and the Christian Moral Tradition

While there are other models for understanding the influence of technologies like communication and information technology, these three approaches—instrumentalism, technological determinism, and cultural materialism—dominate the broad lines that we see within both scholarly and popular debates about how technologies should be used. Notably, there is a good deal of debate outside of theology that centers on which one of these approaches or methods most accurately portrays the nature of technology and its influence on human life. As is typical within the scholarly world, the general presumption is that there can be only one right answer. There must be a winner and a loser,

---

[21] Jaron Lanier, *You Are Not a Gadget: A Manifesto* (New York: Alfred A. Knopf, 2010).

[22] Glenn Greenwald, "NSA Collecting Phone Records of Millions of Verizon Customers Daily," *The Guardian* (June 6, 2013), www.theguardian.com/world/2013/-jun/06/nsa-phone-records-verizon-court-order. Glenn Greenwald, "NSA Prism Program Taps in to User Data of Apple, Google and Others," *The Guardian* (June 7, 2013), www.theguardian.com/world/2013/jun/06/us-tech-giants-nsa-data. Laura Poitras, "The Program," *The New York Times* (August 22, 2012), www.nytimes.com/-2012/08/23/opinion/the-national-security-agencys-domestic-spying-program.html?-_r=1&. Peter Maas, "How Laura Poitras Helped Snowden Spill His Secrets," *The New York Times* (August 13, 2013), www.nytimes.com/2013/08/18/magazine/laura-poitras-snowden.html?pagewanted=all.

so the influence of technology must be best described by instrumentalism, or by determinism, or by cultural materialism. This view is common outside of the academic debate as well, among pundits, journalists, and even theologians for whom technology is a passing interest, but not an area of significant work. It is not unusual to hear complaints about how technology has made this generation of students stupid, materialistic, instrumentalists, or to hear squeals of glee among teachers who believe they have finally figured out the secret to getting students to really engage in classwork by using the next type of listserv, wiki, or online learning module. As far as technology is concerned, we can be a lot like Peter, understanding new realities in terms of previous conclusions, and moving quickly to affirm what corresponds to the familiar.

However, what I find striking about these three different—and supposedly contradictory—approaches to the influence of technology is that none of them is wholly without merit. Indeed, each one is grounded in an important insight into our shared experiences of technologies like social media, smart phones, and digital media. Instrumentalism, for instance, rightly recognizes the importance of freedom and human choice and freedom in creating the world that we live in, both for ourselves and for the larger community. Digital technology has shown itself to be a powerful tool that enables people to extend the range of options available to them as beings who seek to find fulfillment through acting in the world. As Christians, we recognize the inviolability of a well-formed conscience, holding that through formation, serious deliberation, and reasoned judgment, the human person can discover the will of God in a particular situation in the form of right reason. Even though we may be constrained by the realities of the world, we are authentically free to act within our limits, and we hold out hope that through our actions, we will break through any and all limitations. Instrumentalism also upholds the notion of responsibility, by which, in the Christian view, we know ourselves as stewards not only of creation but also of our own search for fullness of being and return to God. Through all of this, we express and create our identities as unique children of God.

Technological determinism, on the other hand, rightly recognizes that our materiality matters. Human beings are embodied creatures who are shaped by the things we do and practices that we engage in. Thus, it is impossible to utilize tools that do not, at some level, shape who we are through the fact of their existence. Glimpses of the concerns behind determinism exist within the Catholic tradition. In recent decades, the Thomistic tradition has developed an account of practices as the foundation of the moral life, suggesting that the formation of virtue is a matter of imitation: We cannot become moral people without actually doing the things that moral people do, nor can we understand or come to love the good without first engaging our bodies and minds in the actions that accomplish good. Even when they deemphasize them, determinists do not deny that human beings make authentic decisions that have real consequences. Rather, they focus on bringing to consciousness and attention the unintentional and unrecognized aspects of our behavior, emphasizing that everything we do influences us in ways that we may not want it to, or even realize.

While I have noted that Catholic social teaching on social communication tends to utilize an instrumentalist approach to technology, elements of determinism are evident throughout other areas of Catholic social thought. In magisterial work on poverty, for instance, Catholics have frequently emphasized global solidarity, in part because they recognize the realities of geographical determinism. Where you were born matters to your long-term prospects for health, education, and economic well-being. As our lives becomes increasingly enacted in and through technology, it makes sense that we would expand our understanding of relevant materiality to encompass technology and its ability to shape large parts of our lives and experiences, and perhaps even determine them.

Finally, cultural materialism rightly recognizes the deeply social nature of the human person. We begin our lives in relation and live them out as parts of groups. So, too, are the technologies that we use born through community effort and extend our reach into the social world. For good or ill, our lives are conditioned by the social structures and shared meanings that we are a part of. While we are able to make decisions and act on our own, all of our thinking and decision-making and actions happen within the context of family, friends, neighbors, church, workplace, city, nation, and globe. This understanding of the fundamentally social nature of the human person is, of course, dear to the Catholic moral tradition. Catholic social thought rejects materialism, but it does share with the materialist an attention to corporate identity, embodiment, and action. For example, integral human development is understood as the responsibility of the whole, often described in terms of the principle of common good achieved only through solidarity. This social nature is a component of the natural law, yet it is also grounded in the inner life of the Trinity, the model for self-giving and love. Social context, the social practices that people engage in, and the social structures people create to support one another are so fundamentally important, the Roman Catholic tradition has spoken of justice as a fundamental part of spreading the gospel. Society and its institutions are not merely the necessary stage upon which individuals live out their lives, but a robust environment that can alternately impair our ability to thrive or enable human flourishing. While there are debates about how it is to be achieved, this tradition has consistently aimed to transform society so that it continues to more closely approximate justice.

Thus, in light of the broader picture of human life that we see in Christian ethics, it is clear that instrumentalism, determinism, and cultural materialism each emphasize and build upon important insights into what it means to be human. Yet, while this affirms the underling reasonableness of all three theories, it also suggests that, from the context of Christian ethics, all three are insufficient when understood as the single method needed to frame moral inquiry because it marginalizes important aspects of human experience and action. The question to ask, then, may not be which of these three approaches best helps us understand the impact of technology in our lives. Rather, the question to ask is how we might draw on each of these methods within our moral analysis so that we can both provide an accurate assessment of what we have done and develop a plan for what we should do next. This will necessarily involve moving beyond the path laid out over the past eighty years in Catholic social teaching on social communications, a tradition that has thrown its lot in with instrumentalism when it comes to communication and information technologies. The key, however, may lie deeper back in the tradition.

Fonts of Moral Wisdom

If we want to move beyond the conflict among these three approaches to the influence of technology to draw fully upon the insights they offer, one fruitful strategy will be to take the lead from fundamental concepts within moral theology, which is a field that has as its bread and butter assessing past action and evaluating options for future action. More specifically, the classic model of intention, the object of the act, and circumstances—the "three fonts of moral wisdom"—can help us examine the appropriateness of these models of technology, and thus provide us a road map for a new model for understanding new and emerging social communication acts and practices.

When speaking about morality within the context of new communication and information technologies, it can be challenging to think in terms of existing moral norms, principles, and especially rules. As technologies emerge, we engage in new activities and develop new practices that sometimes map accurately onto existing moral standards, but often they just appear to do so, making it easy to misjudge the core morality of an action. (Some examples of this will be offered in the final section of this article.) In the grand scheme of things, the goal of life is fullness of being of the human person that leads to union with God in the beatific vision. At times, this would have been referred to as perfection, and more recently, as integral human development. While ultimately depending on the gift of grace, we do our part to contribute to fullness of being through accomplishing acts that enhance both our own and other people's development. Yet it is exceedingly rare that our actions are absolutely destructive of the human person or absolutely enhancing, absolutely moral or absolutely immoral.

Rather, in most cases our actions are mixed, imperfectly good. Thus, where it might sound strange to describe communication or information activities as being "moral" or "immoral"—outside of simple cases of lying or slander—it doesn't sound strange at all to say that an event or system of communication can, to a lessor or greater degree, enable people to achieve the fullness of the being as children of God.

As has been noted, the three fonts framework provides a means for parsing actions in order to consider the extent to which they enhance fullness of being and achieve this goodness. Deriving from the Thomistic model of the four-fold goodness of the act, the three fonts suggest that to fully understand a past or future action, we need to examine three interrelated aspects: the intention (i.e., the end/*finis operantis*), the means (i.e., the object/*finis operis),* and the circumstances.[23] An analysis of circumstances is the most complex when considering the use and role of technology. The "intention" is the goal that we seek to attain through carrying out a particular action; it is what drives us to act in the first place. The "means" refers to the thing that is being done in order to achieve the intention. It is what is sometimes referred to as the "act-in-itself." (Recall that the dominant Catholic instrumentalist view tends not to place the good or bad of technology in the technology-itself.) In contrast, "circumstances" is a somewhat amorphous category that can, at times, be quite sprawling, especially in relationship to technology.

In the broad sense, circumstances are the conditions that provide a context for the action, the "specific facts of the case or the relevant data of the moral setting in which the act takes place."[24] A key part of the category of circumstances of an action is the consequences. The consequences are the concrete, objective results of the means that were chosen to achieve the intention. Yet, within the Catholic tradition, consequences do not exhaust the relevant circumstances. Circumstances would also include a whole host of situation-specific factors that exert influence on which means are chosen to achieve the desired end. It is the "who, what, where, and when" of the situation. When setting Internet connectivity prices, for instance, it would be a relevant circumstance that a company is the sole provider in a rural area, a factor that might tempt the company to choose a means that would take advantage of potential customers' limited freedom. Finally, some have suggested that the alternative means available to the actor but have not been chosen are relevant aspects of the circumstances.[25] Our ability to

---

[23] The three fonts of moral wisdom comprise the three morally determinant parts of the "fourfold goodness" of an act. See Thomas Aquinas, *Summa Theologica*, trans. Fathers of the Dominican Province, 2nd and rev. ed., 1920, online ed., 2003; II-II, q. 18, a. 4, www.newadvent.org/summa/2018.htm#article2.

[24] Russell B. Connors and Patrick T. McCormick, *Character, Choices & Community* (Mahwah: Paulist Press, 1998), 50.

[25] Connors and McCormick, *Character, Choices & Community*, 51f.

do good is dependent on freedom and opportunities we have to act in particular ways. Thus, assessing the quality of actions must always be done in light of the possible means available to the actor.

What is notable here is that, except in a few cases, the Roman Catholic tradition maintains that actions are not understood as completely good, choice-worthy, or even reasonable unless all aspects of the action promote fullness of being.[26] Actions that are good are those that start with a good intention, use a means that is appropriate both to the nature of the human person and to the particular circumstances at hand in light of the options available, and result in the most positive effect on integral human development as possible. Realistically speaking, most of the things we do fall short of perfection in one or more of these areas. Yet, these actions are also suffused with goodness. The goal of life is to transform the "not so good" into the "pretty darned good," creating habits of reliable action along the way.

Models of Technology Influence in Light of the Three Fonts

If we reflect on the models for the influence of technology in light of the three fonts of moral wisdom, it becomes a bit more clear why, despite their unique insights, a moral theologian might find that each of the three approaches to the influence of technology would ultimately fall short of providing a singular framework for accurately assessing past social communication acts or a plan for future ones.

Consider, for instance, instrumentalism. Instrumentalism argues that the influence of a technology is dependent upon the person who uses them and the way in which they are used. Mapped onto the three fonts, instrumentalism conceptualizes the influence of technologically mediated actions primarily in terms of the intention of the communicator. In the language of communication, this ties most strongly to the content portion of the messaging. Where social communication is successful, it is because communicators sought to enhance people's lives and sent out messages that fit those intentions. Where there are problems, they exist either because communicators had bad intentions that failed to live up to the good, and so created questionable content, or created content that failed to embody the good intentions they had. One could think, here, of advertisers who entice people to buy products that do not enhance goodness or who mean well but use degrading imagery. For the instrumentalist, good content flowing from rightly pointed intentions leads to good effects.

In contrast, technological determinism—the belief that engagement with a particular technology can shape the human person independent of intentionality—understands the influence of technologically mediated actions in terms of the means—the technology itself.

[26] *ST,* II-II q. 18, a. 1, and q. 20, a. 2.

More specifically, determinists focus on the many and disparate unintended consequences that accompany the adoption and deployment of any technology, which are ultimately more formative than the intended actions and circumstances. One might think here, for instance, of the transformation of human conversational patterns—moving from responsive, time intensive, and disclosive modes to controlled, efficient, and inauthentic—that has resulted from the physical and material experience of digital messaging that scholars like Sherry Turkle describe.[27] Determinists can sometimes come off as cagey or imprecise because they can gloss over the known positive uses of technologies, emphasizing instead the profound dangers of potential or systemic results, especially those that are slow developing, subtle, and below consciousness. Thinkers who use other approaches, such as instrumentalism would not deny that technologies have certain typical consequences. It is rare, however, for instrumentalists to recognize consequences that are independent of the intention. But from the determinist perspective, the significance and moral species of a technology comes not from what we mean to do, but effects that flow from its usual use.

For its part, cultural materialism understands the influence of technologically mediated actions in terms of the circumstances of the communication or information event. In other words, it holds that the primary influence of technology is found not as much in technologies themselves as in the social context, the preexisting interests, rationality schemes, and broader social practices of the cultures in which technologies exist. More particularly, cultural materialism emphasizes the way in which broader culture deploys technology to support existing cultural goals. As such, it can question the relevance of freedom and autonomy, suggesting that the range of options that we are afforded is already constricted in order to give manipulation the appearance of being meaningful choice while still serving social goals. In our contemporary communication environment, for instance, the cultural materialist would note how our online experience is shaped by algorithms created by the platform we use, the searches we have done, and the demographics that we demonstrate, to the point that the prices we may pay for things may end up higher as a result of who we are.[28] Here, the significance and moral species of a technology are largely a factor of

[27] Sherry Turkle, *Alone Together: Why We Expect More from Technology and Less from Each Other* (New York: Basic Books, 2011). For a brief outline of the primary argument of the book, see Sherry Turkle, "The Flight From Conversation," *The New York Times,* April 201, 2012, http://www.nytimes.com/2012/04/22/opinion/sunday/the-flight-from-conversation.html?_r=5&pagewanted=all&&pagewanted=print.

[28] See, for instance, Dana Mattioli, "On Orbitz, Mac Users Steered to Pricier Hotels," *The Wall Street Journal* (August 23, 2012), http://online.wsj.com/articles/SB10001424052702304458604577488822667325882.

the circumstances that originally shaped the technology and continues to shape how we use it.

Setting the models of tech influence in the context of the traditional hermeneutic of the three fonts of moral wisdom reveals that all three of these approaches are valuable in that they inform different parts of the complex decision-making process about technology and media use. It also shows that using any one of them alone—be it instrumentalism, determinism, or cultural materialism—leaves out important considerations when evaluating the moral significance of past practices or planning new ones. Strongly set in any one perspective, we might fail to account for information that is critical for assessing which path most fully achieves the good. But if we allow them to mutually correct the limitations found in the others, utilizing the insights of all three approaches would enable us to more fully understand the impact of our communication.

Catholic Social Teaching on Social Communication in Light of the Three Fonts Approach

As noted previously, the single body of significant theological work on communication technology that is available to Christian ethicists is Catholic social teaching on social communication. Since 1936, two encyclicals, two pastoral instructions, one conciliar decree, two major sets of pastoral guidelines, forty-eight annual World Communications Day addresses, and at least ten minor documents—more than 210,000 words—have been written by various popes and offices of the Vatican on the theological, moral, and social implications of various mass communication technologies. As one part of the much larger tradition of Catholic social teaching, one might expect work on social communications to contain the same kinds of thorough descriptions of intentions, means, cultural circumstances, and systemic contexts that characterize work on other topics. One might consider, for instance, the depth of engagement with the economic particularities in the U.S. Catholic Bishops' letter *Economic Justice for All*.[29] Or one might consider the close reading of global capital markets that Pope Benedict offers in *Caritas in veritate* and his 2013 World Day of Peace message,[30] or the beautiful reflections of Pope John XXIII on the experience of living under threat of nuclear war in *Pacem in terris*,[31] or the

[29] United States Catholic Bishops, *Economic Justice for All* (1986), www.usccb.org/-upload/economic_justice_for_all.pdf.

[30] Pope Benedict XVI, *Caritas in veritate* (June 29, 2009), www.vatican.va/holy_father/benedict_xvi/encyclicals/documents/hf_ben-xvi_enc_20090629_caritas-in-veritate_en.html. *Blessed are the Peacemakers,* Message for The World Day of Peace (January 1, 2013), www.vatican.va/holy_father/benedict_xvi/messages/peace/documents/hf_ben-xvi_mes_20121208_xlvi-world-day-peace_en.html.

[31] Pope John XXIII, *Pacem in terris* (April 11, 1963), www.vatican.va/holy_father/john_xxiii/encyclicals/documents/hf_j-xxiii_enc_11041963_pacem_en.html.

work of Paul VI on the experience of poverty in *Populorum progressio*, or of Pope John Paul II on the existential turmoil of living in the modern age in *Redemptor hominis*,[32] or Pope Francis' observations on economic exclusion in *Evangelii gaudium*.[33] Each of these works evinces a realistic and savvy understanding of the influences of social and material context on life and society, an understanding that enabled pointed critique as well as solid recommendations for future action. One might argue whether or not the descriptions within the documents of Catholic social teaching are as accurate as they could be, but they clearly exist.

In contrast, Catholic social teaching on social communication does not provide substantial or regular examples of how we might do robust and thorough analysis of the theological and moral implications of technology.

As I noted, official Catholic documents on social communication played a significant role in the development of media during the twentieth century by adopting an instrumentalist perspective to promote the idea that that media receive their theological significance and moral species from the messages that they are used to convey. This instrumentalist approach formed the backbone of the Vatican's approach to communication throughout the twentieth century and provided a useful hermeneutic for examining mass media technologies like film, television, and radio.

As one would expect of an instrumentalist approach, the documents provide excellent engagement with issues of intentionality and the "means of social communication," where means is understood not as technologies, but rather as the messages that are communicated. This emphasis forms the core of Catholic social teaching on social communication: exhorting people to say good things in good ways for good reasons. In places, documents emphasize forming communicators to become better stewards of the tools of communication.[34] In

---

32 Pope Paul VI, *Populorum progressio* (March 26, 1967), www.vatican.va/holy_father/paul_vi/encyclicals/documents/hf_p-vi_enc_26031967_populorum_en.html. Pope John Paul II, *Redemptor hominis* (March 4, 1979), www.vatican.va/holy_father/john_paul_ii/encyclicals/documents/hf_jp-ii_enc_04031979_redemptor-hominis_en.html.

33 Pope Francis, *Evangelii gaudium* (November 24, 2013), http://w2.vatican.va/content/francesco/en/apost_exhortations/documents/papa-francesco_esortazione-ap_20131124_evangelii-gaudium.html.

34 For instance, Second Vatican Council, *Inter mirifica* (1963), nos. 8-12, 3–5, www.vatican.va/archive/hist_councils/ii_vatican_council/documents/vat-ii_decree_-19631204_inter-mirifica_en.html; Congregation for Catholic Education, *Guide to the Training of Future Priests Concerning the Instruments of Social Communication* (1986), www.vatican.va/roman_curia/pontifical_councils/pccs/documents/rc_pc_-pccs_doc_19031986_ guide-for-future-priests_en.html; Pontifical Council for Social

other places, the documents emphasize forming audiences to be able to identify the bad intentions of some creators, as well as the manipulative and nefarious messages that some communicators create.[35] Only through such training, for instance, will communicators desire to put forth positive programming with honest, uplifting messages. Only through such training will audiences become discerning viewers who can easily identify political, social, or consumer propaganda or can tell the difference between portrayals of immoral activity meant to titillate audiences from those that are necessary to teach moral lessons.

While this body of work does provide great insights into the intention and reception of messages through various media, as is typical of instrumentalist approaches, it tends not to pay significant attention to the broader factors associated with impact of the material practice of communicating or the systemic issues of social context beyond the intended and received messages. For instance, a full account of the moral character of communication practices would be well served by consideration of the deterministic aspects of the constitutive characteristics of the technological means we use to communicate. The areas of concern are numerous, such as the effect of anonymity on authenticity, the impact of broad adoption of cell phones across age groups and how family interaction and relational patterns are reconfigured, the development of new trends in journalism like "clickbait" and "churnalism," the ways in which ubiquitous entertainment and gaming culture is influencing liturgical engagement, how technology use by children will affect their development, and the ongoing creation of gated communities of information.

A full account of the moral character of technology and media practices would also be well served by a cultural materialist consideration of the systemic aspects of communication industries and the ways in which they shape technologies to support particular social values, goals, and meaning structures rather than the user's own purposes. This might include exploration of the power dynamics that are involved in contemporary media ownership and consolidation, the expansion of for-profit "knowledge cartels" and control of scholarly in-

---

Communications, *Aetatis novae* (1992), nos. 20-21, www. vatican.va/roman_curia/pontifical_councils/pccs/documents/rc_pc_pccs_doc_2202 1992_aetatis_en.html; Pontifical Council for Social Communications, *Ethics in Advertising*, 15-19.

[35] Pope Pius XII, *Miranda prorsus* (1957), Pt. 1, no. 12, www.vatican.va/holy_father/pius_xii/encyclicals/documents/hf_p-xii_enc_08091957_miranda-prorsus.-en.html; Pontifical Council for Social Communications, *100 Years of Cinema: Training In The Interpretation Of The Motion Picture Medium* (1996), www.vatican.va/roman_curia/pontifical_councils/pccs/documents/rc_pc_pccs_doc_19960101_100-cinema_en.html. Pontifical Council for Social Communications, *The Church and Internet* (2002), nos. 11- 12, www.vatican.va/roman_curia/pontifical_councils/pccs/-documents/rc_pc_pccs_doc_20020228_church-internet_en.html.

formation, the rise of data mining and predictive analytics at the service of marketing, dynamics of the digital divide (especially in the global context), and the expansion of surveillance, censorship, and filtering. All of these are significant influences on the impact of social communications on persons and societies, and considerations like these should find their way into contemporary work on the ethics of technology.

To defend, for a moment, the approach of Catholic social teaching on social communication, it could be argued that the literary form of official pronouncements and addresses limits the possibility for a thorough and nuanced approach to technology of the kind that I am suggesting. Most of the documents released over the past two decades have been the annual World Communication Day addresses. These have gained quite a bit of notoriety over the past few years in the popular press, but at an average of about 1500 words, they have little room for nuance and depth. One has to go back at least ten years to find documents in the 4,000-5,000 word range, such as the Pontifical Council for Social Communication's 2000 document *Ethics in Communication,* 2002's *Ethics and Internet* and *Church and Internet,* or Pope John Paul II's final Apostolic Letter, 2005's *The Rapid Development.*

These documents did engage some determinist and cultural considerations, albeit only briefly. *Ethics in Communication* mentions ideas as various as message fragmentation, media influence in education, and global inequity in communication technology.[36] *Ethics and Internet* and *Church and Internet* raise concerns about censorship in a few lines, but follow-up work has not been done to see if these concerns are the case, despite significant political, social, and technological changes around the world.[37] *Ethics in Internet* critiques straw-men anarchist libertarians, yet forgoes wrestling with the complexities of regulating the global Internet system.[38] Going back farther, *Aetatis novae* covers cultural, social, political, and economic contexts of communication in a mere two paragraphs, and *Pornography and Violence in the Communications Media* discusses the economic and political structure of mass media in a single paragraph.[39] The only document that really

---

36 Pontifical Council for Social Communications, *Ethics in Communications* (2000), nos. 29, 17, and 14, www.vatican.va/roman_curia/pontifical_councils/pccs/documents/rc_pc_pccs_doc_20000530_ethics-communications_en.html.

37 Pontifical Council for Social Communications, *Ethics and Internet* (2002), no. 12, http://www.vatican.va/roman_curia/pontifical_councils/pccs/documents/rc_pc_pccs_doc_20020228_ethics-internet_en.html; *The Church and Internet,* no. 11.

38 Pontifical Council for Social Communications, *Ethics and Internet*, no. 8.

39 Pontifical Council for Social Communications, *Aetatis novae* (1992), nos. 4-5, www.vatican.va/roman_curia/pontifical_councils/pccs/documents/rc_pc_pccs_doc_-22021992_aetatis_en.html. Pontifical Council for Social Communications, "Pornography and Violence in the Communications Media: A Pastoral Response" (1989), no.

moves beyond the instrumentalist approach in any significant way is 1971's *Communio et progressio*.[40] But this advantage is also its chief liability: At nearly 20,000 words, it is of limited interest for most readers.

That being said, these longer documents did pretty well to mention material or cultural aspects at all. The range of social factors and use patterns did not vary significantly in the early days of film and television. One sat down in front of a moving picture in an intentional manner to take in a story or message that was created and distributed by a major corporation. But the advent of the Internet, mobile technologies, and user generated content have created myriad ways to use technologies for communication and expression on platforms as varied as Facebook, 4Square, Wordpress, YouTube, Flicker, Pinterest, 4chan, and Sound-Cloud. Just as the Vatican's preferred format got shorter, the complexity grew.

And to be fair, it does seem that recent documents do at least recognize the critical nature of attending to material and social conditions for communication. For instance, the 2013 World Communication Day Address notes that:

> Social networks are the result of human interaction, but for their part they also reshape the dynamics of communication which builds relationships: a considered understanding of this environment is therefore the prerequisite for a significant presence there.[41]

Clearly, there is a growing awareness of the social aspects of communication here.

However, if this awareness is growing, it is also fair to say that it is not yet mature. Despite this mention of social dynamics, the address does not go on to offer a considered understanding of the issues in a way that a social materialist would recognize. For instance, at the start of the fifth paragraph, the document states that "the challenge facing social networks is how to be truly inclusive."[42] On the face of it, this statement makes sense: it certainly will be a challenge to get social networks to be inclusive. Yet, in the absence of a discussion of the dynamics in society and on the Internet that mitigate against this happening, the statement rings hollow.

20, www.vatican.va/roman_curia/pontifcal_councils/pccs/documents/rc_pc_pccs_-doc_07051989_pornography_en.html.

[40] See, for instance, Pontifical Council for Social Communications, *Communio et progressio,* nos. 33-47.

[41] Pope Benedict XVI, "Social Networks: Portals of Truth and Faith; New Spaces for Evangelization" (2013), no. 5, www.vatican.va/holy_father/benedict_xvi/messages/-communications/documents/hf_ben-xvi_mes_20130124_47th-world-communications-day_en.html.

[42] Pope Benedict XVI, "Social Networks," no. 5.

The reality is that as they exist now, social networks are anything but inclusive. Indeed, many social networks exist for the sole point of being exclusive: to be places where people of like mind gather to share similar perspectives without the need to engage people who are different. There are social networks that put this bias front and center, such as the social networking platform Netropolitan, which is aimed squarely at the wealthy, requiring a $9,000 joining fee and $3,000 annual fees.[43] On social networks that are not structurally exclusive, the anonymity of the web affords the opportunity to marginalize and belittle those who are different. An October 2014 study by the Pew Research Center reported that "fully 73% of adult Internet users have seen someone be harassed in some way online and 40% have personally experienced it."[44] The most common form of harassment is the use of offensive names, but also includes purposeful embarrassment, physical threats, and stalking.

As it stands, technological factors (anonymity) and cultural factors (classism/racism/sexism) mitigate against the transformation of these social practices through actions intended to embody Christian love through heartfelt messaging. To suggest otherwise rings as naïve and romantic as Microsoft CEO Satya Nadella's 2014 comment that women will achieve pay equality not by asking for raises, but rather by trusting the system to reward them accordingly.[45] Thus, while the Pope Benedict's comment is true—being inclusive is a great challenge—the address does not provide sufficient analysis to either describe just how complex the situation really is or provide a roadmap for its transformation. Lack of regular attention to aspects of means and circumstances limits the sizable body of Catholic social teaching on social communications from providing a helpful tutorial for effective moral analysis of technology.

Avoiding the "Peter Moment"
A Broader View for Fuller Understanding

Employing a robust analysis of intention, means, and circumstances that draws on the insights of the instrumentalist, determinist, and cultural materialist approaches to technology will enable moral theologians to offer more fruitful analyses of the impact of our gadget use on persons and communities. At this point, I'd offer two examples of the ways in which this fuller approach might lead us to different

---

43 Amanda Kooser, "Social Network for Rich People Costs $9,000 to Join" (September 17, 2014), www.cnet.com/news/social-network-for-rich-people-costs-9000-to-join/.

44 Pew Research Center, "Online Harassment" (October 2014), 3, www.pewinternet.org/2014/10/22/online-harassment/.

45 Selina Larson, "Microsoft CEO Satya Nadella to Women: Don't Ask for a Raise, Trust Karma," *ReadWrite* (October 9, 2014), http://readwrite.com/2014/10/09/nadella-women-dont-ask-for-raise.

conclusions than the "tried and true," single approach method that is commonly used. Instead of examining issues that have received a great deal of attention in the press (i.e., worker justice, NSA surveillance, or drones), let us consider two small-scale, everyday practices that a typical teen or young adult is likely to engage in. One will consider the act of the teen or young adult, the other will consider the act of a teacher who instructs those teens and young adults.

One example of what it might be like to broaden our approach to technology to consider intentionality, technological means, and social context can be found in the question of the appropriate means for ending a relationship. During their high school and college years, most American youth engage in some way in the social practice of dating. Whatever the professed intention, dating serves as a way for people to become familiar with social protocols, explore what it is like to create deep relationships with different kinds of people, and ultimately identify someone to enter into a loving, long-term relationship with. Unfortunately, this exciting process of discovery carries with it the much less exciting experience of the break-up, where an unsuccessful relationship is ended, either mutually or unilaterally. Feelings, expectations, and investment of many different kinds lend even the most amicable break-up the potential for a great deal of emotional pain. This pain can be exacerbated through callous treatment of one party by the other, but it can also be mitigated through careful attention to the needs and emotional state of the other. But even with the best of intentions, the end of a relationship is often difficult.

Unfortunately, relationships have not become any easier with the advancement of digital information and communication technology. In the age of "play dates," "helicopter parenting," and a pervasive sense of unease with the state of safety for children, youth have fewer locations for unsupervised interaction with one another. With ubiquitous adoption of devices by youth, cell phones and social media have rapidly started to function in the same ways that malt shops, roller rinks, shopping malls, and arcades did for previous generations. As youth technology use researcher danah boyd puts it, "teens are looking for a place of their own to make sense of the world beyond their bedrooms. Social media has enabled them to participate in and help create… [new] networked publics" where they can interact with one another, even when stuck at home with parents.[46] Teens and young adults

[46] danah boyd, *It's Complicated* (New Haven: Yale University Press, 2014), 5; "Why Youth (Heart) Social Network Sites: the Role of Networked Publics in Teenage Social Life," in *Youth, Identity, and Digital Media,* ed. David Buckingham (Cambridge, MA: MIT Press, 2007). On "hiding in plain sight," see Laura M. Holson, "Text Generation Gap: U R 2 Old (JK)," *The New York Times* (March 9, 2008), www.nytimes.com/-2008/03/09/business/09cell.html?pagewanted=all&_r=0.

use technology to engage in a wide variety of social interactions, including, naturally, dating and romantic relationships.[47] Indeed, technology use has even extended solidly into the sexual aspects of teen and young adult relationships. While findings vary among studies, recent studies have found that 27.6% of 14-19 year olds and 44% of 18-24 year old cell phone owners have received sexually suggestive or explicit messages or images on their devices.[48] Thus, these networked spaces are not simple by any means. In their digital lives, teens and young adults are working though the same complex and fraught aspects of growing up that they do offline.

In this social context, it might come as no surprise that young people use technology to accomplish the difficult task of ending a relationship. The advantages of using a text message or social media post are presumably quite apparent: The complicated business of making one's self vulnerable and of facing another's pain are significantly mitigated when you remove the face to face and dialogical components of the process. If "breaking up is hard to do," doing it digitally makes it much easier, However, this raises potential moral questions. At the very least, use of a private medium like text messaging would seem be an expression of negligence, violating the basic requirement of solicitude.[49] The act may arise out of a lack of prudential judgment about the appropriate course of action to uphold care for the other, more a failure of good intention rather than the presence of a bad intention. It may also arise out of fear of what needs to be done due to the emotional pain that might be experienced through the face-to-face conversation, thus an intentional keeping at arms length.[50]

However, the choice to break up over a public medium like a social network site adds to these failures, at the very least, an additional violation of the dignity of the other through making one's private life into a public matter, even when done out of ignorance.[51] At its worse, it

---

[47] For particularly thoughtful, ethnography based treatment of teen dating in the digital age, see danah boyd, "Friendship," 79-116 and C. J. Pascoe, "Intimacy," 117-148 in *Hanging Out, Messing Around, and Geeking Out,* ed. Mizuko Ito (Cambridge, MA: MIT Press, 2010).

[48] Jeff R. Temple, et al., "Teen Sexting and Its Association with Sexual Behaviors," *Archives of Pediatric and Adolescent Medicine,* 166:9 (2012), http://archpedi.jamanetwork.com/article.aspx?articleid=1212181; Amanda Lenhart and Maeve Duggan, "Couples, the Internet, and Social Media," Pew Research Center (February 11, 2014), 18, www.pewinternet.org/files/2014/02/PIP_Couples_and_Technology-FIN_0211-14.pdf. On differences in study findings, see Bianca Klettke, David J. Halliford, and David J. Mellor, "Sexting Prevalence and Correlates: A Systematic Literature Review," *Clinical Psychology Review,* 34 (2014); 44-53.

[49] As in Aquinas, *Summa Theologica*, II-II, q. 54, a. 13.

[50] As in Aquinas, *Summa Theologica*, II-II, q. 125, a. 1.

[51] The right to privacy has been affirmed throughout Catholic social teaching on social communication. See Pontifical Council for Social Communications, *Communio et progressio,* no. 42. Originally discussed under the rubric of the right to information afforded the public through the mass media, in the Internet era, this would conceivably

can easily become the kind of cruelty and derision aimed at humiliation that forms the foundation of bullying.[52] Given this assessment, ending a relationship in any way other than through a face-to-face conversation appears as a less than morally laudable action grounded in either a failed intention or the choice of a inadequate means for embodying a good intention. Such evaluation might lead us to create a concrete moral norm that "one ought not to break up with someone online."

While this norm sounds clear and sensible, a fuller description of the social world of current teens and young adults reveals that it may be inadequate to assess the moral character of breaking up over mediated channels. Several aspects are particularly instructive. First, the kind of strong distinction between "online" and "face-to-face" that many adults make—and that underlies any claim that one is "more authentic" than the other—does not exist for youth. "For most teens, social media do not constitute an alternative or 'virtual world'. They are simply another method to connect with their friends and peers in a way that feels seamless with their everyday lives."[53] Mediated emotional interactions are not disconnected from unmediated interactions, and thus participate as equals in the broader relational context.

Second, as a result, using social media as part of the breakup process can engage positive functions in relational lives.[54] Social media can be used to communicate through broader, overlapping friend networks and indirect communication channels in ways that are understood as more sensitive because they are less direct. By managing exposure to postings and news feeds, both parties involved in the end of relationship can manage their anxiety levels in ways that face to face encounters do not allow. And narrating one's experience through social networks affords both parties many opportunities for validation from their peers in times where support is particularly important, as well as exit the relationship smoothly by slowly releasing bonds with former significant others. As the determinist would affirm, social media has changed the practice of rationality. As a result, our description of both the actor's intentions and the fit between means and intention may be in need of revision.

A third aspect of the social world of current teens and young adults that is relevant to assessment of the choice to break up with someone digitally—particularly through social media—concerns the particular character of current online culture. It likely comes as no surprise, but women experience higher levels of harassment throughout their social

---

extend to non-journalistic communication posted on public sites. See also Second Vatican Council, *Inter mirifica*, no. 5.

52 As in Aquinas, *Summa Theologica*, II-II, q. 159, a. 2 and q. 75, a. 1.

53 boyd, "Friendship," 84.

54 Pascoe, "Intimacy," 135-141, 146.

media experiences. As noted previously, harassment is a common experience among Internet users, with 40% of adults having experienced some form of it personally. Among young adults, that number is higher, with a full 70% of Internet users ages 18-24 having been harassed online.[55] But women experience much higher rates than men of "particularly severe forms of online harassment," including stalking (26% of female Internet users) and sexual harassment (25% of female Internet users).[56] Within the realm of sexting, while both males and females report similar levels involvement, teen girls experience much more pressure to do so. They are asked to send sexual pictures at a much higher rate (68.4%) than boys (42.1%),[57] and boys more frequently send pictures from girls on to their friends. They also experience significant negative consequences to their reputations for both sending pictures and refusing to send them, while boys do not.[58] Combining these two trends, a particularly heinous form of harassment emerged in 2010. Referred to as "revenge porn," it consists in posting sexually suggestive or naked pictures of women (pictures of males are exceedingly rare) by disgruntled ex-boyfriends (identified posters are almost exclusively male) for the sole purpose of propagating embarrassing images across the web that will shame and harm women.[59] Indeed, between recent celebrity selfie photo hacks and threats of violence against high profile feminist media critics like Anita Sarkeesian, there is growing recognition of the widespread culture of misogyny that has been present for years in the online world, but that the social materialist would likely recognize as endemic to the intellectual, economic, and social patterns of western culture itself.[60]

Given this asymmetry, it is plausible that in addition to being a way to take advantage of the positive aspects that it affords, using social media for the purposes of breaking up with someone may very well, for girls and young women, be best described as an exercise in self-

---

[55] Pew, "Online Harassment," 14.

[56] Pew, "Online Harassment," 15.

[57] Jeff R. Temple, et al., "Teen Sexting and Its Association with Sexual Behaviors." See also, Bianca Klettke, David J. Halliford, and David J. Mellor, "Sexting Prevalence and Correlates," 52.

[58] As Julia R. Lippman and Scott W. Campbell put it in "Damned If You Do, Damned If You Don't... If You're a Girl: Relational and Normative Contexts of Adolescent Sexting in the United States," *Journal of Children and Media* 8:4 (2014), 371.

[59] Dave Lee, "IsAnyoneUp's Hunter Moore: 'The Net's Most Hated Man," *BBC.com* (April 20, 2012), www.bbc.com/news/technology-17784232; Dan Goodin, "Feds arrest 'most hated man on the Internet' in Revenge Porn Hacking Case," *ArsTechnica.com,* January 23, 2014, http://arstechnica.com/tech-policy/2014/01/feds-arrest-most-hated-man-on-the-internet-in-revenge-porn-hacking-case/.

[60] Catherine Buni and Soraya Chemaly, "The Unsafety Net: How Social Media Turned Against Women," *The Atlantic,* October 9, 2014, http://www.theatlantic.com/technology/archive/2014/10/the-unsafety-net-how-social-media-turned-against-women/381261/?single_page=true.

care or self-protection than in failed intention or unfitting means. No matter how a breakup happens, there is always potential for embarrassment and shame. That is as unavoidable now as it has ever been. However, with today's digital tools, there is an increased potential that an ex-boyfriend will respond in a way that has long-term negative consequences for the young woman involved. By making the breakup itself public, a young woman has the primary role of shaping the messaging within her community, mitigating the chance that her ex will be able to use the situation as a launching point for harassment. In a social world characterized by falsehoods, derision, and willful spreading of other people's private and intimate information, it is critical for girls and women to be able to control the stories that are told about them. Breaking up online may be less about a lack of care or an intentional shaming than about initiative and intentionality in relationships that should be mutual but, all too often, are not. While "one ought not to break up with someone online" is clear and catchy, the material and social conditions of the act itself call into question the sufficiency of the underlying assumptions that support it.

A second example of how we might broaden our approach to technology beyond questions of intentionality to include the technological means and social context can be found in the question of what one might, as a college professor, ask of those whom we invite to learn and explore as part of the assignments in a course. It certainly goes without saying that across the spectrum of learning environments, educators strive not merely to impart information to their students, but to engage them in a process of self-discovery and personal growth such that they pursue not merely information, but integral human development. To do this, teachers sometimes invite students to do work that is very personal, exploring the depth of their experiences in a host of areas. Students in art programs, for instance, are using visual media to explore difficult topics like abuse, loss, and addiction. Students in communication programs are testing the creative waters, trying to find their voices by doing provocative and probing work, be it investigative journalism or shock media. Students in theology classes are invited to explore the complex realities of living spiritually in a consumer culture. Through these kinds of assignments, students develop who they are in addition to what they know.

To this, we might add another factor: Faculty members these days frequently ask their students to use social platforms like YouTube and free online tools like Google Docs as media for both academic work and more exploratory, reflective tasks. The intentions here are often fairly straightforward and unwaveringly good. Using digital tools can enable students to utilize their creativity through the media of photography, video, audio, and blogging. Using new media is a nice break from paper writing and exams, which, in turn, can increase student motivation. And choosing "free" tools for these activities keeps educational costs down. These are all laudable intentions. Providing students interesting assignments and multiple pathways for expression are excellent ways to improve student engagement and, thus, performance. Using technology and new media at the college level seems like a win-win situation.

However, considering the normative technology practices within our broader social context suggests that in order to reap the benefits of technology in education, faculty must attend to much more than simply giving the assignment. One of the most controversial aspects of the social media landscape over the last five years has been privacy. Most recently, in the wake of Edward Snowden's revelations about the National Security Administration in 2012, this concern has centered on government data mining of phone call information and social media accounts. Before that, there was significant concern about data aggregation by social media sites for the purposes of advertising. As problematic as these situations are, there is a deeper concern, namely of we might call the "existential" need for privacy.

In a *Heythrop Journal* article from 2010, political philosopher Hayden Ramsey explores the link between privacy and integral human development. He argues that:

> Privacy is a human need: it is a good necessary for all people if they are to share in basic goods. Privacy, however, does not correspond with any specific basic good. It is not essential for participation in any one good. Rather, privacy is essential for effective participation in every basic human good—possessing privacy is necessary if we are to flourish in respect of health, knowledge, creativity, work, leisure, family, friendship, religion, peace of mind and practical thinking.[61]

Privacy, then, is a necessary precondition for basic human development. Ramsey goes on to offer examples of the links between privacy and different types of development, noting:

> Our needs for education and job training will be satisfied more effectively where our needs for freedom from interference and from observation are also satisfied; we need cultural and spiritual development in order to share in art and religion, but to develop in these ways we need too a measure of solitude; to satisfy our need for linguistic and social skills we also need freedom to grow, security to experiment.... Solitude and freedom from interference with our thinking allow us to build respect for self, others and thinking itself which we will need if we are to plan our own lives reasonably.[62]

---

[61] Hayden Ramsay, "Privacy, Privacies and Basic Needs," *Heythrop Journal* 60 (2010): 294.
[62] Ramsay, "Privacy, Privacies and Basic Needs," 295.

Privacy provides human beings with the space necessary to take our first steps in living our identities in concrete practices, experimenting with alternate selves, and entering into vulnerable spaces without fear of retribution or the cost of public failure. Without privacy, we will find it difficult to become our full selves.

Recognition of this role of privacy is important because there are times when faculty members ask students to explore the deepest parts of themselves, so they can grow into creative, intelligent, and responsible adults. Some professors are mindful of the importance of the full gamut of privacy needs, and they direct students to use closed university learning management systems like Blackboard or set up their own secure sites where students can post their work. Others, however, are not, inviting students to use public fora like YouTube, Wordpress, Instagram, and Stellar to put their work directly in the public forum. Yet, even when faculty set up private channels for submission, much of this work doesn't stay private forever. Many of the tools we use have robust sharing features built in, even if we do not use them for the assignment. Additionally, the culture of sharing that predominates today—that valorizes public collaboration and contribution—makes posting even the most personal work a laudable act. Many students have a very public sense of their lives: if they do something cool, they want to post it for their friends or family. Thus, between the invitation to share within the tools themselves (the means) and the encouragement to share within the student's cultural context (circumstances) students themselves may very well fail to respect the privacy that they themselves need to become their full selves.

Importantly, the stakes are high in a wired society. According to a 2012 study by placement firm CareerBuilder, more than a third of American companies examine social media when researching job candidates.[63] Sixty-five percent say they want to know if candidates present themselves professionally, 51% want to know if it is a good fit for company culture, and 12% say they are looking for reasons not to hire. In the end, 34% of hiring managers who looked at candidates' social media activity chose not to hire them as a result of things they found. The single biggest reason they chose not to hire: 49% they found material that they considered provocative or inappropriate.

Given the reality that self expression could, conceivably, lead to trouble finding a job, we are left with a question: Are faculty members developing responsible assignments for the twenty-first century? The work that students do in our courses might be tremendous, and their

[63] CareerBuilder, "Thirty-seven percent of companies use social networks to research potential job candidates, according to new CareerBuilder Survey," www.careerbuilder.com/share/aboutus/pressreleasesdetail.aspx?id=pr691&sd=4%2F18%2F2012&ed=4%2F18%2F2099.

personal and intellectual growth significant. Indeed, it might be something totally uncharacteristic, a moment on a journey to figuring out who they really are. Yet, in our digital sharing world, that material will follow them for years, and it might harm their employment possibilities. It is important not to have paternalistic concern, yet it is also important to consider whether or not we prepare students for the reality that what they see as a small part of their educational experience, carried out in the freedom and privacy of the university community, will—if ever entered into the public web—be part of a public profile that will be connected to them for years. Given the high stakes—both personal and professional—faculty members must do serious work—both technical and pedagogical—to ensure that what we ask students to do does not lead to problems down the line.

Conclusion

As we traverse the second decade of the twentieth century—forty years into the digital era—we know that contemporary information and communication technology poses complex problems that require more thorough analysis than would have been done a century ago. We know that while the Pope writes beautiful tweets, they are unlikely to have a positive spiritual effect when sandwiched in between updates from Fox News, Bacardi Rum, the Gap, and Nikki Minaj. And we know that if a young child wanders off from the park after you stop paying attention to watch a video on your cell phone, the fact that you were watching a lecture on the Eucharist will not make it all better. Thus, it is incumbent upon scholars to approach questions of technology and media with the same kind of sophisticated, multivalent analysis that we use when we approach any other moral question. Goals of the communicator, content of the message, material engagement with particular communication technologies, personal messaging practices and habits, and broader social realities—intent, means, circumstance, and consequences—all of these are critical parts of the communication event. Each one helps us understand one part of the whole process of messaging and the culture in which it is realized. If we, as moral theologians, want to understand the ways in which contemporary communication technologies are transforming individuals and communities as well as plan how to use communication technologies in ways that lead to integral human development and a global common good, it is incumbent upon us to understand each of these factors and draw all of them—be they instrumental, determinist, or cultural materialist—into our picture of communication as we work to help create students, churches, and communities in the twenty-first century.

CONTRIBUTORS

Jana M. Bennett is Associate Professor of Theology and Ethics at the University of Dayton. Her books include *Water is Thicker than Blood: An Augustinian Theology of Marriage and Singleness* (New York: Oxford, 2008), and *Aquinas on the Web? Doing Theology in an Internet Age* (London: Continuum, 2012). She is also the author of numerous articles about feminism, disability, and technology. She is currently at work on a book about single adult Christians, especially non-vowed Christians, and their particular vocations in the church.

James F. Caccamo is Associate Professor of Theology and Chair of the Department of Theology and Religious Studies at Saint Joseph's University (Philadelphia). A former computer programmer, Jim's work focuses on the moral implications of technology and media practices. He is the co-author of *Living Worship*, an interactive app for teaching liturgy in seminary settings, and contributor to the USCCB and Orthodox Archdiocese of America's "Internet and Mobile Safety Guide" (faithandsaftey.org). He has published on tech ethics in *Journal of Business Ethics*, *Liturgy*, *Josephinum Journal of Theology*, and the *National Catholic Reporter*.

Nadia Delicata is a Lecturer in Moral Theology at the Faculty of Theology, University of Malta. Her primary area of interest is Christianity and culture, with a focus on challenges to Christian formation in a digital age. In her work, both published and in progress, she brings together a media ecology hermeneutic and the thought of contemporary philosophers and cultural theorists, with early and patristic grammatical and rhetorical theology, to allow the latter to inform strategies of Christian formation in a digital context.

Patrick Flanagan is Assistant Professor in the Department of Theology and Religious Studies at St. John's University, New York. His main research interests lie in the areas of information technology ethics, marketplace morality, and healthcare ethics. He co-authored *Good Business: Catholic Social Teaching at Work in the Marketplace* (Anselm Academic, 2014) which applies the themes of Catholic social teaching to the corporate world. He has published in the *Journal of Business Ethics, Journal of Religious and Theological Information,* and *Chicago Studies.* In addition to serving as an editor for the *Journal of Religion and Business Ethics*, he serves as lead editor for a special annual edition of the *Journal of Business Ethics* in conjunction with the International Vincentian Business Ethics Conference Promoting Business Ethics. Presently, he is working on a book project on virtuous navigation of the Web vis-à-vis the seven deadly sins.

Mary E. Hess is Professor of Educational Leadership and Chair of the Leadership Division at Luther Seminary, in St. Paul, MN. Her research focuses on the intersections of learning, new media, and religious community. Recent books include *Teaching Reflectively in Theological Contexts: Promises and Contradictions*, edited with Stephen Brookfield (Ashgate, 2008) and *Engaging Technology in Theological Education: All That We Can't Leave Behind* (Rowman & Littlefield, 2005). A past president of the Religious Education Association, she publishes widely in educational journals, has written the blog *Tensegrities* since 2003, and is a consultant with the Wabash Center for Teaching and Learning in Theology and Religion.

Kara N. Slade is a PhD student in Christian theology and ethics in the Graduate Program in Religion at Duke University. A former specialist in the dynamics of nonlinear and complex systems, she earned the BSE, MS, and PhD in mechanical engineering and materials science at Duke's Pratt School of Engineering before joining the National Aeronautics and Space Administration as a research engineer. Her research interests include the ethics of technology, bioethics, and theological anthropology. Ordained as a priest in the Episcopal Church, she also currently serves as Vicar of St. David's Episcopal Church in Laurinburg, NC.

Matthew John Paul Tan is the Felice and Margredel Zaccari Lecturer in Theology and Philosophy in Campion College Australia. He has published articles in the *Heythrop Journal*, as well as *Politics, Religion & Ideology*. He is the author of *Justice, Unity and the Hidden Christ: the Theopolitical Complex to the Social Justice Approach to Ecumenism in Vatican II* (Eugene: Pickwick Publications 2014), and he is also editor of the theological blog, *The Divine Wedgie.*

Joseph Wolyniak is a Visiting Scholar in the Department of Religious Studies at the University of Denver and D. Phil. candidate in theology at the University of Oxford (Harris Manchester College). A 2012 Episcopal Church Foundation Fellow, he is the vice chair of The Episcopal Church's Executive Council Committee on Science, Technology & Faith, founding member of the Scholar-Priest Initiative in The Episcopal Church and Anglican Church of Canada, and a Theologian-in-Residence at the Church of the Ascension (Denver, CO).

JOURNAL • OF

M • O • R • A • L

THEOLOGY

Upcoming Issues

Open to all Submissions
Volume 4, Number 2 (June 2015)
Editor: David Matzko McCarthy

Disability
Volume 5, Number 1 (January 2016)
Editor: Miguel J. Romero
and David Matzko McCarthy

Open to all Submissions
Volume 5, Number 2 (June 2016)
Editor: David Matzko McCarthy
and Jason King

***Populorum Progressio*: 50 Years**
Volume 6, Number 1 (January 2017)
Editor: Mari Rapela Heidt
and Matthew A. Shadle

Open to all Submissions
Volume 6, Number 2 (June 2017)
Editor: Jason King

Articles available to view or download at:

www.msmary.edu/jmt

The

Journal of Moral Theology

is proudly sponsored by the

Fr. James M. Forker Professorship of Catholic Social Teaching

and the

College of Liberal Arts

at

Mount St. Mary's University

MOUNT ST. MARY'S UNIVERSITY

College of Liberal Arts